GUINNESS WORLD RECORDS 2010

GUINNESS WORLD RECORDS

GAMER'S EDITION

British Library Cataloguing-in-Publication Data: a catalogue record for this book is available from the British Library.

ISBN:
978-1-4053-5525-4

Check the official *GWR Gamer's Edition* website **www.guinnessworldrecords.com/gamers** regularly for record-breaking gaming news as it happens, plus exclusive interviews and competitions.

ACCREDITATION: Guinness World Records Limited has a very thorough accreditation system for records verification. However, while every effort is made to ensure accuracy, Guinness World Records Limited cannot be held responsible for any errors contained in this work. Feedback from our readers on any point of accuracy is always welcomed.

Guinness World Records Limited does not claim to own any right, title or interest in the trademarks of others reproduced in this book.

© 2010 Guinness World Records Ltd, a Jim Pattison Group company

EDITOR-IN-CHIEF
Craig Glenday

MANAGING EDITORS
Matt Boulton, Ben Way

GAMING EDITOR
Gaz Deaves

EDITORIAL TEAM
Rob Cave, Rob Dimery, Alex Meloy

INDEX
Chris Bernstein

DIRECTOR OF PUBLISHING
Mina Patria

PRODUCTION MANAGER
Jane Boatfield

PRODUCTION ASSISTANT
Erica Holmes-Attivor

BUYING CONSULTANT
Patricia Magill

COLOUR ORIGINATION
FMG, London, UK

PICTURE EDITOR
Michael Whitty

DEPUTY PICTURE EDITOR
Laura Jackson

PICTURE RESEARCHER
Fran Morales

ORIGINAL PHOTOGRAPHY
Paul Michael Hughes

CONCEPT CREATION & LAYOUT
Itonic Design Ltd, Brighton, UK

GAMER'S CONSULTANTS
Pro-Gaming:
Robert Haxton
Hardware:
Ellie Gibson
Shooting Games:
Dan Whitehead
Sports Games:
Wesley Yin-Poole
Action-Adventure Games:
Gaz Deaves
Fighting Games:
Guy Cocker
Party Games:
Chris Schilling
Puzzle Games:
Martyn Carroll
Role-Playing Games:
Simon Parkin
Strategy & Simulation Games:
Craig Shaw
Instant Gaming:
David Crookes

RECORDS MANAGEMENT
VP of Records:
Marco Frigatti (Italy)

Head of Adjudications:
Andrea Bánfi (Hungary)

Records Management Team:
Gaz Deaves (UK)
Danny Girton (USA)
Ralph Hannah (UK)
Kaoru Ishikawa (Japan)
Tzeni Karampoiki (Greece)
Olaf Kuchenbecker (Germany)
Carlos Martínez (Spain)
Talal Omar (Yemen)
Mariamarta Ruano-Graham (Guatemala)
Chris Sheedy (Australia)
Lucia Sinigagliesi (Italy)
Kristian Teufel (Germany)
Aleksander Vipirailenko (Lithuania)
Wu Xiaohong (China)

SALES AND MARKETING
Senior VP Sales & Marketing:
Samantha Fay

Sales & Marketing Director:
Nadine Causey

Licensing Director:
Frank Chambers

US Marketing Director:
Laura Plunkett

Senior National Accounts Manager:
John Pilley

PR Manager:
Amarilis Espinoza

US Marketing Manager:
Philip Robertson

International Licensing Manager:
Beatriz Fernandez

US Licensing Manager:
Jennifer Osbourne

Business Development Managers:
Stuart Claxton (USA)
Erika Ogawa (Japan)

International Marketing Executive:
Justine Bourdariat

Marketing Executive:
Tom Harris

PR Executives:
Karolina Thelin (UK)
Jamie Panas (USA)

Marketing & PR Assistant:
Damian Field (UK)

GUINNESS WORLD RECORDS
Managing Director:
Alistair Richards
VP Finance: Alison Ozanne
Director of IT: Katie Forde
Director of Television:
Rob Molloy
Legal & Business Affairs:
Raymond Marshall
Director of HR: Kelly Garrett
Management Accountant:
Jason Curran
Finance Manager: Neelish Dawett

Digital Content Manager:
Denise Anlander
Accounts Payable Manager:
Laura Hetherington
IT Infrastructure Analyst:
Paul Bentley
Contracts Administrator:
Lisa Gibbs
Television Assistant:
David Chabbi
Office Administrators:
Janet Oatham (UK)
Danielle Pointdujour (USA)

ABBREVIATIONS & MEASUREMENTS: Guinness World Records Limited uses both metric and imperial measurements. The sole exceptions are for some scientific data where metric measurements only are universally accepted, and for some sports data. Where a specific date is given, the exchange rate is calculated according to the currency values that were in operation at the time. Where only a year date is given, the exchange rate is calculated from December of that year. "One billion" is taken to mean one thousand million.

GENERAL WARNING: Attempting to break records or set new records can be dangerous. Appropriate advice should be taken first and all record attempts are undertaken at the participant's risk. In no circumstances will Guinness World Records Limited have any liability for death or injury suffered in any record attempt. Guinness World Records Limited has complete discretion over whether or not to include any particular records in the book. Being a Guinness World Record holder does not guarantee you a place in the book.

GUINNESS WORLD RECORDS 2010

GUINNESS WORLD RECORDS

GAMER'S EDITION

CONTENTS

TO TRACK DOWN YOUR FAVOURITE GAMES, JUST TURN TO THE INDEX ON P.212.

Handy hints show you the quickest route to your favourite games

The very best images available from the latest record-breaking games bring each spread to life in dramatic style

Quotes from big names in gaming and industry professionals give insights into the top games

Key records are highlighted and illustrated

NEW AND UPDATED RECORDS

Each year in Gamer's Edition, we strive to bring you either completely new or updated records, to keep the book as fresh and current as we possibly can. Where we've done this, you will see the following icons before the record title:

NEW RECORD

UPDATED RECORD

Of course, we've included some classic old records as well, because sometimes oldies are goodies.

685... the number of games name-checked in *Gamer's Edition 2010*, which means there should be something for every gamer in this book, whatever your preference.

Clear, easy-to-read headings make finding your way through the book a breeze

Amazing number facts bring a new dimension to gaming feats

Dynamic double-page images introduce each new section of the book in stunning style

Fascinating gaming trivia and fantastic facts add extra fun to every page

ACCURACY

As with all Guinness World Records books, every effort has been made to bring to you the most accurate and up-to-date records. If, however, you believe that you know of a more impressive achievement or a higher score, please let us know. We rely on your help to keep our books as fresh and as accurate as possible. Visit www.guinnessworld records.com/gamers to find out how you can contribute...

Text that appears in **bold** type refers to an official Guinness World Record.

WELCOME TO GAMER'S 2010

! GET INVOLVED IN NEXT YEAR'S BOOK – TURN TO P.8 TO SEE HOW.

FASTEST MOBILE GAMING RIG

The launch of last year's *Gamer's Edition* was itself a record-breaking event as members of the *Gamer's Edition* staff braved the iciest of weather conditions to set the record for the fastest mobile gaming rig. The rig, which was built and driven by Edd China (UK), achieved a top speed of 57 mph (92 km/h) while the three passengers played home consoles in London, UK, on 11 February 2009.

IT HAS BEEN A GREAT 12 MONTHS FOR VIDEOGAMES – GREAT NEW GAMES, GREAT NEW RECORDS AND A GREAT NEW LOOK FOR GWR GAMER'S EDITION.

What an incredible year we've had at *Guinness World Records Gamer's Edition*! Since the 2009 book came out, we've been travelling the globe adjudicating at the most amazing gaming events, handing out prized *Gamer's Edition* certificates and generally meeting the great and the good of the gaming world.

Whatever the record-breaking attempt, we've been on hand to make sure that all the rules were followed and that there was no foul play. Just about every kind of videogame-themed event has been covered, from game-playing marathons to high-score attempts to gaming-themed fancy dress gatherings. Take a look over the page to find out how you can become a record-breaker and turn the page again for some great examples of this year's adjudications.

For those of you who've read the book over the past couple of years, you'll have noticed that we've made a few changes in this 2010 edition, which we hope you'll enjoy.

The book is still packed with the usual exciting mix of records, facts and figures, and hundreds of great images exploding out of the pages, but we've also taken on board your comments and made the whole book clearer and easier to navigate.

Perhaps the most important change is that instead of dedicating a two-page spread to each game, as we've done in previous books, this year we've divided the book up into genres and sub-genres, much like we do in our main *Guinness World Records* book, which means that each spread features loads more of your favourite videogames.

Another feature of this year's *Gamer's Edition* is that we've tried to give you pointers towards games that you might not know, but are so good that you really should try them. On each spread, you'll find a "Ten Games You Should Play In This Genre" table, showing you what our expert writers think are the best

NEW RECORD ● UPDATED RECORD

« *Crammed full of small, highly readable facts, records and mini-interviews… there's something there for practically anyone who's ever tickled a joypad.*

The Guardian *review of* Gamer's Edition 2009 »»

GUINNESS WORLD RECORDS 2009 GAMER'S EDITION
IN BOOKSTORES NOW!

GUINNESS WORLD RECORDS 2009 GAMER'S EDITION

GAMER THE GAMER'S BIBLE "If you're a gamer, you need this on your shelf GAMER EDITI

GUINNESS
WORLD RECORDS

LIL POISON VISITS GWR

In February 2009, the **world's youngest professional gamer** Lil Poison (aka Victor De Leon III) called in at the offices of Guinness World Records in London, UK, to help us celebrate the launch of *Gamer's Edition 2009*. Now a venerable 11 years old, Lil Poison started playing videogames at the age of two and has been a record holder since 2005.

games in each sub-genre. In each table you'll find some big name games and also some more obscure ones that you may not have heard of.

In *Gamer's Edition 2009*, we published our list of the top 50 games, as voted for by our expert writers and *Gamer's Edition* staff. The list received lots of comments from readers and industry commentators alike, and let's just say that not everyone agreed with our choices. The reaction was great; we love it when you give us your opinions, because it shows that you're getting involved and are really passionate about videogames. So this year, we invited you to tell us what *your* favourite

MEETING MIYAMOTO

A highlight of an amazing year for *Gamer's Edition* had to be meeting the legendary Shigeru Miyamoto (Japan) at the E3 convention in Los Angeles, USA, back in June. Nintendo's General Manager of EAD is the man behind some of the all-time great videogame characters, including Donkey Kong, Mario and Link from *The Legend of Zelda*, and was the driving force behind the Nintendo Wii. Here, we see Miyamoto brandishing his certificate for the **best-selling videogame of all time** – *Wii Sports*, with over 45.7 million copies sold. You can read a full profile of the man dubbed "the father of modern videogames" on pages 102 and 103.

games are, and more than 13,000 of you accepted our invitation and voted online. We count down the results from page 186 onwards, and although we won't spoil it for you now, suffice it to say that your views differ somewhat from those of our experts...

More than ever, this year's book is all about giving you, the reader, what you want to see in the *Gamer's Edition*. So, if there's something you like, something you don't agree with, or a record that you want to break, get in touch and let us know all about it.

DO YOU AGREE?

On each spread, our expert writers have listed their recommendations for the Top Ten games you should try in that sub-genre. Now, we know that whenever videogames are assembled in a list like this, a heated discussion (or argument!) isn't far behind, so there's a chance that you may not agree with what our writers have said. No problem, we're always happy to let you have your say, just log on to the Gamer's Edition website – www.guinness worldrecords.com/ gamers – and let us know about your own Top Ten and any gems you think we should have included.

GUINNESS WORLD RECORDS 2009

! TURN RIGHT OVER TO LEARN MORE ABOUT GWR ADJUDICATIONS.

HOW TO BE A RECORD-BREAKER

NEW RECORD

UPDATED RECORD

HIGHEST SCORE ON TEENAGE MUTANT NINJA TURTLES: TURTLES IN TIME

Holder: DAVID PRICE (USA) Comic book fan David Price punched, kicked and fought his way to a record high score of 212 points on the arcade version of the classic beat-em-up *Teenage Mutant Ninja Turtles: Turtles in Time* (Konami, 1991). David used a single credit to reach this score at the New York Comic Con, New York City, New York, USA, on 7 February 2009, where he was presented with his certificate by GWR's Laura Plunkett.

SO YOU WANT TO BREAK A GAMING RECORD? IF YOU THINK YOU'VE GOT WHAT IT TAKES TO MAKE IT INTO NEXT YEAR'S GAMER'S EDITION, HERE'S A RUN DOWN OF WHAT YOU NEED TO DO...

1. PICK A RECORD
Decide what you're going to do, and make sure you can do it.

2. DO YOUR RESEARCH
There are some world record attempts that we don't recognize for various reasons, so it's worth checking that we'll accept your record. It'd be a shame to miss out on a Guinness World Record because of a technicality.

3. GO TO THE WEBSITE
Go to www.guinnessworldrecords. com/gamers and click on "Set a Record". Tell us who you are and what you're planning to do. We'll send you an agreement to sign that sets out how we approve records and what happens if you're successful.

4. WAIT FOR THE RULES
We usually send out guidelines that specify how you should attempt your record. This includes matters such as game settings, difficulty levels and break-time allowances for marathons. The guidelines are there to ensure a level playing field for everyone.

5. ATTEMPT THE RECORD
For us to consider your attempt as valid, you'll need to convince us that your claim is for real. We insist on the following as a minimum:

● EVIDENCE
A recording in which you describe your record, show us your full set up and the whole of your attempt, from the moment you turn on your system to when you complete the challenge.

● WITNESSES
At least one, but preferably two, independent witnesses. One of your witnesses will need to be a gaming expert – someone from your local videogames store would be fine.

6. SEND US PROOF
Once you have attempted your record, you will need to let us know how you got on. See the box on the facing page for a list of the sort of information we require as evidence.

7. LEAVE IT TO US
Leave the rest to us, but remember that our word is final. In most cases, we'll approve your record based on the evidence you send us, but sometimes we may ask for more info, or even invite you to attend an official Guinness World Records adjudication to verify your claim in person.

8. RECEIVE CONFIRMATION
Finally, if you have been successful, we send you a *Gamer's Edition* certificate celebrating your record-breaking achievement. You bask in the glory of being a genuine Guinness World Record holder!

138... the number of claims we have received for the **longest videogames marathon on an FPS** since the *2009 Gamer's Edition* went to press – none beat the Frag Dolls' 24 hr 4 min.

SEND US THE PROOF

For us to consider your record, you'll need to send us hard copies of the following:

> **The footage –** A recording (DVD format) of the entire record attempt from start to finish. Make sure it's as high quality as possible – we may reject your claim if the footage isn't clear enough.

> **Witness statements –** We need a signed statement from each of your witnesses that details exactly what they saw you do, including times, scores, dates and the location where your attempt took place. Each statement needs to be on letterheaded paper from the witness's company, and must include their contact details.

> **Photos –** You'll need to include some photographs of the attempt in progress, and of the venue where it took place.

> **Screenshots –** If your record is of an in-game achievement, you can support your entry with screenshots. While we don't use these as evidence (they're too easy to tamper with), we may use them to illustrate your achievement on our website or in the book if we approve it.

> **Any other supporting evidence –** If there's anything else that you'd like to submit that you think will help us determine that your claim is the real deal, feel free to include it, but bear in mind we can't return anything you send us.

INVITE AN ADJUDICATOR

> Arrange for an adjudicator to attend your record attempt and you'll enjoy a unique and rewarding GWR experience...

Instant confirmation that you're an official Guinness World Record holder (if you're successful)...

International media coverage for your record attempt...

A full write-up about your record on our website...

Expert support from a member of our Adjudications Team...

One of our adjudicators will also be present on the day to do interviews and press conferences.

> Please note that while attempting a Guinness World Record is free, GWR charges a fee for adjudicators to attend record attempts. To find out more about this premium service, visit www.guinnessworld records.com.

Gamer's Edition adjudicator Damian Field was on hand to oversee an attempt at the **largest air guitar ensemble** record organized by EA to mark the launch of Brütal Legend during the Download Festival, in Donington Park, UK, on 13 June 2009.

Adjudicator Kristian Teufel presents a record certificate to Zak Bennett (UK), who remained unbeaten for 108 matches of Street Fighter IV at HMV Oxford Street in London, UK, on 20 February 2009 (see p.108).

Danny Johnson (USA, centre) receives his certificate for setting the highest score on Guitar Hero 3: Legends of Rock from members of our US team in New York City, New York, USA, at celebrations for the launch of Gamer's Edition 2009 on 4 February 2009.

ADJUDICATIONS

!

INSPIRED TO ATTEMPT A WORLD RECORD? TURN BACK A PAGE TO SEE WHAT YOU NEED TO DO...

« *If I'm feeling down, I can just look at my collection and remember where I got things from. It really cheers me up.*
Record-breaking Pokémon collector Lisa Courtney

»

IN 2009, WHEREVER A VIDEOGAME RECORD ATTEMPT TOOK PLACE, WE WERE THERE. HERE'S A SELECTION OF THE RECORDS WE'VE ADJUDICATED THIS YEAR...

* MOST POPULAR ONLINE CONSOLE SERVICE

Xbox LIVE has over 20 million active subscribers, which represents 67% of the total install base as of May 2009. At E3 2009, held in Los Angeles, USA, on 1 June 2009, *Gamer's Edition*'s Matt Boulton (far left) and Gaz Deaves (far right) presented a certificate marking the achievement to Xbox Live's General Manager, Marc Whitten (centre right), and the service's Director of Programming, Larry Hryb, who is perhaps better known as resident blogger "Major Nelson" (centre left).

* MOST KILLS IN COUNTER-STRIKE IN 12 HOURS

Bjørn "Threat" Pers (Sweden) proudly displays his certificate awarded for the most kills scored against human opponents on *Counter-Strike 1.6*. Bjørn achieved 518 kills in 12 hours at DreamHack Summer 2009, in Jönköping, Sweden, which took place on 14 June 2009.

* LARGEST COLLECTION OF POKÉMON MEMORABILIA

In the 13 years to 13 June 2009, Lisa Courtney (UK) amassed a record-breaking collection of 12,113 different items of Pokémon memorabilia. Lisa's favourite item is a doll of the Pokémon Absol that she bought from eBay. Her collection includes items from the UK, USA, France and, of course, Japan. She has made several trips to Japan for the specific purpose of collecting Pokémon merchandise, each time sending between eight and 12 boxes full back to the UK.

67I... the **most kills on** *Quake III Arena* **in one hour**, achieved by the USA's Johnathan "Fatal1ty" Wendel at the Copenhagen eSports Challenge in Denmark on 13 April 2009.

GUINNESS WORLD RECORDS

The **most players in a 24-hour** Guitar Hero **relay** is 594, achieved by players from Activision Italy and gamers from the city of Verona, Italy, on 11-12 September 2009. The marathon axe-wielding session saw teams competing at different locations across Europe as part of celebrations marking the launch of Guitar Hero 5. GWR's Aleksandr Vypirailenko was on hand to ensure fair play.

Adjudicator Justine Bourdariat witnessed the **longest** Guitar Hero World Tour **marathon**, which lasted 24 hr 2 min and was achieved by Simo Piispanen, Aku Valmu, Jaakko Kokkonen and Simo Matti Liimatainen at Assembly Winter 2009, in Tampere, Finland, on 21 February 2009.

* MOST PEOPLE DRESSED AS VIDEOGAME CHARACTERS

Gamer's Edition officials were in attendance at the MCM Expo, held at Excel in London, UK, on 23 May 2009, to witness the largest gathering of people dressed as videogame characters, which featured 376 enthusiastic participants.

These certificates will take pride of place in our homes to show all who enter that we are the very best in the world at something.

Ready-Up.net's Kirsten Kearney celebrates achieving the racing game marathon record

* NEW RECORD
* UPDATED RECORD

* LONGEST VIDEOGAME MARATHON PLAYING A RACING GAME

Members of the Ready-Up.net editorial team – Dan Bendon, Simon Brown, Kirsten Kearney, Martin Robertson, Fran Shergold and Sharon Tang (all UK) – played *Burnout Paradise* for 24 hours non-stop at ESC Games, Glasgow, UK, from 18 to 19 April 2009. Kirsten is pictured (right) receiving the team's certificate from GWR's Karolina Thelin.

CERTIFICATE

The longest marathon playing a racing game lasted 24 hours and was achieved by the staff of Ready-Up at ESC Games, Glasgow, UK from 18-19 April 2009.

GAMING AWARDS ROUND-UP

! HEAD ON OVER TO OUR PRO-GAMING REVIEW ON P.22 TO CHECK OUT THE STAR PLAYERS.

EVERY YEAR, GAMES CRITICS AND FANS AROUND THE WORLD GATHER TO HONOUR THE LATEST HIT GAMES. HERE ARE THE HIGHLIGHTS OF THE RECENT AWARDS SEASON

BAFTA VIDEO GAMES AWARDS 2009

AWARD	GAME/WINNER
Best Game	Super Mario Galaxy
Action & Adventure	Fable II
Artistic Achievement	LittleBigPlanet
Casual	Boom Blox
Gameplay	Call of Duty 4: Modern Warfare
Handheld	Professor Layton and the Curious Village
Multiplayer	Left 4 Dead
Original Score	Dead Space
Sports	Race Driver: Grid
Strategy	Sid Meier's Civilization Revolution
Story & Character	Call of Duty 4: Modern Warfare
Technical Achievement	Spore
Use of Audio	Dead Space
Academy Fellowship	Nolan Bushnell

"Uncharted 2 was unequivocally that special something.
PlayStation: The Official Magazine's Rob Smith on Uncharted 2 (right)

GAME CRITICS AWARDS: BEST OF E3 2009

AWARD	GAME
Best of Show	Uncharted 2: Among Thieves
Best Original Game	Scribblenauts
Best Console Game	Uncharted 2: Among Thieves
Best PC Game	Star Wars: The Old Republic
Best Handheld Game	Scribblenauts
Best Hardware/Peripheral	Project Natal
Best Action Game	Modern Warfare 2
Best Action/Adventure Game	Uncharted 2: Among Thieves
Best Role Playing Game	Mass Effect 2
Best Racing Game	Split/Second
Best Sports Game	Fight Night Round 4
Best Fighting Game	Tatsunoko vs. Capcom: Ultimate All-Stars
Best Strategy Game	Supreme Commander 2
Best Social/Casual/Puzzle Game	DJ Hero
Best Online Multiplayer	Left 4 Dead 2

"We have a philosophy that we make games for everybody...
Nintendo's Rob Lowe (far left), accepting the BAFTA for Best Game

GOLDEN JOYSTICK AWARDS 2009

AWARD	GAME/WINNER
Family Game of the Year	LittleBigPlanet
Bliss Handheld Game of the Year	Grand Theft Auto: Chinatown Wars
Retailer of the Year	GAME
Mobile Game of the Year	Metal Gear Solid Touch
Nintendo Game of the Year	Call of Duty: World at War
MSN Multiplayer Game of the Year	Call of Duty: World at War
The Rampage Soundtrack of the Year	Guitar Hero World Tour
Xbox Game of the Year	Gears of War 2
Amiqus Games UK Developer of the Year	Jagex
PC Game of the Year	Fallout 3
PlayStation Game of the Year	Killzone 2
Publisher of the Year	Activision Blizzard
Online Game of the Year	Left 4 Dead
Shortist One to Watch	Call of Duty: Modern Warfare 2
Ultimate Game of the Year, together with Zavvi.co.uk	Fallout 3

TRIVIA

◢ Organized by the Academy of Interactive Arts and Sciences, the Interactive Achievement Awards are the videogames equivalent of the Oscars®, voted on solely by people who work in the industry. Online shooter Left 4 Dead scooped the prize for Computer Game of the Year at the 2009 event. Doug Lombardi (above), Vice President of Marketing at Valve, accepted the award for the company.

SPIKE VIDEO GAME AWARDS 2008

AWARD	GAME/WINNER
Game of the Year	Grand Theft Auto IV
Best Action-Adventure Game	Grand Theft Auto IV
Studio of the Year	Media Molecule
Gamer God	Will Wright
Best Shooter	Gears of War 2
Best Music Game	Rock Band 2
Best Soundtrack	Rock Band 2
Best RPG	Fallout 3
Best Team Sports Game	NHL 09
Best Individual Sports Game	Shaun White Snowboarding
Best Xbox 360 Game	Gears of War 2
Best PS3 Game	LittleBigPlanet
Best Wii Game	Boom Blox
Best PC Game	Left 4 Dead
Best Multiplayer Game	Left 4 Dead
Best Fighting Game	SoulCalibur IV
Best Handheld Game	Professor Layton and the Curious Village
Best Driving Game	Burnout Paradise
Best Graphics	Metal Gear Solid 4: Guns of the Patriots
Best Original Score	Metal Gear Solid 4: Guns of the Patriots

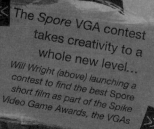

« The Spore VGA contest takes creativity to a whole new level...
Will Wright (above) launching a contest to find the best Spore short film as part of the Spike Video Game Awards, the VGAs.

GAMES OF THE YEAR: TOP 3

! FROM OUR GAMES OF THE YEAR TO YOUR TOP SERIES EVER – CHECK OUT PP.186–95.

A VINTAGE 2009 SPOILED GAMERS WITH SOME INCREDIBLE OFFERINGS, AND THIS YEAR'S CHART PICKS OUT 10 TITLES DESTINED FOR TRUE GREATNESS

« *It was another roller coaster of quiet, creeping build-up and then thunderous rushes of action, diverse in presentation and surprising in its variety.*
Kotaku.com review of Modern Warfare 2 »

* NEW RECORD
▪ UPDATED RECORD

MODERN WARFARE 2

(Activision, 2009)
Infinity Ward's shooter is so big that almost a dozen games were pushed back from a 2009 release into 2010 to avoid competing with it. The series' well-paced single-player action and frequent "OMG!" moments are only surpassed by the depth and playability of the multiplayer components, which will keep *Modern Warfare 2* relevant well into next year.

89.86%... the GameRankings average review score achieved by *The Beatles: Rock Band*, a figure backed up by fellow aggregator Metacritic, which gave the game 89%.

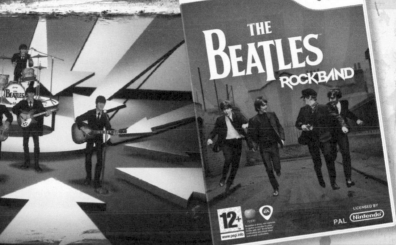

2

THE BEATLES: ROCK BAND

(MTV Games, 2009)
Harmonix took the band simulation genre to the next level with this digital tribute to the Fab Four. Unique features that are specific to the Beatles' legacy include a three-part vocal harmony system and Beatles-themed instruments, cementing *Rock Band*'s position as the thinking person's rhythm game.

3

HALO 3: ODST

(Microsoft, 2009)
With the single-player element acting as a side story to *Halo 3*'s main event, *ODST* sees the player assume the role of an Orbital Drop Shock Trooper (below), rather than the Master Chief. The game, which includes the complete *Halo 3* multiplayer experience and all the original downloadable content, is a must-have for fans of the series and a welcome rejuvenation of Xbox Live's most popular exclusive shooter.

TOP 10 GAMES: 4 TO 10

! TURN TO P.24 TO CHECK OUT THE BEST NEW RELEASES FOR YOUR FAVOURITE PLATFORMS.

4 FIFA 10

(EA, 2009)
Ever the fan favourite, *FIFA* has finally surpassed its rival *Pro Evolution Soccer* in critical reception as well as sales figures. Each annual update brings gamers closer to the experience of a real football game, with increasingly lifelike players, more realistic animations and just enough gameplay tweaks to keep fans coming back, year after year. Highlights of the latest edition include "Virtual Pro", a system that allows gamers to create their own soccer player and guide him through the various season modes available in the game.

5 ASSASSIN'S CREED II

(Ubisoft, 2009)
Ubisoft Montreal's latest open-world sneak-em-up builds admirably on the successes and failures of its prequel. A stronger plot, more stealth and less repetitive gameplay prove to be a winning formula in the game's new setting of Renaissance Italy. New features include the player's ability to operate in water, which is particularly important in the canal-veined setting of Venice, where players can swim, travel in small boats and drag unsuspecting enemies under the water. Players can also now take to the air, using the flying machine built by new ally, and all round Renaissance genius, Leonardo da Vinci.

6 UNCHARTED 2: AMONG THIEVES

(Sony, 2009)
The return of the intrepid Nathan Drake was always going to be hotly anticipated by fans of the PlayStation 3 exclusive, and developer Naughty Dog has more than delivered the goods in this second outing. The addition of both co-operative and competitive modes this time around makes for a mouthwatering multiplayer offering, while all-new stealth segments further enrich the single-player campaign. Together with a brand-new mystery to unravel, based around the historical explorer Marco Polo, *Uncharted 2* is essential gaming for any self-respecting action-adventure fan.

* **NEW RECORD**
* **UPDATED RECORD**

450... the staggering number of Ubisoft personnel involved in the development of *Assassin's Creed II* – almost three times as many as worked on the first game.

GUINNESS WORLD RECORDS

×02 ×03 ×01   00024210 3

8 **LEFT 4 DEAD 2**
(Valve, 2009)
The zombie apocalypse hits New Orleans in Valve's frantic survival horror shooter. The trademark mix of spooky environments, colourful characters and terrifying boss fights returns in style for another slice of tense co-op action.

7 **NEW SUPER MARIO BROS. WII**
(Nintendo, 2009)
This new take on the 25-year-old formula sees the world's most famous plumber team up for some "co-opetition": up to four players tackle the game's 2D platforming levels together as both allies and rivals. With such strong affection for the Mushroom Kingdom from both Nintendo and gamers, *New Super Mario Bros. Wii* was always guaranteed to be a smash hit.

9 **BORDERLANDS**
(2K Games, 2009)
Veteran shooter developer Gearbox's attempt to marry shooting and looting is one of only two non-sequels in this year's list. *Borderlands'* millions of combat options and 60-plus hours of play provide one of the most refreshing and addictive gaming experiences of the year. And, being the first title in a planned series, it may well have a sequel of its own in next year's chart.

10 **SCRIBBLENAUTS**
(Warner Bros. Interactive Entertainment, 2009)
While it's let down a little by its skittish controls, there's no denying the importance of 5th Cell's groundbreaking puzzler. With a dictionary of at least 20,000 recognized words, and the motto "write anything, solve everything", there's never been a game that has put such a strong emphasis on players using their imaginations. The result bodes extremely well for future releases from the developer.

FACT

Borderlands, the apocalyptic first-person shooter from developer Gearbox, features a random content creation system capable of generating literally millions of weapon variations. The system also affects the behaviour of in-game enemies, so that players can never tell exactly how they will react or attack – which should keep them on their toes!

TRIVIA

Deciding on a game's box art is always a tricky business, with multinational releases calling for multicultural considerations. However, Valve's Left 4 Dead 2 appears to have run into more problems than most. The new artwork (above left) was supposed to feature the original thumbless hand minus two torn-off fingers, but this was deemed too gory for the USA so the fingers were hastily reinstated, albeit folded over. However, the hand still caused problems for the UK, where the resulting reverse "V" gesture is considered offensive. To fix the issue, the whole hand had to be turned around on the UK cover, so that the palm faces towards the viewer – which ironically, given the game's ultra-violent content, results in a gesture of peace.

YEAR IN REVIEW: OCT TO MAR

! FAST FORWARD TO P.40 TO LOOK INTO THE FUTURE OF GAMING.

OCTOBER 2008

▸ Richard Garriott (pictured), the creator of *Ultima and Tabula Rasa*, became the first game developer to travel into space. His trip lasted 10 days and cost $30 million (£18.2 million).

▸ Sony recalled millions of copies of *LittleBigPlanet* after Muslim groups complained that the soundtrack featured phrases from the Qu'ran.

▸ Will Wright, the brains behind *The Sims* and *Spore*, gave $3,000 (£1,820) to John McCain's campaign to become US President. Supporters of Barack Obama's campaign included *Guitar Hero* creator Alex Rigopulos, who donated $32,900 (£19,960).

▸ A spokesperson for the New York Police Department condemned *Saints Row 2*, claiming the game was "encouraging depravity and immorality while glorifying criminal behaviour".

■ **NEW RECORD**
□ **UPDATED RECORD**

> *We tried to make it feel less like an incursion and more like a war… you're part of something bigger.*
>
> Rod Fergusson, Senior Producer on Gears of War 2, explaining the difference between the original game and its sequel »

NOVEMBER 2008

▸ *Gears of War 2* sold more than 2 million copies worldwide during its opening weekend launch (pictured). A record 15 million hours of gameplay were racked up and players unlocked over 19 million Achievements.

▸ 2D Boy, developer of PC title *World of Goo*, calculated that only one in 10 players of the game had actually bought it, while the rest were using illegal copies.

▸ Sony announced that the number of PlayStation Network users had reached 14 million.

DECEMBER 2008

▸ Research firm Nielsen reported that US gamers spent more time playing the PS2 (pictured) than any other home console in 2008. Leading the charge for current generation consoles was the Xbox 360, which was next on the list, followed by the Wii.

▸ EA's *FIFA 09* took the Christmas No.1 spot in the UK games charts, narrowly beating *Call of Duty: World at War* into second place.

▸ Sony launched its free online community *PlayStation Home*. More than 3.4 million PS3 owners joined within the first month.

▸ The Nintendo Wii was revealed to be the most searched-for item on online auction site eBay.

JANUARY 2009

> *EVE Online* player "Xabier" caused a financial crisis after running off with ISK 80 billion of in-game currency. Xabier had been an employee of Dynasty Banking, which gave him access to other players' investments.

> ELSPA reported 83 million games were sold in the UK during 2008, bringing the total amount spent to £1.9 billion ($3.13 billion). *FIFA 09* (pictured) was the best-selling UK title, with 2 million copies shifted in just three months.

> Scientists at Oxford University, UK, suggested that *Tetris* could combat the effects of post-traumatic stress disorder.

> Movie director Uwe Boll, best known for his adaptations of videogames such as *Alone in the Dark* and *House of the Dead*, received the less-than-coveted Worst Career Achievement lifetime award at the anti-Oscar® "Razzies".

TRIVIA

> On 13 November 2008, Blizzard launched new expansion pack World of Warcraft: Wrath of the Lich King *(above)*. It became the fastest-selling PC game of all time, with 2.8 million copies sold in the first 24 hours of release.

> Wrath of the Lich King *raised the level cap in WoW from 70 to 80. The first player to reach level 80 was "Nymh", playing on the French-language server Drek'thar. Nymh spent 27 hours grinding monsters in the Grizzly Hills area to achieve the goal.*

> On 16 March 2009, the MMORPG EverQuest *celebrated its 10th anniversary, and Publisher Sony Online Entertainment marked the occasion by hosting a series of in-game events.*

FEBRUARY 2009

> Nintendo welcomed the decision of a Japanese court to ban sales of the R4 and R4i cards (pictured) often used to store pirated DS games.

> Dermatologists identified a condition they named PlayStation Palmar Hidradenitis, or "PlayStationitis" for short. Symptoms include painful sores on the hands caused by sweat produced while gaming.

> Nintendo and SEGA announced that, following the success of *Mario and Sonic at the Olympic Games*, the long-time rivals were to meet up again in *Mario and Sonic at the Olympic Winter Games*.

> Rockstar released the first *Grand Theft Auto IV* expansion pack, *The Lost and Damned*. It received rave reviews and Microsoft claimed it broke the record for downloadable content sales on Xbox Live.

MARCH 2009

> Nintendo boss Satoru Iwata unveiled a new *Zelda* game for the DS – *The Legend of Zelda: Spirit Tracks* (pictured) – at the Game Developers Conference in San Francisco, USA.

> The number of *Halo 3* matches played online reached 1 billion, which is equivalent to 64,109 years of playtime.

> Metallica drummer Lars Ulrich admitted that his children are better than him at *Guitar Hero* – even when it comes to playing his own songs.

> The National Center for the History of Electronic Games opened in Rochester, New York, USA. The museum, said to be the first of its kind, exhibits more than 15,000 items.

> David Hayter, who provides the voice of Solid Snake in the *Metal Gear* series, set up his own production company – Dark Hero Studios. The company's first project is *Demonology*, a movie inspired by Hayter's own experience of attending an international school in Japan.

YEAR IN REVIEW: APR TO SEP

! DON'T BECOME A COUCH CASUALTY! TURN TO P.132 FOR TOP GAMING HEALTH TIPS.

The Pirate Bay

APRIL 2009

▣ The founders of The Pirate Bay (logo pictured), a website that allows users to share music, movie and videogame files, were sentenced to a year in prison by a Swedish court. They were also ordered to pay $4.5 million (£3 million) in damages.
▣ Scientists at Huddersfield University (UK) found that racing games cause more agitation and aggression in players than shooters. That's life in the fast lane for you...
▣ The British Army launched *Start Thinking, Soldier*, a free, web-based, point n click Flash game designed to attract new recruits into the military.
▣ A six-year-old Norwegian boy asked permission from King Harald V to change his name to Sonic X, after the famous videogame hedgehog. The King refused to grant the boy's request immediately, and told the youth to wait until he was 18.
▣ Konami cancelled plans to publish *Six Days in Fallujah*, a videogame based on the Iraq war, following protests from soldiers' relatives and anti-war campaigners.

▣ NEW RECORD
▢ UPDATED RECORD

MAY 2009

▣ Edinburgh Zoo (UK) officials renamed their wolverine "Logan" to celebrate the release of the *X-Men Origins: Wolverine* videogame (pictured).
▣ 3D Realms, the studio working on long-awaited shooter *Duke Nukem Forever*, shut down due to financial difficulties. The game had been in development for over a decade.
▣ The head of the UK's Serious Organised Crime Agency claimed prisoners were using PlayStations to communicate with the outside world and commit crimes. The Prison Service denied the allegations.
▣ To celebrate the launch of *BIG Family Games*, THQ delivered a specially commissioned gold-plated Nintendo Wii to Buckingham Palace.
▣ Ex-metaller Ozzy Osbourne (UK) signed up to star in heavy metal-themed game *Brütal Legend* alongside Motörhead frontman Lemmy Kilmister (UK).

JUNE 2009

▣ Nintendo announced *DS Classroom* (pictured), a piece of software that allows teachers to communicate with up to 50 DS handhelds at once. It also allows students to send test answers directly to their teacher's PC.
▣ Scottish developer T-Enterprise cancelled plans to produce a game set in the Guantánamo Bay, Cuba, detention facility after being accused of glamorizing terrorism. Former Guantánamo prisoner Moazzam Begg (UK) had been hired as a consultant on the proposed game.
▣ At E3 2009, Shigeru Miyamoto (Japan) demonstrated *New Super Mario Bros. Wii*, the first Mario game to feature a four-player co-op mode, while Nintendo President Satoru Iwata (Japan) showed off Wii Vitality, a sensor that slips on to the user's finger and tracks his or her heart rate.
▣ US President Barack Obama encouraged parents to get their children to "step away from videogames and spend more time playing outside".
▣ EA Sports boss Peter Moore (UK) challenged President Obama to try out fitness title *EA Sports Active*, promising: "I guarantee you'll need aides saying 'Yes You Can!' to finish your first workout!"

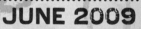

41,000... the number of people who attended the 2009 Electronic Entertainment Expo, better known as E3, in June 2009.

AUGUST 2009

> Sony stole the show at the GamesCom convention in Cologne, unveiling a thinner, lighter console – the PS3 "slim". The company also announced plans to release PSP Minis, games limited to 100 MB and costing under $7 (£4.20) each.
> Microsoft's big GamesCom reveal was the announcement that *Fable III* was in development. The third instalment in the series will let players govern the kingdom of Albion, deciding whether to be a benevolent ruler or a tyrant.
> The Blizzard fan convention, BlizzCon, was held in Anaheim, California, USA. All of the 20,000 tickets available for the two-day event, priced at $125 (£74) each, sold out in just eight minutes.
> Sony revealed that over 1 million people had used PS3 music service VidZone in the eight weeks since launch, streaming more than 100 million videos. "Boom Boom Pow" by The Black Eyed Peas (pictured) was the most popular video, but Michael Jackson dominated the chart, with six top 10 songs.

JULY 2009

> Microsoft revealed that seven Japanese animation studios were working on a series of anime shorts titled *Halo Legends* (pictured).
> More than 28,000 German gamers signed a petition against a proposed government ban on videogames with violent content, or "killerspiele", while a further 400 took part in a protest march through the city of Karlsruhe.
> British psychiatrist Dr Richard Graham announced plans to offer in-game addiction therapy to young *World of Warcraft* players. He claimed some fans were spending up to 16 hours a day on the game, neglecting their studies and social lives in the process.
> Activision priced *Call of Duty: Modern Warfare 2* at $60 (£36) in the US and £55 ($88) in the UK. The company blamed the high UK price tag on a weak pound and record development costs.
> Sam Raimi, director of the *Spider-Man* films, signed up to direct the big-screen adaptation of Blizzard's *World of Warcraft*.

SEPTEMBER 2009

> Courtney Love, the widow of Kurt Cobain (both USA), threatened to sue Activision over the Nirvana singer's appearance as an unlockable playable character in *Guitar Hero 5*. Cobain's former bandmates also said they were dismayed that his avatar (pictured) could perform other artists' songs.
> At the Tokyo Game Show, Microsoft showed how Project Natal's motion-sensing technology could be used to play *Katamari Damacy*. Not to be outdone, Sony revealed at the same event that *Resident Evil 5: The Director's Cut* would be playable with its own new PS3 motion controller, dubbed the "PlayStation Wand".
> *Tomb Raider* creator Toby Gard said goodbye to Eidos and Lara Croft, the character he designed nearly 13 years ago, to pursue new challenges.
> The PS3 "slim" arrived in stores and was an instant hit. More than 150,000 units were sold in Japan during the first week, while UK sales rose by 999% in just seven days. By the end of the month, over 1 million PS3 "slim" consoles had been sold worldwide.

PRO-GAMING REVIEW

MANY PRO-GAMERS CUT THEIR TEETH ON SHOOTER TITLES – CHECK THEM OUT FROM P.44.

★ NEW RECORD
■ UPDATED RECORD

AT THE CORE OF ELECTRONIC SPORTS IS THE PHILOSOPHY THAT NO MATTER WHO OR WHERE YOU ARE IN THE WORLD, EVERYONE HAS THE POTENTIAL TO BE A VIDEOGAMES WORLD CHAMPION

■ FIRST FEMALE PRO-GAMER TO WIN A KESPA MATCH

Holder:
SEO JI-SOO (TOSSGIRL)
(South Korea) Although Korea's renowned pro-gaming scene has seen a number of competitions for female players in the past, the only woman currently active in the male-dominated Shinhan Bank Proleague is Seo Ji-Soo (ToSsGirL). She is signed to team STX SouL and boasts an impressive Actions Per Minute average of 360. In 2008's Gom Averatec-Intel Classic Season 2, ToSsGirL defeated pro-gamer Modern 2-0 in a *StarCraft* match, becoming the first female gamer ever to win a KeSPA-sanctioned tournament match.

The past year has been tough for electronic sports (eSports), with initiatives worldwide being hampered by the global economic slowdown. eSports remains heavily reliant on the financial backing of software and hardware firms and, when their marketing budgets tighten, eSports feels the pinch. One established tournament to succumb to the funding gap was the Electronic Sports World Cup (ESWC), which had run major championships since 2003. In response, a spokesperson admitted that "the current global economic context is not favourable".

Economic frailties were also behind the sudden demise in 2008 of the Championship Gaming Series (CGS). Having sustained two seasons, aired on major international TV networks, the CGS had represented a real attempt to market eSports to a worldwide audience. Before the collapse, contracted CGS players were receiving monthly salaries ranging from $2,500 to $3,300 (£1,500 to £2,000).

It's not all doom and gloom, though. The prospects for premier eSports event the World Cyber Games (WCG) in Chengdu, China, look secure, with the eighth annual event taking place in November 2009 and featuring the world's most talented gamers playing well-known PC and Xbox 360 games.

One of the longest-serving games in tournament line-ups, including the WCG's, is the team-based first-person shooter (FPS) *Counter-Strike*, whose continued presence at worldwide tournaments is testimony to the game's ongoing appeal. Despite this, *Call of Duty 4* has picked up a respectable following of its own, and it is interesting that a second team-based FPS has broken through where duelling FPS games, such as

LAN PARTIES

eSports events regularly employ LANs (Local Area Networks) to enable a large number of people to play online together at the same time – but they're not just used for pro-gaming. LAN parties, where people get together to indulge in a long weekend of gaming for fun, have a proud tradition, and people travel great distances to attend them. Hamar in Norway, for example, normally boasts a population of 29,211, but this swells to 33,393 when the annual LAN party is on – a population rise of around 17%.

Unreal Tournament 3 and *Quake 4*, have failed to inspire a major competitive scene. It remains to be seen whether the growing success of *Quake Live!* can reverse this trend.

EA's *FIFA* series is another perennial eSports hit, with numerous online leagues and major tournaments based around the series' money-spinning annual releases. Meanwhile, real-time strategy action

« *I work out a lot – you know, being physically fit and making sure your neurotransmitters are working properly…*
Johnathan "Fatal1ty" Wendel »

$150,000 (£84,400)... prize money offered by the CyberAthlete Professional League in 2005, the **largest cash prize in a professional videogame tournament**.

OVERVIEW

> The near-universal penetration of computer and console technology, in conjunction with the growth of the Internet, has created a global gaming infrastructure tapped into by millions of people every day. The challenge for the eSports community is to mould this resource into a competitive spectacle, where the best players are given recognition as true sporting champions.

is still dominated by *Warcraft III* and *StarCraft*, despite their age. While the forthcoming release of *StarCraft II* looks set to address the issue, the transition between the two titles will be a seminal moment for eSports, especially in Asia, where the televized Shinhan Bank Proleague is followed by thousands of fans.

In the wider world of eSports, there are literally hundreds of teams, each with their own ambitions, capabilities and traditions. These teams operate by recruiting and supporting talented gamers to play under their banner. The team can then market their shared success to the wider business world. The most financially secure teams are found in South Korea, but because of their tight domestic focus they lack the global profile of Western teams.

Fnatic, Mousesports and Team Dignitas are a few of the prominent Western teams, but it is SK Gaming (Sweden) that remains the most influential. SK Gaming receives global

DREAMHACK

The **largest LAN party** took place between 29 November and 1 December 2007 at DreamHack AB Winter in Jönköping, Sweden. It consisted of 10,544 unique computers and 11,060 participants. At a previous DreamHack, held on 27 November 2004, the Swedish Microsoft-Unisys team set a record for the **most action gamers playing on a single server**, with 1,073 gamers playing *Counter-Strike* on just one Unisys ES7000 server. More recently, DreamHack Summer 2009 played host to another *Counter-Strike* record: **most kills scored against human opponents on *Counter-Strike 1.6***. This was achieved by Bjørn "Threat" Pers (Sweden), who amassed an impressive 518 kills at the Jönköping event, held on 14 June 2009.

EXPERT

> Robert "Moyes" Haxton has been involved in competitive gaming for nine years. Having taken part in championships across the globe, he now works for Team Dignitas, one of the world's premier eSports teams, specializing in real-time strategy games.

TRIVIA

> In addition to the standard PC and console games, the World Cyber Games 2009 features competitions for two mobile phone games: *Asphalt 4* and *Wise Star 2*. This is double the number seen at the 2008 event.

> The PC format dominates the world of professional gaming, accounting for eight out of the 12 titles featured at the World Cyber Games 2009, which include *Warcraft III*, *StarCraft* and *FIFA 09*.

> The growing popularity of rhythm games has resulted in the inclusion of a *Guitar Hero* category in the World Cyber Games since 2008.

ESPORTS — THE KEY PLAYERS

JOHNATHAN "FATALITY" WENDEL (USA)
With world titles in five different games, as certified by Guinness World Records, American Johnathan Wendel has temporarily halted his phenomenally successful playing career to concentrate on his licensing deals with hardware manufacturers, who use his patented player name on their products. He has been a spokesman for the late Championship Gaming Series and regularly features as a commentator at eSports events.

MANUEL "GRUBBY" SCHENKHUIZEN (Netherlands)
There are plenty of big names within the highly competitive world of *Warcraft III*, but few come much bigger than Manuel "Grubby" Schenkhuizen, whose name reverberates across the world of eSports. He has secured major titles every year since 2004 and, with estimated career prize

winnings of $160,000 (£96,600), has been one of the few to significantly benefit from gaming financially. It is his ability to remain at the forefront of an incredibly competitive community, for such a long period of time that truly inspires professional gamers.

DAVID "ZACCUBUS" TREACY (UK)
Few have shown the same dedication to eSports as the UK's David "Zaccubus" Treacy. At 24, he continues to commit himself to pro-gaming, despite the competitive decline of the First Person Shooters with which he made his name – *Unreal Tournament 2004*, *Painkiller* and *Quake*.

LEE JAE-DONG (N.DIE_JAEDONG) (South Korea)
The top-ranked Korean *StarCraft* pro-gamer as of August 2009, and current Ongame.net champion, n.Die_Jaedong boasts an Action Per Minute average of 600, which equates to 10 mouse clicks or movements every second. The star player for the Hwaseung OZ team, he has gained a reputation as a legend-killer by beating many elite players.

recognition from professional gamers and its website acts as a community page that draws a vast number of hits each month and informs the views of both serious and casual gamers alike.

No one can doubt the growing influence of the eSports movement, but technology, design studios, governing bodies, event organizers and gamers themselves still have plenty of work to do before its full potential can be realized. However, there is no reason why, one day, eSports cannot go on to rival more traditional sports, with large prize funds, mainstream media attention and spectacular championships that captivate the world.

PROJECT
NATAL

XBOX 360

While the Wii boasted the **first motion-sensitive controllers**, Microsoft's forthcoming Project Natal for Xbox 360 seeks to do away with them altogether, offering the most advanced controller-free gaming experience.

CONTENTS:

BEST OF PS3

! WHAT ABOUT SONY'S HANDHELD PLATFORM? CHECK OUT P.36 FOR ALL THINGS PSP.

SONY HAD A VERY BUSY YEAR IN 2009, WITH THE LONG-AWAITED ARRIVAL OF THE PS3 "SLIM" AND AN INCREASINGLY RICH VARIETY OF WORLD-CLASS PLATFORM-EXCLUSIVE GAMES

PS3 SLIM

CPU: Cell Broadband Engine
HDD SIZE: 120 GB
MEMORY: 256 MB XDR
PS2 COMPATIBILITY: No
COLOUR: Black
USB 2.0 PORTS: 2
WI-FI: Yes
HDMI CABLE INCLUDED: Yes

« *The quality of games you can make on PS3 is so much higher.*
Gran Turismo creator Kazunori Yamauchi »

SYSTEM UPDATES

▷ *On 18 August 2009, Sony unveiled the much-anticipated PS3 "slim" at Gamescom 2009 in Cologne, Germany.*

▷ *At the same event, Sony also announced that it had signed up over 27 million users worldwide to its online community gaming service PlayStation Network.*

▷ *Sony launched a wireless keypad for PS3 on 28 November 2008. The keypad clips on to the top of DualShock 3 and Sixaxis controllers and features a compact QWERTY keyboard. It also has shortcut buttons for quick access to the message inbox and text chat.*

KILLZONE 2

Publisher: Sony
Release date: 27 February 2009
Sony's answer to *Halo 3* was a huge hit when it finally reached the shops in February 2009. In *Killzone 2*, the elite operatives of the ISA battle the Helghast once again, but this time they must fight on the enemy's home planet. The game features highly advanced AI, detailed and destructible environments and some spectacular special effects. An essential addition to the collection for any first-person-shooter fan.

✳ NEW RECORD
▣ UPDATED RECORD

Only On PlayStation. PlayStation.Network
KILLZONE 2

NOBY NOBY BOY
Publisher: Namco Bandai
Release date: 19 February 2009
In *Noby Noby Boy*, players control a character simply named Boy, stretching his cylindrical body around the planets of the solar system. There are hours of fun to be had experimenting with Boy's stretchy form – you can even loop him through holes or tie him in a knot. The lengths players stretch Boy to are uploaded via the Internet, and a persistent character, Girl, grows accordingly. Each time Girl reaches a new point in the solar system, new levels are unlocked. It might all sound a bit confusing, but once you give *Noby Noby Boy* a try, you're sure to be hooked.

EYEPET
Publisher: Sony **Release date:** 23 October 2009
This platform-exclusive, developed at Sony's London Studio, is designed to showcase the true power of the PlayStation Eye camera peripheral for PS3. *EyePet* brings a virtual pet into your home or, more accurately, brings your home into the world of a virtual pet. An Augmented Reality (AR) game, the PlayStation Eye captures footage of you and your house and displays it on screen in real time alongside a monkey-like pet you can interact with. Ideal for anyone who isn't allowed to have a real pet at home.

PLAYSTATION HOME
Publisher: Sony **Release date:** 11 December 2008
Not a game in itself, PlayStation Home allows users with a PlayStation Network account to create their own customizable avatar and virtual apartment. They can then explore a virtual community (or Home World), interact with other PS3 users via voice or text chat, watch videos advertising upcoming games, and even shop for virtual items and play mini games.

TRIVIA

> The highlight of Sony's E3 2009 conference was the unveiling of a new motion-sensitive controller. It features a glowing, colour-changing ball that the PlayStation Eye camera uses to track movement.

> In July 2008, Sony introduced the "Trophy" system as part of the platform's operating system update. Trophies come in four grades – bronze, silver, gold and platinum – and reward players for their in-game achievements. Players can even upload their trophy haul to their PlayStation Network account to compare with their friends.

> On 30 April 2009, David Reeves retired as president of Sony Computer Entertainment Europe. He had been with the company for 14 years, during which time he helped to sell millions of consoles. He also visited 66 of the 106 countries where the PlayStation is available. "I am going to spend my time now trying to repay society for all I have taken from it," Reeves said on retiring. "If your children are wondering why their ski instructor is very elderly, your car mechanic has a bad back, or the social worker keeps bringing you PSP games, then it could just be me!"

BEST OF WII

! FOR NINTENDO ON THE MOVE, CHECK OUT BEST OF DS ON P.34.

ONE OF THE WII'S MAJOR ATTRACTIONS IS THE NUMBER OF EXCLUSIVE TITLES AVAILABLE FOR IT – HERE, WE TAKE A LOOK AT A FEW OF THE GAMES DESTINED FOR BIG THINGS IN 2010

SYSTEM UPDATES

> The hardware spec of the Wii has not changed since the console launched in November 2006. However, in June 2009, Nintendo announced a new glossy black model for Japan, dubbed KURO Wii – "kuro" meaning "black" in Japanese. The new unit (pictured) was priced at 25,000¥ (around £160/$265), the same price at which the original white console was launched.

> In October 2008, Nintendo finally addressed the issue of the Wii's limited storage capacity. Company president Satoru Iwata announced a new firmware update that would allow users to download WiiWare and Virtual Console games directly to an SD card. In addition, the size of SD cards that could be used would no longer be limited to 2 GB. The update was released in Japan on 25 March 2009.

- NEW RECORD
- UPDATED RECORD

WII

CPU: PowerPC-based "Broadway" processor
FLASH RAM SIZE: 512 MB
MEMORY:
64 MB GDDR3 RAM
GAMECUBE COMPATIBILITY: Yes
COLOUR: White (black model in Japan only)
USB 2.0 PORTS: 2
WI-FI: Yes

POWER

A

HOME

1

2

Wii

POWER

RESET

EJECT

Wii

Nintendo

« Life is a videogame. No matter how good you get, you are always zapped in the end.
Shigeru Miyamoto, game designer

50 MILLION... the number of Wii consoles sold as of March 2009, as announced by Nintendo president Satoru Iwata at the company's 2009 GDC keynote.

LITTLE KING'S STORY

Publisher: Rising Star Games **Release date:** 24 April 2009
Members of the development team behind this RPG worked on titles such as *Harvest Moon, No More Heroes* and *Final Fantasy XII*, and their talent shines through in *Little King's Story*. Gameplay is a combination of real-time strategy, adventure and simulation elements. As the King, players command their subjects to dig for treasure, construct buildings, fight off enemies and expand their territory. The game has a unique fantasy feel to it and storybook-style visuals. The control and menu systems are straightforward enough for casual gamers to get to grips with, but there's real depth here for serious RPG buffs, too.

MADWORLD

Publisher: SEGA
Release date: 10 March 2009
Inspired by the graphic-novel style of Frank Miller's *Sin City* (2005) movie, developer Platinum Games went black and white with their well received Wii offering, *MadWorld*. The game is fairly unique as Wii titles go, featuring an uncharacteristically high level of bloody violence and a main character, Jack Cayman, who wields a retractable chainsaw in place of his right arm. Assuming the role of Jack, players must fight for their survival in a deadly game show called *Death Watch*.

WII MOTIONPLUS

Nintendo continues to develop new peripherals for the Wii, such as MotionPlus. This small rectangular device clips on to the base of the Wii Remote and allows the console to track player movements with incredible accuracy. The MotionPlus peripheral detects the slightest tilt, turn and twist of the Remote so that gameplay feels more realistic than ever.

NEW SUPER MARIO BROS. WII

Publisher: Nintendo
Release date: 4 November 2009
This game is designed to add a new twist to a classic series by allowing up to four people to play together. In *New Super Mario Bros. Wii*, players can cooperate or compete as they explore side-scrolling 2D worlds. They can even pick their fellow players up, saving them from danger or else throwing them straight into it. There are new items to play with, too, such as the propeller suit, which allows players to float through the air by shaking the Remote. *New Super Mario Bros. Wii* offers an ingenious new take on the games that made Nintendo so successful in the first place.

TRIVIA

▶ During a private press conference held at E3 2009, Shigeru Miyamoto confirmed a second *Zelda* title for the Wii was in development. He did not reveal the name of the game, but did show the audience an example of early concept art.

▶ With New Play Control!, Nintendo hopes to bring classic GameCube titles to a new audience by revamping them for the Wii. One example is Donkey Kong Jungle Beat. The original game required a set of bongo controllers, but the new version uses the Remote and Nunchuk. In short, New Play Control! offers a great way to take a trip down memory lane or introduce younger gamers to what they missed.

▶ Despite difficult economic times, Nintendo enjoyed bumper sales in 2008. Data trackers NPD declared the Wii was the first home entertainment console to be purchased by upwards of 10 million Americans in a single year. The DS came in second, with 9.95 million handhelds sold.

BEST OF XBOX 360

! TO FIND OUT WHAT OUR READERS CONSIDER TO BE THEIR TOP 50 GAMES, TURN TO PP.186–195.

MICROSOFT HAS HAD ANOTHER SUCCESSFUL YEAR IN 2009, WITH EXCLUSIVE DOWNLOADABLE EXPANSIONS, MUCH-ANTICIPATED SEQUELS AND EVEN SOME ONLINE GAMES THAT LET YOUR NXE AVATAR JOIN IN

XBOX 360 ELITE

CPU: IBM PowerPC Custom Core
HDD SIZE: 120 GB
MEMORY: 512 MB GDDR3 RAM
XBOX COMPATIBILITY: Yes, for over 450 titles
COLOUR: Black
USB 2.0 PORTS: 3
WI-FI: No (add-on available separately)
HEADSET INCLUDED: Yes
ETHERNET CABLE INCLUDED: Yes
HDMI CABLE INCLUDED: Yes
XBOX LIVE MEMBERSHIP: Silver, plus one-month Gold trial

XBOX 360 ARCADE

CPU: IBM PowerPC Custom Core
HDD SIZE: None (includes a 256 MB memory unit)
MEMORY: 512 MB GDDR3 RAM
XBOX COMPATIBILITY: No
COLOUR: White
USB 2.0 PORTS: 3
WI-FI: No (add-on available separately)
HEADSET INCLUDED: No
ETHERNET CABLE INCLUDED: No
HDMI CABLE INCLUDED: No
XBOX LIVE MEMBERSHIP: Silver, plus one-month Gold trial

✳ NEW RECORD
▶ UPDATED RECORD

363,850... the highest Gamerscore on Xbox 360, held by Raymond "Stallion83" Cox (USA) as of 15 September 2009.

SYSTEM UPDATES

▷ On 19 November 2008, Microsoft launched the New Xbox Experience (NXE) update for the Xbox 360 dashboard. NXE allows 360 owners to create customizable avatars, host virtual parties and play community-created games.

▷ At E3 2009, Microsoft announced Xbox LIVE Primetime, a series of games where Xbox LIVE members can play in live contests against each other using their avatars. The games are styled in the form of live television shows, with the action taking place at set times to mimic the live format.

1 VS 100

Publisher: Microsoft
Release date: 8 May 2009
The first Xbox LIVE Primetime title to be played by the public was a beta version of the popular Endemol game show *1 vs 100*. The game, free for Xbox LIVE Gold members, allows players to pit themselves, via their NXE avatars, against each other as either the "1" or as part of the mob, with successful contestants taking home Microsoft Points. Despite only being a beta version, the game broke the record for the **most contestants on a single episode of a game show**, with a total of 114,000 players logged in for one session in July 2009.

GEARS OF WAR 2

Publisher: Microsoft **Release date:** 7 November 2008
"Bigger, better and more badass" is how *Gears of War* designer Cliff Bleszinski describes the second instalment in this blockbuster shooter series. It sees hero Marcus Fenix fighting off the Locust threat once again, using an array of even more powerful weapons. Highlights of *Gears 2* include improved co-op play, chainsaw duels and the option to use enemies' bodies as shields. More than 2 million copies were sold during the game's first weekend on sale, and during the same period 1.5 million *Gears 2* fans racked up 15 million hours of gameplay on Xbox LIVE.

« *Every day, there's a live host giving out real prizes based on questions that they wrote that morning.*
Xbox LIVE's Marc Whitten on Xbox LIVE Primetime

FORZA MOTORSPORT 3

Publisher: Microsoft **Release date:** 23 October 2009
According to Microsoft, *Forza Motorsport 3* is the defining racing game of this console generation and the best driving simulator available. It is certainly one of the most realistic, with superb vehicle handling and stunning high-definition visuals that run at 60 frames per second. There's plenty of content for racing fans to lap up, including 100 tracks and 400 cars from 50 different manufacturers. In fact, there's so much to *Forza 3* that the game comes on two discs – enough racing action to satisfy even the most dedicated petrolheads.

TRIVIA

▷ A big surprise of 2009 was the announcement that the Metal Gear Solid series would be coming to Xbox 360 for the first time. Solid Snake is having a break, though – Metal Gear Solid: Rising stars the cyborg Raiden.

▷ The Lost and Damned, the first of the Xbox 360-exclusive expansion packs for GTA IV, made its debut as a download in February 2009 to much critical acclaim. The expansion pack is estimated to have sold 1 million downloads in its first month on sale.

▷ Released in November 2008, the Netflicks application allows Xbox LIVE Gold members in the USA to stream thousands of movies. Microsoft estimates that the application has been downloaded over 1 million times.

▷ Kodu, a game-development tool for Xbox 360, was launched in June 2009, and is intended to teach younger players the basics of videogame programming.

BEST OF PC

! FOR MORE PC-SPECIFIC GAMING, CHECK OUT THE SHOOTERS ON P.50.

SYSTEM UPDATES

> The launch of Windows 7 in October 2009 brought about some marginal improvements in visual performance over its Vista predecessor. The new operating system offers updated graphics handling through Direct 3D 11 plus support for multi-touch screens, allowing developers and gamers to take advantage of these new features in games such as Ubisoft's new real-time strategy game, R.U.S.E.

> Hardware manufacturer Asus released the W70vp laptop, with an 18.4-inch screen and Intel Core 2 Duo T9600 processor. At The Gathering LAN party in Hamar, Norway, in April 2009, a modified version was tested and confirmed as the world's fastest overclocked laptop, with a score of 20,342 in the 3DMark06 PC performance benchmarking tool.

ALTHOUGH SOME HARDCORE GAMERS LIKE TO BUILD THEIR OWN MACHINES, THERE ARE MANY FIRMS OFFERING HIGH-END CUSTOM HARDWARE OFF THE SHELF – AND ALIENWARE, ESTABLISHED IN 1996, IS ONE OF THE BIGGEST PLAYERS

ALIENWARE ALX X-58

OS: Windows Vista Home Premium 64-bit
CPU: 3.86GHz Overclocked Intel™ Core i7-975 Extreme Edition
MEMORY: 12 GB, 1600 MHz DDR3
GRAPHICS: 1,792 MB NIVIDIA® GeForce® GTX 295
HARD DRIVES: 7,200 RPM, 64 MB cache, 1 TB storage / 10,000 RPM, 16 MB cache, 2 TB storage
OPTICAL DRIVE: 4x dual-layer Blu-ray burner
NETWORKING: Dual integrated Gigabit Ethernet RJ-45
CASE: Black and chrome
COOLING SYSTEM: Liquid
PRICE: From £2,099 ($1,267)

400,000... the number of copies of *Spore* downloaded illegally in 2008, making it the year's most pirated videogame – an incredible feat, since it was only released in September.

[ ]

GUINNESS WORLD RECORDS

THE SIMS 3

Publisher: EA **Release date:** 2 June 2009

The first two *Sims* titles proved highly popular and the third instalment is no exception – 1.4 million copies were shifted in the first week on sale, making *The Sims 3* EA's fastest-selling PC game in history. During the same period, fans downloaded 7 million pieces of player-created content from *The Sims 3* website. Highlights of the game include the ability to make the characters appear more realistic than ever, thanks to the enhanced Create-a-Sim tool. In addition, players have the option to roam around neighbourhoods seamlessly for the first time. The game, released as both a standard edition and a collector's edition, might not have revolutionized the series, but there's definitely enough new content to ensure fans will come back for more.

WORLD OF WARCRAFT: WRATH OF THE LICH KING

Publisher: Blizzard **Release date:** 13 November 2008

Over four years since its release, *World of Warcraft* still dominates the massively multiplayer online gaming landscape. Blizzard's second expansion pack, *Wrath of the Lich King*, gives players a whole new continent to explore – the forbidding, frozen wasteland of Northrend. The game also introduces a new class, the Death Knight, along with an achievements system and improved player-vs-player options, while the level cap has also been increased to 80. All in all, it's a quality add-on that *WOW* buffs will want to get their teeth into while looking forward to the next instalment, *Cataclysm*, which is due in late 2010.

PLANTS VS. ZOMBIES

Publisher: PopCap
Release date: 5 May 2009

PopCap has been established for years as a leading publisher of casual PC games, having enjoyed great success with blockbusters such as *Peggle* and *Bejeweled*. More recently, *Plants vs. Zombies* has been a big hit, too, thanks to its accessible yet addictive gameplay. It's a tower defence game, in which players must prevent hordes of zombies from making it up their front garden path and through their front door. This is done by planting a variety of mutant flowers and foliage, which keep the zombies at bay. *Plants vs. Zombies* is simple to pick up but its incredible depth means it is also very difficult to put down.

« Initially the expectation was 50 machines a month, maybe 100, and we don't have to work for anybody...

Alienware co-founder Nelson Gonzalez on early expectations for his now multi-million-earning PC hardware company

»

TRIVIA

Videogame piracy continues to plague the PC gaming industry. That includes developers such as Crytek, whose 2007 shooter Crysis was widely copied and illegally downloaded. As a result, company president Cevat Yerli has said the studio will not produce any more PC exclusives in the future.

PC gamers are renowned for adapting their equipment, and outrageously modded PC cases, such as Aleksander Kolesnikov's "Wheel Case", pictured below, are not uncommon. Also subject to idle fingers are the games themselves – in May 2009, GameSpy published a list of the most bizarre mods available. In the top spot is Cat-Life, a mod that allows users to play classic shooter Half-Life from the perspective of a cat. Runners-up include Left 4 Dead mods that feature voiceovers from Bill Cosby and WWE wrestler Macho Man Randy Savage, plus a naughty new spell for Oblivion inspired by the 1992 movie Basic Instinct.

✳ **NEW RECORD**
● **UPDATED RECORD**

! FOR MORE DOUBLE-SCREEN GAMING, CHECK OUT DR. KAWASHIMA'S BRAIN TRAINING ON P.145.

HARDWARE /

BEST OF DS

THE NINTENDO DS SUCCESS STORY CONTINUED INTO 2009, WITH THE US AND EUROPEAN LAUNCHES OF THE HANDHELD'S LATEST UPDATE – THE SLIMMER, SLICKER, CAMERA-LADEN DSI

* NEW RECORD
▢ UPDATED RECORD

NINTENDO DS LITE

WEIGHT: 218 grams
PHYSICAL DIMENSIONS: length 133 mm, height 73.9 mm, depth 21.5 mm
CPU: ARM7 and ARM9 processors
HDD SIZE: 256 KB Flash memory
SD CARD SLOT: No
MEMORY: 4 MB RAM
BATTERY: 1000 mAh (15–19 hours)
GBA COMPATIBLE: Yes
WI-FI: Yes

NINTENDO DSI

WEIGHT: 214 grams
PHYSICAL DIMENSIONS: length 137 mm, height 74.9 mm, depth 18.9 mm
CPU: ARM7 and ARM9 processors
HDD SIZE: 256 MB Flash memory
SD CARD SLOT: Yes
MEMORY: 16 MB RAM
BATTERY: 840 mAh (9–14 hours)
GBA COMPATIBLE: No
WI-FI: Yes

SYSTEM UPDATES

▷ The Nintendo DSi launched in Japan on 1 November 2008. The handheld went on sale in the USA, Europe and Australia the following April. Like the original DS and DS Lite, it features dual screens and is operated using a stylus. However, the DSi is thinner and lighter, while its screens are bigger and brighter. It also has two motion-detecting cameras and in-built Flash memory. Unlike previous iterations, the DSi also has a region-locking system, which means it cannot be used to play games imported from other countries.

I MILLION... the number of copies of *Pokémon Platinum* sold in Japan during the game's first two days on sale, in September 2008, making it the **fastest-selling DS title**.

GRAND THEFT AUTO: CHINATOWN WARS

Publisher: Rockstar **Release date:** 17 March 2009

Critics doubted whether Rockstar could create a *GTA* game for the DS that was as expansive as those on other consoles. However, *Grand Theft Auto: Chinatown Wars* is a triumph, pushing the handheld's technical capabilities to the limit and offering a huge, immersive gameworld to explore. Players take on the role of Huang Lee as he becomes involved with the Triads of Liberty City, uncovering crime and corruption along the way. The game features touch-screen controls, a GPS map system and an extensive collection of mini games. Fans of the series won't be disappointed.

CHRONO TRIGGER

Publisher: Square Enix **Release date:** 6 February 2009

The original SNES version of *Chrono Trigger* was released in 1995, but never made it to PAL regions. Nearly 15 years on, the game finally got a global release in the form of a revamped DS version, which manages to maintain the feel and style of its predecessor. The hero, a young boy called Crono, finds himself travelling through time on a swashbuckling mission to save the world. An epic storyline, sweeping score and unique battle system combine to produce an RPG that still stands up as a classic of the genre.

AIR TRAFFIC CHAOS

Publisher: Majesco

Release date: 9 September 2008

The premise might not seem overly exciting, but *Air Traffic Chaos* somehow manages to be one of the most addictive DS games ever made. Players take on the role of a busy air-traffic controller tasked with managing take-offs, assigning gates and overseeing landings safely, all the while taking into account different weather conditions. Fiendishly difficult at times but also highly rewarding, it is the ideal game to while away long journeys – unless, perhaps, you're on a plane.

[Nintendo] puts in smart nips and tucks to its already-svelte handheld while adding a raft of useful multimedia features.

PC World magazine on Nintendo's new DSi handheld

SHOP TILL YOU DROP

Nintendo launched the new DSi Shop alongside the DSi handheld at the end of 2008. It's an online service that allows users to browse, buy and download specially designed software, known as DSiWare. Thanks to the DSi's expanded Flash memory, applications can be saved directly to the handheld itself.

There are plenty of DSiWare games to choose from, such as *WarioWare: Snapped!*, which is played using the DSi's two motion-sensitive cameras. Other applications include software that lets users make their own animated cartoons, and combine photos to create mini-movies. The DSi Shop also offers the Nintendo DSi Browser, which gives gamers quick and easy Internet access.

FACT

1 In June 2009, Nintendo unveiled DS Classroom, a new piece of software designed for use in schools. It allows teachers to communicate with up to 50 Nintendo DS units using a PC. Students taking part in class tests on their handhelds can send answers straight to their teacher's computer screen. DS Classroom was initially only announced for Japan, where some schools were already using DS consoles as teaching aids on an unofficial basis. If it proves successful, though, DS Classroom could eventually be released in Europe and the USA.

TRIVIA

2 Although released in Japan in September 2008, Nintendo's new Pokémon Platinum only reached US and European shores in March 2009 and May 2009, respectively. Set in the fictional Sinnoh region, the game stars renegade Pokemon Giratina. New features include the Wi-Fi Plaza, which allows up to 20 players to connect online to trade, battle and play mini games, and the Vs. Recorder, which allows players to save and review videos of their battles. There's also the new Distortion World, where the rules of time and space don't apply.

BEST OF PSP

THE SONY PSP IS CONSIDERED TO BE ONE OF THE COOLEST GADGETS EVER MADE – CHECK OUT THE LATEST, GREATEST TITLES FOR GAMING ON THE MOVE

FOR MORE POCKET-SIZED CLASSICS, SEE BEST OF MOBILE PHONES ON P.38.

* NEW RECORD ■ UPDATED RECORD

SYSTEM UPDATES

▷ *The PSP-3000 was launched in October 2008. The updated handheld boasts an enhanced LCD screen that provides higher-quality images, crisper colours and greater definition when used in natural light conditions. Other new features include a built-in microphone for use with applications such as Skype.*

▷ *Sony unveiled the PSP Go at E3 in June 2009. It's the smallest, lightest model to date. Instead of a UMD drive, it has 16 GB of internal Flash memory for storing games, music and movies. The PSP Go also has a unique sliding display, Bluetooth support and a Memory Stick Micro port.*

PSP-3000

WEIGHT: 189 grams
PHYSICAL DIMENSIONS: Length 169.4 mm, height 71.4 mm, depth 18.6 mm
CPU: PSP CPU
HDD SIZE: N/A
MEMORY STICK SLOT: Pro Duo
MEMORY: 64 MB
BATTERY: 1200 mAh (4.5–7 hours)
UMD DRIVE: Yes
MICROPHONE: Yes
WI-FI: Yes

PSP GO

WEIGHT: 158 grams
PHYSICAL DIMENSIONS: Length 128 mm, height 69 mm, depth 16.5 mm
CPU: PSP CPU
HDD SIZE: 16 GB
MEMORY STICK SLOT: Micro
MEMORY: 64 MB
BATTERY: 1200 mAh (3–6 hours)
UMD DRIVE: No
MICROPHONE: Yes
WI-FI: Yes

3.5 MILLION... the number of *Monster Hunter Freedom Unite* games sold in Japan as of 8 July 2009, according to the game's publisher Capcom.

MONSTER HUNTER FREEDOM UNITE

Publisher: Capcom
Release date: 27 March 2008
In Japan, *Monster Hunter* is hugely popular, out-selling both *Pokémon* and *Wii Fit* during 2008. The series has also increased its following in the West with the release of *Monster Hunter Freedom Unite*. Players choose their preferred weapons and armour then embark on epic quests, journeying through forests, swamps and deserts to hunt down fierce monsters. *Monster Hunter* has become a social gaming phenomenon, as up to four players can share their adventures via the PSP's ad hoc mode. However, there's also a single-player option, in which solo gamers are accompanied by an AI-controlled sidekick known as a "Felyne Fighter".

RESISTANCE: RETRIBUTION

Publisher: Sony
Release date: 12 March 2009
Not all console games make the transition to handheld successfully, but *Resistance: Retribution* stands out as one of the best shooters available for PSP. It's set in the weeks following the original PS3 game and sees players take on the role of James Grayson, a former British Marine. He's on a revenge mission to destroy the Chimera and eventually joins the European resistance, otherwise known as the Maquis. Gameplay takes place from a third-person perspective and there's a unique targeting system designed specially for the PSP. Classic weapons such as the Auger and LAARK make an appearance, and there are five multiplayer game modes for up to eight players.

> « *We could put it out at any time, or we could carry on working on it. There's always something to polish.* »
> Kazunori Yamauchi, Gran Turismo creator

GRAN TURISMO

Publisher: Sony **Release date:** 1 October 2009
The PSP version of *Gran Turismo* was first announced at E3 in May 2004, but five years on, fans were still waiting for the game to cross the starting line. According to series creator Kazunori Yamauchi (Japan), the delay was due to the time the development team had to spend on other titles such as *GT Prologue*. However, Yamauchi promised the PSP version would be worth the wait. The game features more than 800 vehicles from manufacturers such as Ferrari and Nissan and over 30 tracks. Also, for the first time in the series, players have the option to share and trade vehicles.

! TURN BACK TO P.24 FOR A DETAILED LOOK AT MODERN GAMING HARDWARE.

BEST OF MOBILE PHONES

SYSTEM UPDATES

> In October 2008, Nokia launched the N85, a new N-Gage compatible smartphone. It came with an 8 GB Micro SD card pre-loaded with demos for more than a dozen games, including Tetris, FIFA 08 and The Sims 2: Pets.

> The iPhone 3GS was unveiled on 8 June 2009. Apple executive Philip Schiller described it as "the fastest, most powerful iPhone yet". New features include a 3-megapixel autofocus camera, video recording, built-in compass, longer battery life and improved 3D graphics. The iPhone 3GS is available in black or white, with storage capacity of 16 GB or 32 GB.

MOBILE PHONE GAMING IN 2009 WAS DOMINATED BY A MASSIVE INCREASE IN RELEASES FOR THE iPHONE AND iPOD TOUCH, BUT OTHER MOBILE PHONE PLATFORMS ARE STILL IN THE FIGHT

« *Better than the DS, better than the PSP.*
ngmoco co-founder Neil Young gives his opinion of the iPhone »

✳ **NEW RECORD**
◉ **UPDATED RECORD**

IPHONE 3GS

WEIGHT: 135 grams
PHYSICAL DIMENSIONS: Length 115.5 mm, width 62.1 mm, depth 12.3 mm
INTERNAL MEMORY: 16 GB or 32 GB
SD CARD SLOT: No
BLUETOOTH: Yes
CAMERA: 3 megapixels
GAMES: App Store software
COLOURS: White or black
STAND-BY TIME: Up to 300 hours
TALK TIME: Up to 12 hours

NOKIA N85

WEIGHT: 128 grams
PHYSICAL DIMENSIONS: Length 103 mm, width 50 mm, depth 16 mm
INTERNAL MEMORY: 85 MB
SD CARD SLOT: Micro SD up to 8 GB
BLUETOOTH: Yes
CAMERA: 5 megapixels
GAMES: N-Gage software
COLOURS: Copper, black
STAND-BY TIME: Up to 363 hours
TALK TIME: Up to 7 hours

21,178... the number of game and entertainment applications available for the iPhone and iPod Touch via Apple's App Store as of 10 September 2009.

GUINNESS WORLD RECORDS: THE VIDEOGAME

Platform: iPhone **Publisher:** TT Games
Release date: 25 July 2009

Think you've got what it takes to be a record-breaker? Find out now, by taking on one of the 36 mini-game challenges featured on TT Games' latest foray into the world of iPhone gaming. As you would expect, the game makes the most of the iPhone's touch-screen interface, with players encouraged to tap and slide their way to greatness. The diversity of the challenges is key here, from most melons smashed to growing the longest fingernails, and the game has something for all.

DOOM RESURRECTION

Platform: iPhone **Publisher:** id Software
Release date: 26 June 2009

id Software's classic first-person shooter series made an impressive debut on the iPhone with *Doom Resurrection*. The game features eight levels built from scratch and an all-new storyline. With the help of a robot sidekick, players must take on an army of demons as they try to invade a Martian research facility. Firing, reloading, dodging and weapon-switching is all done by tapping the screen. The detailed 3D levels are fast-paced and action-packed, and there are some seriously tough bosses to face. *Doom Resurrection* is proof that you don't need a PC to enjoy a good blast of FPS gaming.

WORD-FU

Platform: iPhone **Publisher:** ngmoco
Release date: 27 February 2009

Combine martial arts with wordplay and what do you get? *Word-Fu*, of course, a game that tests players' spelling skills to the limit. Shaking the iPhone rolls nine dice with letters on each side. Players must then use the touch screen to spell out as many words as possible before the time runs out. The goal is to score 5,000 points in a single round, thereby earning the coveted black belt. It's as simple as it sounds – and surprisingly addictive, too.

TAP TAP REVENGE 2

Platform: iPhone
Publisher: Tapulous
Release date: 3 March 2009

Like rhythm games *Rock Band* and *Guitar Hero*, the *Tap Tap* titles feature coloured notes scrolling down the screen in time to music. Players have to tap the balls at the right moment to score points, and sometimes shake the iPhone to match the beat. Along with a new Career Achievements system, *Tap Tap Revenge 2* boasts more than 150 songs, as well as Facebook integration and online options. There have also been a number of *Tap Tap Revenge* spin-off games, featuring songs from artists such as Nine Inch Nails, Weezer, Coldplay and Lady Gaga.

FUTURE GAMING

! GETTING AHEAD OF OURSELVES? THEN TURN BACK TO P.18 TO DISCOVER WHAT WENT ON LAST YEAR.

AS WE LOOK AHEAD TO A FUTURE OF HANDS-FREE AND SERVER-POWERED GAMING, IT SEEMS THE DAYS OF HARDWARE-HEAVY GAMEPLAY COULD SOON BE A THING OF THE PAST

CLOUD GAMING

> *One of the most exciting new gaming technologies to come out of 2009 was "cloud computing". This allows users to stream games directly into their homes via the Internet (the cloud), rather than having to buy or download physical copies. All the data-heavy computing takes place in vast server farms hundreds of miles away, delivering to users the smooth, lag-free gameplay they crave.*

GAIKAI

In July 2009, renowned games designer David Perry demonstrated his latest project, Gaikai: a streaming, browser-based games-on-demand service to rival OnLive. He posted a video showing Blizzard's *World of Warcraft* running as normal on a PC, but powered by a remote server 800 miles (1,287 km) away. Perry's aim with Gaikai is "to make games available everywhere with just one click", doing away with the need for expensive hardware and software upgrades. According to Perry, the system – due in late 2009 – will be easier to use and cheaper to run than rival services.

ONLIVE

Scheduled for launch in late 2009, the PC games-on-demand service OnLive is designed to allow users to play high-end games on low-spec PCs and Macs. The games will be powered by remote servers, and the only limit on resolution quality will be the speed of the user's Internet connection. Gamers without a PC will be able to access the OnLive service via the MicroConsole (left), a small book-sized unit that does the job of the PC and displays the games on the user's TV. Companies signed up to support OnLive so far include Atari, Codemasters, Eidos, EA, THQ, Ubisoft and Warner Bros.

> By removing the reliance on expensive, short-lived hardware, we are dramatically shifting the economics of the industry.
>
> OnLive founder and CEO Steve Perlman

GUINNESS WORLD RECORDS

MOTION GAMING

> With the all-consuming success of the Wii, it was only a matter of time before other platforms jumped on the motion-sensing bandwagon and developed their own waggly controllers. It all kicked off at E3 2009, with Microsoft and Sony announcing rival systems, albeit with very different takes on the concept.

SONY PLAYSTATION 3 MOTION CONTROLLER

So far, Sony's new motion-sensing controller, dubbed the "PlayStation Wand", uses a combination of the already available PlayStation Eye webcam and a Wii Remote-style controller featuring a glowing orb on one end (above). As the player moves the controller, the camera tracks the position of the orb and translates the movement into the game. The orb can also simulate in-game effects, such as a muzzle flash from a gun.

* **NEW RECORD**

● **UPDATED RECORD**

PROJECT NATAL

Perhaps the most ambitious announcement of E3 2009 was Microsoft's Project Natal for Xbox 360. Promising "controller-free gaming", Natal is a camera attachment that can recognize where gamers are in 3D space, allowing them to use their whole bodies to control their games. Demos at the show included a version of *Burnout Paradise* that can be controlled by the player holding an imaginary steering wheel, and *Milo & Kate*, which features a slightly unsettling virtual boy with whom the user can have simple conversations. Slated for release in 2010, Microsoft has stated that the launch of Natal will see a "great launch line-up" and be treated as a large-scale, high-profile event "like the launch of Xbox 360".

REJECTS GALLERY

The path to gaming greatness can quickly become a road to ruin littered with the discarded shells of failed consoles: for every runaway success (PlayStation), there is also an unmitigated disaster (sorry, Dreamcast). Here we pay tribute to some of gaming's biggest failures.

GIZMONDO

GPS functionality and a flagship London (UK) store couldn't save this doomed handheld (right).
Why it failed: Launching in 2005 at the same time as the PSP was always a big ask, but with management spending more time crashing rare sports cars than selling consoles, the Gizmondo never had a hope.

PHANTOM

A PC-based console that was appropriately named, given the fact that it never materialized (prototype pictured left).

Why it failed: Despite a prototype appearing at E3 2004, where the system was vaunted as a real challenger to the big boys, the Phantom was never released, due to funding difficulties. It remains on hold.

VIRTUAL BOY

Nintendo's premature attempt to bring virtual reality into homes in 1995 (right).
Why it failed: A very heavy, eyestrain-inducing binocular 3D headset that made the user look like some kind of alien invader from Mars.

RECORD-BREAKING GAMES

"How do you make something better when your last game is called the best ever? We want to bring fans a new experience that will make them say, 'Wow, you blew me away again.'"

Vince Zampella, head of Infinity Ward, discussing *Modern Warfare 2* (below)

CONTENTS:

SHOOTING GAMES

With 24.84 million copies sold, *Halo* is the **best-selling first-person shooter (FPS) franchise ever**. Pictured is the latest in the series, *Halo 3: ODST*, which has a new take on part of the *Halo 3* story.

CONTENTS:

INTRODUCTION

IF YOU LIKE SHOOTER-BASED TITLES, CHECK OUT ACTION-ADVENTURE GAMES ON P.84.

KEY GAME
KILLZONE 2

Sony's *Killzone 2* is widely viewed as a contender for the title of "*Halo* killer" – a game that challenges the Xbox title in the greatest shooter stakes. With a Metacritic average score of 91/100, achieved across over 70 reviews, the game's atmospheric visuals, intense gameplay and masterful multiplayer mode push the boundaries of what can be achieved with the shooter genre.

THE SHOOTER GENRE CAN LAY CLAIM TO AT LEAST ONE OF THE VERY FIRST COMPUTER GAMES EVER CREATED, MAKING IT THE GREAT-GRANDDADDY OF THE GAMING SCENE

Conceived in 1961, *Spacewar!* featured two spaceships trying to gun each other down – a simple formula that confirmed something that boys have known for generations: playing at chasing and shooting is great fun.

This idea was fleshed out further in 1973 when a group of students at NASA added guns to their prototype 3D maze game, *Mazewars*, and invented the first-person shooter (FPS). Tomohiro Nishikado's seminal *Space Invaders* descended into the public consciousness in 1978 and, bolstered by a *Star Wars*-inspired sci-fi craze, helped to make shooting the default template for arcade action. The early 1980s saw an explosion in gaming, with shoot-em-ups becoming increasingly advanced and innovative. *Defender* introduced horizontal scrolling, while *Xevious* provided more than one weapon to play with.

By 1985, titles such as *Gradius*, *Commando* and *Space Harrier* were far in advance of the static monochrome screen of *Space Invaders*. Concepts such as extra lives, power-ups and high score tables embellished the shooter framework, giving gamers different ways and reasons to play. The likes of *Ikari Warriors* and *R-Type* continued to evolve the genre through the late 1980s, but innovations towards the end of the decade came in the form of tweaks rather than great leaps forward.

That all changed in 1992 when id Software unleashed *Wolfenstein 3D* on PC gamers. Building on the idea behind *Mazewars*, the game dropped players into a labyrinthine Nazi stronghold filled with soldiers and attack dogs. *Doom* swiftly followed in 1993 and the modern FPS was born. The following years saw the FPS become the dominant form of shooter, as gamers went crazy for the immersive worlds that the increasingly powerful home computer 3D hardware could conjure up. *Star Wars* went FPS with *Dark Forces* in 1995, allowing players more physical freedom, while id raised the bar yet again with *Quake* in 1996. *Half-Life* arrived in 1998, making clever use of

> « *Trying to recapture the magic that was felt when players first stepped out onto Halo... is not unlike trying to get lightning into a bottle.*
> Xbox 360 *magazine* »

TIMELINE

1961
Created for the PDP-1, *Spacewar!* features two starships, "the needle" and "the wedge", which battle it out in space in the **first ever shooter**.

1978
Taito's *Space Invaders* (left) hits the arcades, becoming the **first arcade shooter** and, later, the **longest-running videogame series in history**.

1984
Nintendo's light-gun shooter *Duck Hunt* revolutionizes home-console gaming, allowing players to use a NES gun peripheral to shoot on-screen targets.

1986

Inspired by Sylvester Stallone's *Rambo* (1985), *Ikari Warriors* (left) is the **first arcade shooter to use a rotary joystick** and becomes an instant classic.

TALKING TO...

GREG THOMPSON, DEVELOPER OF MAZEWARS, 1973

In the early 1970s, a group of students on work experience at NASA's computer department tried their hand at creating a game. The result was *Mazewars*, a game in which two players chased each other around a 3D labyrinth trying to shoot one another – the first example of what we now know as the first-person shooter. Greg Thompson, one of the team responsible for developing the game, explains...

Why did you include the shooting, rather than just make a straight maze game?

It came from thinking how we could make the program more interesting. It came to us that a natural progression was to avoid something else also in the game, in this case bullets the other player could shoot down the halls toward the other player. Once you had bullets to avoid and something to keep score, the game was on.

When games like *Wolfenstein 3D* and *Doom* came out, what was your reaction?

They seemed like natural progressions, being able to take advantage of new technology combined with expanded gaming features. We wanted to embellish the *Mazewars* game at the time but were limited by available technology – however, there are no limits to one's imagination.

Were you any good at the game?

I was only so-so, although I had implemented a few cheat keys to help myself. One would let me knock out a wall in only my copy of the maze. This allowed me to walk through walls other players thought still existed. Even with these assists, there were many players that were clearly better than myself.

> Dan Whitehead first began making excited "pew pew" noises on the ZX Spectrum in the 1980s. He started writing professionally in 1991 and has since contributed to magazines such as Planet PlayStation, Official Xbox Magazine *and* Retro Gamer. *He also writes regularly for the Eurogamer website. He still loves to exercise his trigger finger in games such as* Left 4 Dead, Halo 3 *and* Killzone 2 *but has learned to cut down on the "pew pew" noises.*

OVERVIEW

> *It can be hard to pin down "shooters" as a genre, since so many games involve shooting in some form. For the purposes of this book, a shooting game is one in which shooting is the dominant gameplay element. From first-person, third-person and online shooters to run and gun and old-fashioned 2D arcade blasting – if the lead is flying, you'll find it in here.*

* NEW RECORD
◗ UPDATED RECORD

the first-person viewpoint to enhance the story as well as the action.

The shift to 3D opened up the opportunities for blasting in other ways as well: 1996 saw both *Tomb Raider* and *Resident Evil* debut on consoles. While neither was technically a shooter, both paved the way for the sort of 3D worlds that would allow third-person shooters (TPS) to flourish. And in 1997, the FPS genre finally made the leap from keyboard to joypad, as *GoldenEye 007* reinvented the shooter for N64 gamers. By the time series like *Halo* and *Killzone* were born, console first-person shooters were on the way to becoming the most popular videogame genre of the 21st century.

Today, with retro blasters available for download while A-list FPS titles dominate the release schedules, we have the cream of all of shooter history at our fingertips. There's never been a better time than now to invest in digital bullets!

FIRST CONSOLE-BASED FIRST-PERSON SHOOTER

Holder: WOLFENSTEIN 3D (id Software, 1993)
A modified version of *Wolfenstein 3D* was the first first-person shooter on a console platform. Previously, the massive computational power required to run an FPS game limited the genre to the PC platform. The game was released for the SNES in Japan on 5 May 1993.

TRIVIA

> *The first light-gun shooting game appeared as early as January 1936, when the Seeburg Corporation, an engineering company that specialized in manufacturing jukeboxes, created the Ray-O-Lite. Capitalizing on the recent development of the light-sensing vacuum tube, Seeburg's game was basically a coin-op version of Nintendo's* Duck Hunt *– but created almost half a century before the console classic.*

1993	1997	1998	2001	2006	2009
Landmark PC title *Doom* introduces three-dimensional graphics to the first-person shooter and courts serious controversy with its ultra-violent on-screen action.	Released on the N64, Bond game *GoldenEye 007* sets the benchmark for multiplayers and, with over 8 million units sold, makes more money than the film.	Valve's *Half-Life* takes the gaming world by storm, with records for the **highest-rated shooter** (98% in *PC Gamer*) and the **best-selling FPS title for the PC**.	Hotly anticipated launch title *Halo: Combat Evolved* becomes the Xbox console's "killer app", with what is then the most successful launch of an FPS title.	Third-person shooter (TPS) *Gears of War* hits the Xbox 360, scooping the record for **fastest-selling game of 2006** and starting the **best-selling TPS series**.	*Operation Flashpoint: Dragon Rising* takes tactical shooters to a new level, with the most realistic weapons and ballistics ever seen in a videogame.

CONSOLE FPS

! IF YOU'RE A FAN OF *HALO 3*, CHECK OUT P.30 FOR WHAT'S NEW ON THE XBOX 360.

* MOST PLAYERS IN A CONSOLE FPS ONLINE DEATHMATCH

* NEW RECORD
□ UPDATED RECORD

Holder: RESISTANCE 2 (Sony, 2008)
The console first-person shooter that supports the most players in a single online deathmatch is Sony's 2008 release *Resistance 2*, which can have up to 60 participants playing at one time. In order to achieve this impressive feat, the game divides players into numerous teams, all playing on the same map.

Resistance 2 will go down in history as the shooter where most bosses are at least 20 – if not over 300 – times bigger than you are.
1up.com

4 MIN 15 SEC... the time it took Josh "EnsnaredCadaver" Hardy (USA), to complete *Halo 3* level Floodgate without killing any enemies – the **fastest "pacifist"** *Halo 3* speed run.

OVERVIEW

> Although purists insist that the FPS genre belongs on the PC, recently console titles have garnered most of the attention. Early attempts to translate keyboard controls to joypads were of limited success, but with the advent of twin analogue stick controllers, developers could design FPSs with console gamers in mind. The new generation of Internet-enabled consoles has made the FPS genre even more integral to the success of new hardware, with exclusive shooters such as Halo 3 and Killzone 2 showcasing the Xbox 360 and PlayStation 3 respectively.

✳ MOST-PLAYED ONLINE VIDEOGAME

Holder: CALL OF DUTY 4: MODERN WARFARE (Activision, 2007)
Activision's *Call of Duty 4* has been played on Xbox Live by over 13 million gamers since its launch in November 2007, with more than 1.3 million people playing the game on Xbox 360 every day. Pictured are members of Infinity Ward, the game's developers, accepting their certificate at the E3 convention in Los Angeles, California, USA.

MOST CRITICALLY ACCLAIMED CONSOLE FPS

Holder: HALO: COMBAT EVOLVED (Microsoft, 2001)
The first game in the *Halo* series, *Halo: Combat Evolved,* is the highest-rated console FPS of all time, boasting an average rating of 97% on Metacritic and 95% on GameRankings. *Halo* also received many awards, such as Game of the Year from the Academy of Interactive Arts & Sciences.

TRIVIA

> GoldenEye 007, the 1997 James Bond spin-off for the Nintendo 64, continues to feature in lists of the top 100 (if not the top 10) games of all time, scoring highly for its varied objectives, multiplayer options and original stealth gameplay.

TEN GAMES YOU SHOULD PLAY IN THIS GENRE

	GAME
1	GoldenEye 007 (1997)
2	Halo: Combat Evolved (2001)
3	Call of Duty 4 (2007)
4	Killzone 2 (2009)
5	Bioshock (2007)
6	Perfect Dark (2000)
7	TimeSplitters 2 (2002)
8	Halo 3 (2007)
9	Resistance 2 (2008)
10	Medal of Honor: Airborne (2007)

TALKING TO...

BUNGIE STUDIOS, CREATORS OF THE HALO SERIES

What is the secret of a great console FPS?
We have always started by simply making games we want to play. This means that we focus first and foremost on fun, which is a factor of everything from cutting-edge technology to social features to beautiful art to engaging stories. Of course, none of this matters if the controls aren't accessible, tight and intuitive and allow players to jump right in and start having fun.

How do you make sure that the single-player campaign has a good story and action?
Our own internal playtests and gut reactions are the strongest barometer. We also have usability tests and scientific means of assessing various campaign missions and gauging how the story is being received during play.

Where does the motivation to keep topping the last game come from?
We are very much inspired by the passion and responses of our fan community, but the quality bar we aim for with the final product is something that we set and then push to overshoot.

Have we really seen the last of Master Chief?
The *Halo* universe continues to branch out and grow in exciting new ways, but it's probably a safe bet that fans will see John-117 again some day.

FACT

> The TimeSplitters series, of which the 2005 release Future Perfect is the third and most recent entry, is famous for its wacky sense of humour and large cast. The first game boasted 60 characters, while the second had 126. Among the characters on offer in Future Perfect are a cyborg monkey, a dinosaur, a gingerbread man and a giant sock puppet.

PC FPS

! FOR OTHER GREAT PC TITLES SEE THE BEST OF PC SECTION ON P.32.

NEW RECORD
UPDATED RECORD

✳ MOST CRITICALLY ACCLAIMED FIRST-PERSON SHOOTER FRANCHISE

Holder: HALF-LIFE

(Valve Corporation, 1998 to present) Valve's genre-defining *Half-Life*, *Half-Life 2* and compilation *The Orange Box* each carry an average online review score of 96%, making the series the most critically acclaimed PC games franchise in history. Placing players in the role of the FPS genre's least likely action hero, theoretical physicist Gordon Freeman, the game's pacing, action sequences and silent protagonist have proved hugely popular with critics and gamers alike, and deservedly so.

TEN GAMES YOU SHOULD PLAY IN THIS GENRE

	GAME
1	Wolfenstein 3D (1992)
2	Doom (1993)
3	Duke Nukem 3D (1996)
4	Quake (1996)
5	Half-Life (1998)
6	Half-Life 2 (2004)
7	Far Cry (2004)
8	Crysis (2007)
9	Quake II (1997)
10	S.T.A.L.K.E.R. (2007)

Half-Life is the closest thing to a revolutionary step the genre has ever taken.
uk.gamespot.com getting pretty enthusiastic about Half-Life back in 1998

671... the record for **most kills on *Quake III* in one hour of network play**, achieved by professional American gamer Johnathan "fatal1ty" Wendel.

OVERVIEW

First-person shooters (FPS) put the player right in the thick of the action, allowing him to view the game through the eyes of the character so that often only his gun barrel appears on the screen itself. Games typically include a story-driven single-player campaign and an online multiplayer mode. The PC is considered the home of the FPS, with its mouse and keyboard control offering unrivalled precision. The PC was also instrumental in the evolution of multiplayer gaming, with FPS games pioneering local network play as well as Internet connectivity. Increasingly popular, the first-person view has since been co-opted by titles in other genres such as Thief, Deus Ex and Fallout 3.

FIRST BOSS BATTLES IN AN FPS
Holder: WOLFENSTEIN 3D
(Apogee Software, 1992)
Although the practice of throwing players up against powerful boss enemies soon became an FPS cliché, *Wolfenstein 3D* was the first title in the genre to make such battles an integral part of progress. Infamously, the game's final boss was Adolf Hitler himself, sporting a mechanical suit of armour and twin Gatling guns!

LONGEST VIDEOGAME DEVELOPMENT PERIOD
Holder: DUKE NUKEM FOREVER
(Valve Corporation)
With over 11 years passing since its official announcement in 1998, *Duke Nukem Forever* remains trapped in development hell. After a flurry of new screenshots in late 2008, the saga took a sad turn in May 2009, when developer 3D Realms went bust. Publisher Take Two retains the rights, though, so there's still a chance...

* FIRST TRULY 3D FPS
Holder: DESCENT
(Infogrames, 1995)
The first FPS to offer a truly 3D gameworld was *Descent*, which offered six degrees of freedom. With players piloting a small hovering ship through a series of mines, the vast 3D environment was tricky to navigate and some players experienced feelings of nausea when they first played it.

FIRST USE OF 3D FREELOOK IN AN FPS
Holder: MARATHON (Bungie, 1994)
The first commercial FPS to allow players to use the mouse to freely look around a 3D environment was *Marathon*, developed for the Mac by *Halo* creator Bungie in 1994. Earlier FPS games, such as *Doom*, only allowed players to shift their view left or right using the keyboard.

* MOST SUCCESSFUL GAME ENGINE
Holder: UNREAL ENGINE
(Epic Games, 1998)
Now in its third iteration, and with 193 games to its name as of January 2009, Epic's Unreal Engine is the most successful licensed game engine of all time. As the name suggests, it was first created to power the PC first-person shooter title *Unreal*. Games that have since used the technology to power their graphics include the *Harry Potter* series, *X-Men Origins: Wolverine* and *Mass Effect*.

FACT

In order to get *Far Cry* past the censors in Germany, Ubisoft were forced to create a special version of the game for the German market that had its "ragdoll physics" disabled. This feature made bodies react in a more realistic way to being shot, thus making the violence all the more believable. However, players could get round this by reactivating the feature online.

TRIVIA

In id Software's classic first-person shooter *Doom*, the main character carries his weapon in his left hand during gameplay, whereas the game's original cover art shows him to be right-handed.

TACTICAL SHOOTERS

! FOR OTHER MILITARY-STYLE GAMES WITH A TACTICAL FOCUS, TURN TO STEALTH TITLES ON P.92.

■ NEW RECORD
■ UPDATED RECORD

⁕ MOST PROLIFIC TACTICAL SHOOTER FRANCHISE

Holder: TOM CLANCY
(Red Storm/Ubisoft, 1998 to present)
With 17 tactical shooters and 10 expansion discs bearing his name, US author Tom Clancy has endorsed more games in the genre than any other person or brand. Encompassing *Rainbow Six*, *Ghost Recon* and *Ghost Recon: Advanced Warfighter* (pictured), Clancy's reputation for military accuracy and technological detail clearly strikes a chord with tactical fans. As well as tactical shooters, other notable Tom Clancy games include *Splinter Cell*, *HAWX* and *EndWar*.

« *Fighting wars is not so much about killing people as it is about finding things out. The more you know, the more likely you are to win a battle.*

Tom Clancy, mastermind behind many of the greatest tactical shooters »

70... the number of accurately recreated real-life weapons in *Operation Flashpoint: Dragon Rising*, which takes the record for the **most realistic weapons in a videogame**.

OVERVIEW

As first-person shooters became more sophisticated, a sub-genre began to emerge that relied less on non-stop blasting and more on caution and strategy. Tactical shooters, therefore, are far more realistic than other shooters, with more life-like injuries and very different skill requirements. Most are military based and draw upon actual tactics and weaponry used by real armed forces when engaging enemies. Increasingly, these games are designed to be played cooperatively, emphasizing the teamwork required to survive under fire.

as characters, using the voices and likenesses of four real-life soldiers in the game's "Real Heroes" update. None of the soldiers took an active combat role in the game, instead appearing as non-playable characters who answered player's questions about the real US Army.

FIRST VIDEOGAME TO USE SERVING SOLDIERS AS CHARACTERS
Holder: AMERICA'S ARMY
(US Army, 2002; Ubisoft, 2005)
Developed by the US military as a recruitment tool, *America's Army* was the first videogame to use actual serving members of the army

FIRST TACTICAL SHOOTER TO BE USED CLINICALLY
Holder: FULL SPECTRUM WARRIOR (THQ, 2004)
Originally designed as a training tool for the US military, *Full Spectrum Warrior* was later adapted to treat soldiers with Post Traumatic Stress Disorder. In "Virtual Iraq", the game engine is used to generate a non-interactive 3D warzone, through which a therapist is able to guide patients in order to help them confront and overcome the damaging effects of the combat situations that caused their condition.

* FIRST TACTICAL SHOOTER BASED ON A NOVEL
Holder: RAINBOW SIX
(Red Storm Entertainment, 1998)
Developed by author Tom Clancy through his own games company, Red Storm, 1998's *Rainbow Six* is the first tactical shooter to be based on a novel. The game was intended to be released at the same time as the novel, but Clancy was delayed in finishing the book and so the game came out first. The book features several significant plot differences, as parts of the story were revised after the game had been completed.

* FIRST VIDEOGAME TO INSPIRE A HISTORICAL DOCUMENTARY
Holder: BROTHERS IN ARMS: ROAD TO HILL 30 (Ubisoft, 2005)
When the tactical World War II squad shooter *Brothers in Arms* was released in 2005, the History Channel used dynamic battlefield walkthroughs and flythroughs from the game in a documentary of the same name, making it the first videogame to inspire a programme in this way. The documentary tells the story of the 101st Airborne Division, 502nd Parachute Infantry between 6 and 13 June 1944.

FACT

Police Quest: SWAT (Sierra, 1995) is widely believed to be the inspiration for the tactical shooter genre. This realistic strategy-adventure game put players in charge of a police SWAT unit, trying to resolve deadly situations. The game was so strict that players received a ticking off if they tried to skip the opening movie sequence!

TRIVIA

In the SOCOM: U.S. Navy SEALs series of games, SOCOM stands for Special Operations Command, which is a real US military department drawn from the ranks of the Army, Air Force, Navy and Marines that is responsible for covert anti-terrorist missions.

John Clark, the hero of Rainbow Six, has appeared in several Tom Clancy novels. He was played by Liev Schrieber in the 2002 movie The Sum of All Fears. A Rainbow Six movie is in the pipeline for 2010.

The gameworld for PC shooter ArmA: Armed Assault is so realistic and detailed that it is even possible to see a rainbow, given the appropriate weather conditions.

	TEN GAMES YOU SHOULD PLAY IN THIS GENRE
	GAME
1	Rainbow Six: Vegas 2 (2008)
2	Ghost Recon (2001)
3	Ghost Recon: Advanced Warfighter (2006)
4	Brothers in Arms: Road to Hill 30 (2005)
5	America's Army (2002)
6	Operation Flashpoint: Dragon Rising (2009)
7	SOCOM II: US Navy SEALs (2003)
8	ArmA: Armed Assault (2007)
9	Full Spectrum Warrior (2004)
10	Rainbow Six (1998)

THIRD-PERSON SHOOTERS

! IF YOU ENJOY GEARS OF WAR, CHECK OUT P.30 FOR OTHER TOP XBOX 360 TITLES.

✳ MOST CONSOLE PLAYERS ONLINE SIMULTANEOUSLY

Holder: GEARS OF WAR 2 (Microsoft, 2008)
In its first weekend on sale, over 8–9 November 2008, *Gears of War 2* had 1.5 million players logging on to Xbox Live at the same time, the largest number of people ever to play the same console game simultaneously. Players clocked up a staggering 15 million gameplay hours over the weekend, unlocking 19 million Xbox Achievements in the process.

« Rambunctiously entertaining. » uk.gamespot.com reviewing Gears of War 2

TEN GAMES YOU SHOULD PLAY IN THIS GENRE

	GAME
1	Gears of War (2006)
2	Syphon Filter (1999)
3	Psi Ops: The Mindgate Conspiracy (2004)
4	Army of Two (2008)
5	Max Payne (2001)
6	Gears of War 2 (2008)
7	The Club (2008)
8	Syphon Filter: Dark Mirror (2006)
9	Earth Defense Force 2017 (2006)
10	50 Cent: Blood on the Sand (2009)

OVERVIEW

A third-person shooter is one in which the player views his character on-screen, usually from behind or over the shoulder, rather than seeing through his eyes as in an FPS. Third-person shooters frequently make use of stealth elements, or allow players to duck behind cover during firefights. Increasingly, the genre is focusing on co-operative play – Army of Two, for example, is designed for two players working together, while SOCOM: Confrontation is strictly an online multiplayer affair.

MOST PROLIFIC THIRD-PERSON SHOOTER SERIES

Holder: SYPHON FILTER (Sony, 1999 to present)
With a total of eight entries since its debut in 1999, the *Syphon Filter* series holds the record for the most prolific third-person shooter franchise. Following the exploits of Special Agent Gabe Logan, the series has seen particular success on PSP. *Syphon Filter: Dark Mirror* remains in the top 10 most critically acclaimed PSP games of all time – more than three years after its release.

FIRST THIRD-PERSON SHOOTER EXCLUSIVELY MADE FOR CO-OP PLAY

Holder: ARMY OF TWO (EA, 2008)
Though many third-person shooters offer a co-op mode, *Army of Two* is the first to be designed specifically for two players. The core gameplay is based around using one player to distract enemies while the other sneaks up and takes them out. There are 11 co-op manoeuvres, such as playing dead, sharing a riot shield and transferring accumulated "aggro" points.

MOST DESTRUCTIBLE ENVIRONMENT IN A THIRD-PERSON SHOOTER

Holder: RED FACTION: GUERRILLA (THQ, 2009)
Set on Mars, the only things in THQ's *Red Faction: Guerrilla* that cannot be crushed, smashed or blown to pieces are the mountains surrounding the action. Demolition has always played a part in the *Red Faction* series, with the first two FPS titles in the franchise allowing players to blow holes in walls to find new routes. This could initially only be done to specific surfaces but, with the move to next generation hardware, the physics now allow for total destruction.

FASTEST COMPLETION OF LOST PLANET: EXTREME CONDITION

Holder: LASZLO SETA (Hungary)
On 14 January 2009, Laszlo Seta completed separate runs through all levels of Capcom's third-person action game *Lost Planet: Extreme Condition* in just 41 min 35 sec. Laszlo was able to drastically reduce the playing time by avoiding combat wherever possible, and using the game's grapple hook to cover large distances very quickly. "I simply had to master the usage of the grapple hook," he explains. "Especially the move [that] we can call the hook-zip."

FACT

The Xbox's flagship game, Halo: Combat Evolved, was initially created as a third-person shooter, but was redesigned when developer Bungie decided the Xbox controller was better suited to first-person shooter controls.

TRIVIA

Released in 2003, third-person shooter Drake is one of the lesser-known Xbox games, having soon slipped under the radar following review scores ranging from a "high" of 40% down to a disastrous 0%. The zero rating came from Computer Games Magazine, which complained that "aiming at enemies is nearly impossible" – a fatal flaw for any shooter.

Chinese movie director John Woo's 2007 game Stranglehold was a direct sequel to his own 1992 action movie classic. Woo himself appeared as a bartender in both the game and the film.

* **NEW RECORD**
▫ **UPDATED RECORD**

RUN AND GUN SHOOTERS

! IF YOU'RE A FAN OF 2D CLASSICS, CHECK OUT 2D PLATFORMERS ON P.96.

* MOST PROLIFIC RUN AND GUN SHOOTER SERIES

Holder: METAL SLUG (SNK Playmore, 1996)

With 42 separate releases across 14 platforms, *Metal Slug* is the most prolific run and gun series ever. The first game was released on the Neo Geo in 1996, and its sequels went on to appear on the Neo Geo Pocket, Game Boy Advance, PC, SEGA Saturn, PlayStation, PlayStation 2, PSP, Nintendo Wii, Xbox and Xbox 360. The most recent release came in February 2009, with *Metal Slug* 7 hitting the Nintendo DS 13 years after the series began.

One of the incontrovertible truths of videogaming and life in general: exploding things are fun.
IGN.com

1,414,500... the 1987 high score achieved by American Walt Price on Taito's arcade classic *Ikari Warriors*, making it the **longest-standing high score for a run and gun game.**

OVERVIEW

▷ *"Run and gun" is the term commonly used to describe a type of shoot-em-up game in which the player controls a lone, armed character who roams around on foot rather than in a vehicle. Run and gun games are typified by fast, frantic action and can scroll vertically or horizontally across the screen. Traditionally relying on 2D sprite graphics, run and gun flourished between 1985 and 1995, but went into decline with the advent of 3D gaming. Some of its features were absorbed into the third-person shooter, but the genre is now enjoying a mini revival of its own, with many of the classics reappearing on download services such as Xbox Live Arcade and Nintendo's Virtual Console.*

✳ MOST BOSS BATTLES IN A RUN AND GUN GAME

Holder: ALIEN SOLDIER (SEGA, 1995)
With 25 boss battles in 31 levels, the SEGA Megadrive run and gun shooter *Alien Soldier* has the most boss battles per gameplay hour of any title in the genre. The final battle of the game, against the wolf-cyborg hybrid known as Z-Leo, can take over 10 minutes to complete. Other notable bosses in the game include helicopter lizards, giant spiked worms and Wolfgunblood Garopa.

✳ NEW RECORD
◻ UPDATED RECORD

FIRST MOVIE-LICENSED RUN AND GUN GAME

Holder: RAMBO: FIRST BLOOD PART II (SEGA, 1986)
The first run and gun game to use characters from a movie was *Rambo: First Blood Part II* on the SEGA Master System. The game was originally released in Japan under the title *Ashura* and had nothing to do with Sylvester Stallone's action movie. When SEGA released the title in America, it licensed the movie brand and swapped the Asian lead character for a Stallone sprite. In Europe, the game was released in its original form as *Secret Command*, because a *Rambo* game was already being published by Ocean Software.

✳ LONGEST DELAY BETWEEN VIDEOGAME INSTALMENTS

Holder: BIONIC COMMANDO (Capcom, 1987 to present)
Fans of the 1987 run and gun arcade game *Bionic Commando* had to wait a record 21 years and two months for the first direct sequel to the game, which was also called *Bionic Commando* and released in May 2009.

TEN GAMES YOU SHOULD PLAY IN THIS GENRE	
	GAME
1	Metal Slug (1996)
2	Gunstar Heroes (1993)
3	Turrican (1990)
4	Weapon of Choice (2008)
5	Contra III (1992)
6	Green Beret (1985)
7	Vectorman (1995)
8	Bionic Commando (1987)
9	Ikari Warriors (1986)
10	Alien Soldier (1995)

FACT

▷ *With an average score of 74% on the game review aggregator website Metacritic, Weapon of Choice (1998) is the highest professionally rated release on the Xbox Community Games channel. The game is the work of Nathan Fouts, a solo programmer with previous experience working on the Ratchet & Clank series as well as acclaimed PlayStation 3 sci-fi shooter Resistance: Fall of Man.*

TRIVIA

▷ *It took American gamer Jeff Feasel just 17 min 44 sec to complete the entire Bionic Commando campaign on Capcom's 1988 NES version of the game. This is the fastest completion time ever recorded, and it is particularly impressive since the game is notoriously difficult. The game timer runs from the second the start button is pressed to the player's last action of the game, so the pressure is on right from the very beginning.*

▷ *SEGA's Gunstar Heroes, released in 1993, spawned its own soundtrack album, written and performed by Japanese composer Norio Hanzawa and released only in Japan in 1995.*

2D SHOOTERS

! FOR MORE 2D BATTLING, CHECK OUT 2D FIGHTERS ON P.108.

* NEW RECORD
□ UPDATED RECORD

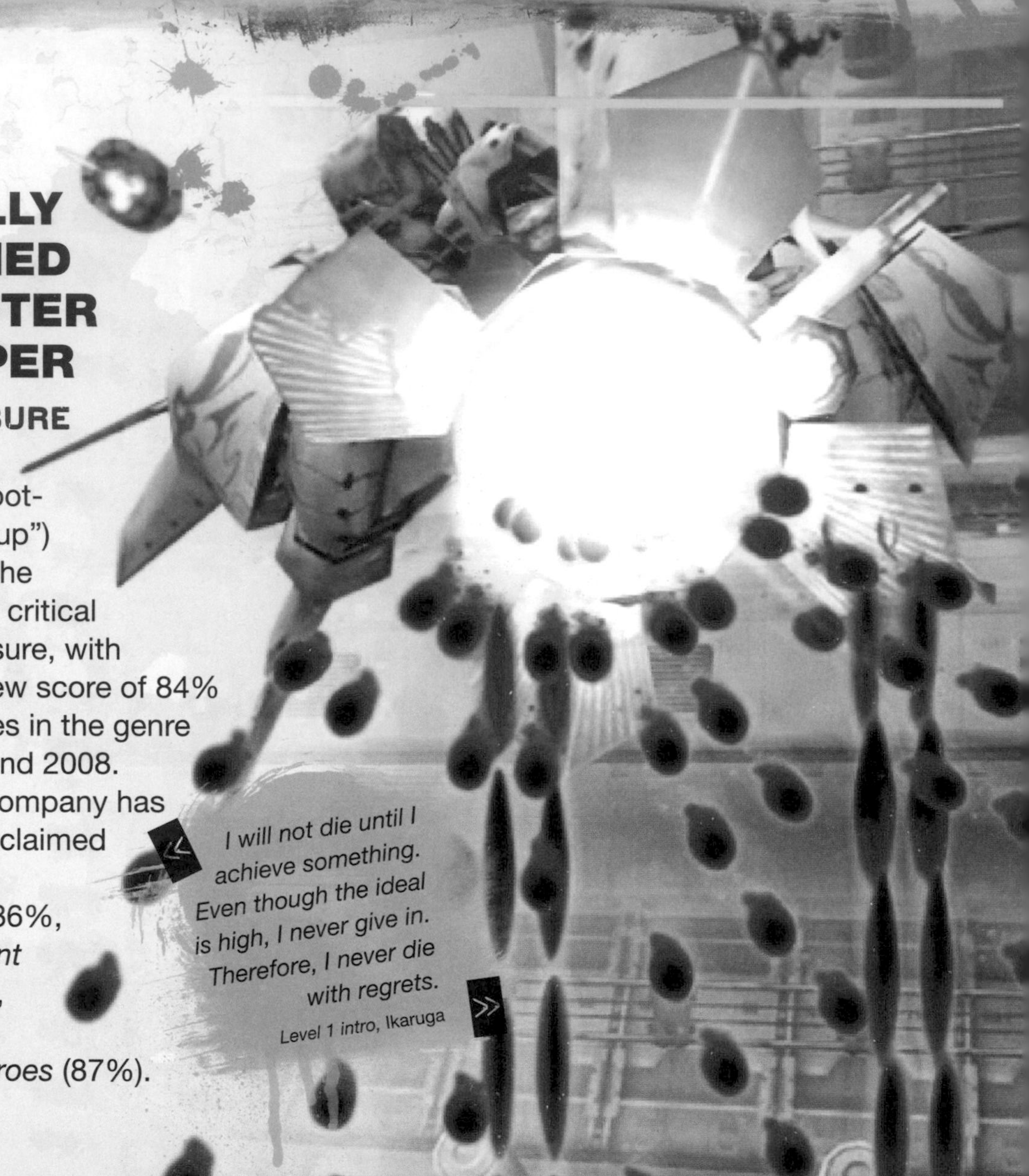

* MOST CRITICALLY ACCLAIMED 2D SHOOTER DEVELOPER

Holder: TREASURE (Japan)

The modern shoot-em-up (or "shmup") developer with the most consistent critical success is Treasure, with an average review score of 84% across eight titles in the genre between 1993 and 2008. The Japanese company has created such acclaimed titles as *Ikaruga* (average score 86%, pictured), *Radiant Silvergun* (92%), *Bangai-O* (85%) and *Gunstar Heroes* (87%).

I will not die until I achieve something. Even though the ideal is high, I never give in. Therefore, I never die with regrets.
Level 1 intro, Ikaruga

TEN GAMES YOU SHOULD PLAY IN THIS GENRE

	GAME			GAME
1	R-Type (1987)	6		Gradius (1985)
2	Ikaruga (2001)	7		Do-Don-Pachi Dai-Fukkatsu (2008)
3	Batsugun (1993)	8		Shoot the Bullet (2005)
4	Bangai-O (2000)	9		Space Giraffe (2007)
5	Gunstar Heroes (1993)	10		Raiden IV (2007)

7... the position given to *R-Type* in the list of Top 10 Toughest Games to Beat, published by IGN.com. (Konami's *Contra* was adjudged to be the toughest game of all time.)

OVERVIEW

> With its roots in *Space Invaders* and *Galaga*, the 2D shoot-em-up genre – or "shmup", as it is known – has the strongest link to the origins of shooting games. Evolving through the 1980s in series such as *R-Type* and *Gradius*, the technological advances of each new generation of hardware allowed games to become faster and more difficult. This led to the rise in the 1990s of "bullet hell" shooters, in which the screen is filled with waves of enemies and projectiles, so progress depends on memorizing intricate patterns of defence and attack. This sub-genre remained a hardcore niche until the online capabilities of services such as Xbox Live made classic titles popular once more.

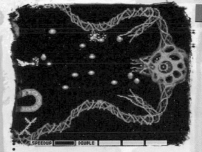

* MOST POPULAR CHEAT CODE

Holder: GRADIUS (Konami, 1985)
The cheat code that has been featured in the most videogames in history is the Konami Code, which debuted in the NES version of *Gradius*, released in 1986, and has been included in 151 games to date. The effect of the code varies from game to game, but in most cases entering the code while the game is paused grants the player most of the game's available power-ups. The same button presses or subtle variations thereof have always been used. For those players who never encountered it, or have simply forgotten about it, the sequence is, of course, Up, Up, Down, Down, Left, Right, Left, Right, B, A.

TRIVIA

> The Japanese PC Engine release of *R-Type* was the first console shooter to be broken up into two separate releases, with players having to wait 10 weeks between the launch of the first cartridge on 25 March 1988 and its follow-up on 3 June of the same year. The game was split because of space restrictions on the credit card-sized carts used by the PC Engine in Japan at the time.

HINTS

> "I think people's scores would noticeably increase if they really started practising flying around in loose circles around the arena. At the earlier difficulty levels, you can almost fly in a regular circle, all the while shooting straight in front of your ship. As you fly, your shots will clear a path right in front of you to fly through!" *Matthew "Blewmeanie" Tompkins, high-score record-holder on Geometry Wars Retro Evolved*[2].

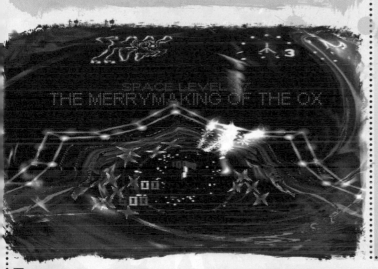

* MOST CRITICALLY DIVISIVE 2D SHOOTER

Holder: SPACE GIRAFFE (Llamasoft, 2007)
The 2D shooter that has attracted the widest spread of review scores, thus dividing games critics with its "love it or hate it" gameplay, is Jeff Minter's *Space Giraffe*, released on Xbox Live Arcade in August 2007. It boasts an unprecedented 80-point gap between highest and lowest critics' score, ranging from a perfect 100% from *Hardcore Gamer Magazine*, which called it "pure addictive fun", to just 2/10 from *Official Xbox Magazine UK* who blasted the game as "damn near unplayable technoslop".

RAREST CONSOLE 2D SHOOTER

Holder: DREAMCAST BANGAI-O PRIZE EDITION (Treasure, 2000)
With only five copies ever distributed, *Dreamcast Bangai-O Prize Edition* is the rarest 2D shooter released for a console. The game was given exclusively to the five winners in a Japanese high-score competition,

hence its incredibly small distribution. Only two copies of the game are thought to have changed hands, with the most recent being snapped up for $500 (£300). Don't worry too much, though – the game itself is exactly the same as the normal edition, and only a golden sticker on the case marks the prize edition as something special.

HIGHEST SCORE ON GEOMETRY WARS EVOLVED[2]

Holder: MATTHEW "BLEWMEANIE" TOMPKINS (USA)
The top score on the Xbox 360 version of *Geometry Wars Evolved*[2] is 869,927,375, which was achieved by Matthew "Blewmeanie" Tompkins (USA) in May 2009.

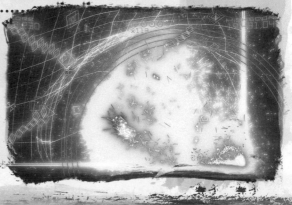

ONLINE SHOOTERS

! IF YOU'RE A MORE SOCIALLY MINDED PLAYER, WHY NOT CHECK OUT MMORPGS, FROM P.156.

Why does this game have the effect of reducing grown men back to moony adolescence?

Agent Scully speaking in The X-Files episode about an online videogame called "First Person Shooter"

TEN GAMES YOU SHOULD PLAY IN THIS GENRE

	GAME
1	Counter-Strike: Source (2004)
2	Unreal Tournament 3 (2007)
3	Team Fortress 2 (2007)
4	Quake Live (2009)
5	Battlefield 1942 (2002)
6	Battlefield 2142 (2008)
7	Warhawk (2007)
8	Left 4 Dead (2008)
9	Star Wars Battlefront (2004)
10	Tribes 2 (2001)

✱ MOST KILLS IN PROFESSIONAL COUNTER-STRIKE TOURNAMENTS

Holder: MTW (Denmark)
As of January 2009, the world's most successful *Counter-Strike* clan is Denmark's mTw. Team members Alexander Holt, Christoffer Sunde, Danny Sorensen, Jonas Svendsen and Muhamed Eid clocked up 5,971 kills in officially recorded competitive *Counter-Strike* matches.

40 HOURS... the duration of the **longest non-stop LAN party**, completed by 274 gamers at Cyber Fusion 2009 in Malaysia. The party featured *Team Fortress 2*, *Quake Live* and *Unreal Tournament 3*.

OVERVIEW

> *Even from the earliest flushes of the first-person shooter, titles such as Doom allowed gamers to link their computers through a local area network (LAN) so that they could play together. As Internet technology improved, this style of multiplayer gaming became increasingly popular and far more accessible. Gameplay evolved in kind, with the traditional last-man-standing "Deathmatch" scenario joined by team-based objectives such as "Capture the Flag". There are now dozens of games designed specifically for this style of play, and dedicated online services to help players team up with other like-minded warriors.*

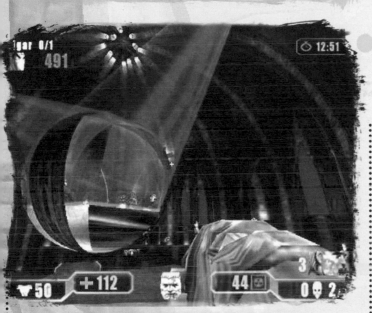

MOST POPULAR ONLINE GAME ON STEAM

Holder: COUNTER–STRIKE: SOURCE (Valve Corporation, 2004)
With daily peaks of around 90,000 players, *Counter-Strike: Source* is consistently the most popular game played on the PC online gaming network Steam. In second place is the original *Counter-Strike*, giving the series as a whole peak daily figures of more than 150,000 gamers.

LONGEST DELAY FOR AN ONLINE GAME SEQUEL

Holder: TEAM FORTRESS
(Valve Corporation, 1999–2007)
The online shooter series with the longest delay between entries is *Team Fortress*, which had an 11-year gap between the first game, released in April 1999, and the second, which came out in 2007.

✳ MOST DIFFICULT ACHIEVEMENT ON LEFT 4 DEAD

"Nothing Special" is zombie shooter *Left 4 Dead*'s toughest achievement, with only 2.2% of players unlocking it. This award requires the player to make it through a campaign with no Survivors taking damage from a Special Infected. The easiest achievement, with 75% of players completing it, is "Drag & Drop", for saving a team-mate from a Smoker before they take damage.

✳ FIRST SHOOTER TO OFFER ONLINE PLAY ONLY

Holder: QUAKE III ARENA
(Activision, 1999)
The first title in an established first-person shooter series to completely abandon the single-player element and focus solely on multiplayer battles was *Quake III Arena*. The game was ported to both PlayStation 2 and Dreamcast consoles, and was followed by the *Team Arena* co-operative expansion pack in 2000. A remake of *Quake III Arena* is underway for Xbox Live Arcade.

✳ **NEW RECORD**
◦ **UPDATED RECORD**

MOST POPULAR TEAM FORTRESS 2 CHARACTER

Holder: THE ENGINEER
Of the nine character classes available in Valve's online shooter *Team Fortress 2*, the Engineer is the character of choice for 15% of all players, which makes him the game's most popular protagonist. This preference may have something to do with the fact that the Engineer has the longest lifespan in the game, surviving for one and a half minutes on average. On the other hand, the least popular character amongst gamers is the Heavy, with only 8% choosing him. This lumbering warrior does have his advantages, though – Heavy players are generally the most effective, averaging 82 kills per hour of gaming.

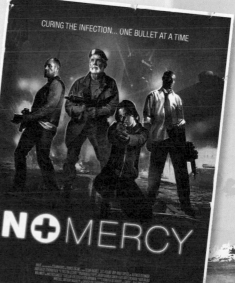

CURING THE INFECTION... ONE BULLET AT A TIME

NO+MERCY

RAIL SHOOTERS

! IF YOU LIKE GAMES WITH PERIPHERALS, TURN TO P.28 AND CHECK OUT THE BEST OF WII.

>> *While it may sound limiting, the idea is to let you focus on shooting and not worry about getting lost or making a misstep and falling down a pit...* >>
IGN.com on rail shooters

TEN GAMES YOU SHOULD PLAY IN THIS GENRE

	GAME
1	Sin and Punishment (2000)
2	Star Fox (1993)
3	Rez (2001)
4	The House of the Dead: OVERKILL (2009)
5	Time Crisis II (1998)
6	Ghost Squad (2004)
7	Panzer Dragoon (1995)
8	Point Blank (1994)
9	Operation Wolf (1987)
10	Duck Hunt (1984)

NEW RECORD
UPDATED RECORD

MOST CRITICALLY ACCLAIMED RAIL SHOOTER

Holder: PANZER DRAGOON ORTA (SEGA, 2002)

With an average approval rating of 91% in online reviews, the rail shooter with the greatest critical reception is *Panzer Dragoon Orta*, a dragon-filled fantasy adventure released for the original Xbox. Beaten into second place is Nintendo's space shooter *Star Fox 64* (1997) with 89%, while a shade back in third is Tetsuya Mizuguchi's *Rez HD* (2008) with 88%.

OVERVIEW

Rail shooters are games that follow a fixed camera path, allowing the player to concentrate solely on aiming and shooting. Sometimes these games are played in third-person perspective with gameplay following a character or vessel into the screen, but the genre can also incorporate light-gun games. First popularized in the early 20th century, when the development of the light-sensing vacuum tube allowed toy guns to "shoot" targets, the modern evolution of these titles use large plastic weapons and tend to debut in the arcade.

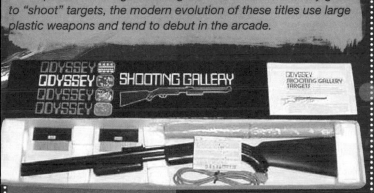

FACT

A peculiar offshoot of the rail shooter sub-genre involves players following a fixed path and taking photographs of wildlife along the way. Notable examples include *Pokémon Snap* on the N64 and Xbox Live Arcade's *Sealife Safari*.

TRIVIA

To regain health in Konami's *Silent Scope* sniper game, players must train their sights on beautiful women sunbathing on rooftops.

* MOST SWEARING IN A VIDEOGAME

Holder: THE HOUSE OF THE DEAD: OVERKILL (SEGA, 2009)
The Wii light-gun game *The House of the Dead: OVERKILL* includes more bad language than any other videogame in history. The game, which is about three hours long, features little dialogue, yet there are 189 uses of the "F" word, which equates to just over one per minute and a total of 3% of all words spoken.

* FIRST HOME-CONSOLE LIGHT GUN

Holder: SHOOTING GALLERY
Created in 1968 by Ralph Baer (USA), and sold commercially in 1972, Shooting Gallery, which was made for the Magnavox Odyssey, was the world's first home-console light gun. A life-sized realistic hunting rifle that had to be cocked before each shot, it also has the distinction of being the **largest home-console light gun**. Only four games were ever released for the gun: *Shootout*, *Dogfight*, *Prehistoric Safari* and *Shooting Gallery*. It is estimated that only 20,000 guns were ever sold.

LONGEST DELAY BETWEEN JAPANESE AND EUROPEAN RELEASES

Holder: SIN AND PUNISHMENT (Nintendo, 2000/2007)
With six years and 10 months between its Japanese debut and official release in Europe, *Sin and Punishment* is the rail shooter with the longest-delayed release. The game was actually developed for the Western market, and features English dialogue, but N64 sales were so low by the time it was completed that it was only ever released in Japan, in November 2000. The game finally came to Europe and America in September 2007 on the Wii Virtual Console, where it can be downloaded for 1200 Wii Points. The Western version still has the Japanese subtitles with the English dialogue.

HIGHEST SCORE ON POINT BLANK

Holder: CHRIS MARTIN (USA)
The record score on the *Point Blank* light-gun arcade machine is 192,338, achieved by US gamer Chris Martin. The score, adjudicated by a referee and accepted by Twin Galaxies, was reached using no continues and represents the maximum possible score in the game. Points are gained for hitting targets and completing tasks, although a record-breaking run such as this also requires the player to get all available bonuses for speed and accuracy.

LONGEST POLICE STAND-OFF WITH A VIDEOGAME PERIPHERAL

In February 2009, a man in Brazil's Distrito Federal carried out a 10-hour stand-off with local police, holding a 60-year-old woman hostage with a SEGA light phaser – the light gun used to play rail shooters such as *Gangster Town*, *Hang On* and *Missile Defence 3D* on the Master System. Thankfully, the incident ended without the woman being harmed.

* FIRST COMBINED LIGHT-GUN/FPS CONTROLLER

Holder: GUNCON 3
Supplied with the PlayStation 3 version of *Time Crisis 4*, the GunCon 3 is a hand-gun peripheral that features a unique two-handed control scheme. Mounted under the barrel is an extension that carries an analogue stick and two shoulder buttons for use by the player's left hand. This enables the first-person shooter sections of the game, which require the player to move a character around the levels. Unlike the GunCon and GunCon 2 before it, the third version supports today's almost obligatory LCD and plasma screens.

SPORTS & RACING GAMES

CONTENTS:

The **best-selling sports series of all time** is EA's *Madden NFL*, which sold 70 million units worldwide between its launch in 1988 and April 2009. Its nearest rival is EA's own 65-million-selling *FIFA* series.

IF YOU ENJOY THE REAL-LIFE EXPERIENCE, TURN TO P.170 FOR MORE SIMS.

INTRODUCTION

■ NEW RECORD
□ UPDATED RECORD

WITH SPORTS AND RACING SIMS GROWING EVER MORE REALISTIC, THERE'S NEVER BEEN A BETTER TIME FOR GAMERS TO LIVE OUT THEIR SPORTING DREAMS – ON THE PITCH OR ON THE TRACK

KEY GAME
GRAN TURISMO

With the first instalment released on the PlayStation over a decade ago, the *Gran Turismo* series has had plenty of time to establish itself as the pre-eminent racing simulator. An exclusively PlayStation affair, the secret behind the series' success is its vast array of licensed vehicles, realistic handling and an incredible game engine that puts players in the driving seat like no other sim of its kind. *GT5* introduces the NASCAR and WRC competitions for the first time.

Whether you want to bend it like Beckham, take on Tiger Woods or smash Lewis Hamilton's lap times, there's a game out there that will allow you to do just that. In fact, sports and racing games have existed almost as long as videogames themselves, with the first sports title, *Tennis for Two*, created by American physicist William Higinbotham as long ago as 1958. However, the game that really sparked the genre into life was the 1970s Atari classic *Pong*, an addictive and highly competitive tennis sim that inspired a generation of game designers.

In the 1980s, it was the arcades that saw the greatest innovations. Namco's F1 racer *Pole Position*, highly realistic for its time, became the most popular coin-op of 1983, paving the way for SEGA's even more impressive *OutRun*, created by legendary Japanese developer Yu Suzuki. The game was a sure-fire hit with its moving cockpit-style cabinet, easy-on-the-eye graphics and instantly memorable soundtrack.

Yet, while these games flourished in the arcades, it wasn't until the late 1980s, with the release of the SNES and Sega Mega Drive, that the genre got going in the home. *Virtua Racing*, SEGA's 1992 F1 racer, was one of the first driving games to use proper polygons, and SEGA kept its foot on the pedal with follow-ups *Daytona USA* and *SEGA Rally*. Meanwhile, Nintendo's more cartoonish *Super Mario Kart* was also hugely popular (and now enjoys phenomenal success on the Nintendo Wii).

While gamers were enjoying some truly impressive racing titles, pitch-based games were also taking off. In 1988, US developer Electronic Arts (EA) released *John Madden Football,* introducing the world to American football through what is now the **longest-running and most successful sports franchise**. Next came the first instalment of its *FIFA* series in 1993, which saw spirited competition from Sensible's *Sensible Soccer*, a title that captured gamers' imaginations with its novel bird's-eye perspective and user-friendly gameplay.

We concentrate on what are the core values for a racing game, and try to elevate those standards up as high as we possibly can.
GT5 *creator Kazunori Yamauchi discussing the Gran Turismo ethos*

TIMELINE

1958 American scientist William Higinbotham creates the **first tennis simulation**, *Tennis for Two* (right), for an oscilloscope.

1986 SEGA's coin-op racer *OutRun* hits the arcades, bringing with it a moving cabinet and a soundtrack that's still enjoyed by fans today.

1988 EA's *John Madden Football* (right) hits the Commodore and Apple II, and spawns the **most successful sports series ever**, with worldwide series sales of 70 million.

1992 Nintendo's *Super Mario Kart* changes the face of racing games forever, and becomes one of the rare titles that can justify the purchase of the console it's made for.

31... the number of Electronic Arts (EA) titles that achieved over 1 million sales in the year to 31 March 2009, up from a "mere" 27 the previous year.

OVERVIEW

> The sports and racing genre can generally be divided into three sub-groups: ball sports, race driving and extreme sports. The first ranges from tennis, golf and soccer to more US-oriented sports such as basketball and ice hockey. These games tend to focus on creating realistic virtual sims, with the player taking on the role of his favourite stars and teams, or else trying to beat them. Driving games, on the other hand, are much more varied, with highly successful arcade and street racers such as OutRun and Need for Speed providing fun-first action, and hardcore sims such as Forza 2 inspiring wannabe Lewis Hamiltons. Finally, in a league of their own are the extreme sports, with skateboarding and snowboarding titles designed for those adrenalin junkies out there!

Soon after, Konami entered the fray, first with *International Superstar Soccer* and then *Pro Evolution Soccer*, the game that has become *FIFA*'s fiercest rival.

Since those days, Microsoft's Xbox and Sony's PlayStation have given developers the power to make ever more realistic sims, with fans able to experience every twist and turn in increasingly minute detail. And the results have certainly gone down well: EA's street racing franchise *Need for Speed* has sold almost 100 million copies, while Sony's PlayStation exclusive *Gran Turismo* boasts sales of 50 million across the series. Elsewhere, Codemasters'

GRID, Turn 10's *Forza* and Bizarre's *Project Gotham Racing* have also proved popular with petrol heads.

Away from racing, EA enjoys continued success with its *Madden*, *FIFA* and *Tiger Woods PGA Tour* series, though it's kept on its toes by yearly offerings from Konami and 2K. Developers are also looking beyond conventional sports, with skate- and snowboarding games catering to extreme sports fans and "street" versions of soccer and basketball offering variations on a theme.

Perhaps the most important recent innovation in the sports arena, however, has been Nintendo's pioneering Wii console. Launched

KEY GAME
TONY HAWK

Former professional skateboarder Tony Hawk is the talent behind one of the first games to put extreme sports on the videogames map. The phenomenally successful *Tony Hawk Pro Skater* arrived on the PlayStation in 1999 and has since spawned 14 sequels and spin-offs across almost every platform.

In 2006, the console came with *Wii Sports*, a collection of golf, bowling, boxing, tennis and baseball games. The title revolutionized gameplay, with players using the Wii's Remote and Nunchuck controllers to simulate the physical actions required to play the actual sports. Perhaps more than any other genre, then, sports and racing sims are now closer than ever to replicating the real-life experience, a goal that remains the holy grail for sports developers and gamers alike.

EXPERT

> As deputy editor of VideoGamer.com, Wesley Yin-Poole spends his days previewing and reviewing the hottest new games as well as quizzing the creators themselves in high-profile interviews. A self-proclaimed sports game fanatic who recently switched from Pro Evolution Soccer to ГІГА, Wesley also specializes in racing games, particularly Criterion's street racer Burnout.

TRIVIA

> Many modern-day sports and racing games aim to be as realistic as possible, but that hasn't always been the case. Big Head Mode – where on-screen characters were given over-sized heads – was popular in many sports games in the 1990s, including *International Superstar Soccer* and *NBA Jam*.

> Although rally driver Colin McRae died tragically in a 2007 helicopter accident, his name lives on in Codemasters' *Colin McRae: DiRT 2*, released in 2009.

KEY GAME
FIFA

Launched into a fiercely competitive soccer games market, EA's *FIFA International Soccer* had the edge over its rivals with the only FIFA licence. The 1995 version was the first to feature real club teams, while the players followed in 1996. The more tricks-focused *Street* version hit the market in 2005.

1995	1997	2003	2006	2008	2009
Konami challenges EA's *FIFA* with its *Winning Eleven* for the PlayStation, a game that would later become better known in Europe as the mighty *Pro Evolution Soccer*.	Sony's first *Gran Turismo* impresses PlayStation owners with its incredible graphics, and soon takes the record for **best-selling PlayStation-exclusive game**.	EA's series defining *Need for Speed: Underground* moves the **best-selling racing franchise** away from the world of semi-professional racing with a "street" makeover.	Nintendo wows the gaming world with the release of its motion-sensitive Wii console and launch game *Wii Sports* – a title that changes the way sports games are played.	EA releases its latest soccer instalment, *FIFA 09*, which stuns gamers with an all-new level of sporting realism and a genre-first 10-on-10 multiplayer option.	The hotly anticipated *Tiger Woods PGA Tour 10* hits the Wii and puts players in total control with the console's innovative new MotionPlus control system.

SOCCER

! FOR THE US VERSION OF "THE BEAUTIFUL GAME", TURN RIGHT OVER TO AMERICAN SPORTS 1.

* LARGEST MULTIPLAYER SPORTS GAME

Holder: FIFA 09 (EA, 2008)
Allowing up to 20 gamers to play a match together, EA's *FIFA 09* can accommodate more players than any other sports game. In online 10-versus-10 matches, each player assumes one of the 10 outfield positions on his team and plays there for the duration of the game. The only player not available is the goalkeeper.

* NEW RECORD
● UPDATED RECORD

OVERVIEW

> *There are two kinds of soccer title out there – games where the player participates in the on-pitch action, and management-style games where the player dictates the game from the sidelines. It's a clear two-horse race in the action sub-genre, with the critically acclaimed* FIFA *and* PES (Pro Evolution Soccer) *series both offering ever-more realistic simulations each year. Meanwhile,* Football Manager *and* Championship Manager *are the key players on the management side.*

« *The [soccer] season has begun and that can only mean one thing – the grudge match between FIFA and PES is ready to kick off...*

TotalVideoGames.com *on the 2009 releases of the feuding soccer series* »

1.2 MILLION... the number of copies of *FIFA 09* sold by EA in the game's first week of release in October 2008, making it the **fastest-selling title in the FIFA series**.

TALKING TO...

CURRENT FIFA INTERACTIVE WORLD CUP HOLDER BRUCE GRANNEC (FRANCE)

Frenchman Bruce Grannec won the FIFA Interactive World Cup (FIWC) competition in Barcelona, Spain, on 2 May 2009. Playing as Manchester United, Bruce beat Mexican Ruben Zerecero (also playing as Manchester United) 3-1 in the final, securing a $20,000 (£12,100) prize, a Kia Soul car and an invite to the FIFA World Player Gala in Zurich.

How long have you been playing *FIFA*?
Basically, I was a *PES* player but I heard a lot of good comments about *FIFA 08*, so I bought *FIFA 09* to see if it was as good as I'd heard. I quickly saw that the game was better, so I decided to compete on *FIFA 09* and I have had a lot of fun.

How much time do you spend practising your skills?
I practise around four, five hours a week and a little bit more before big events like the FIWC. With soccer games, you do not have to practise a lot to reach a good level. In fact, I think that you need many of the skills you need to be a good player on the grass, like vision and mental toughness.

What's the best team and why?
Without a doubt, the best team is Manchester United. This team is complete, with no big failings. The players are also the best. Christiano Ronaldo often made the difference.

How does it feel to be the best?
Obviously, I feel proud but I also have the feeling of having accomplished something. I take it like an award, for hard work. I'll use these winnings for me and my family.

TEN GAMES YOU SHOULD PLAY IN THIS GENRE

	GAME
1	Mario Strikers Charged Football (2007)
2	UEFA Euro 2008 (2008)
3	Championship Manager 2 (1995)
4	FIFA International Soccer (1993)
5	Kick Off 2 (1990)
6	ISS Deluxe (1995)
7	Football Manager 2009 (2008)
8	Sensible Soccer (1992)
9	PES 2005 (2005)
10	FIFA 09 (2008)

* FIRST VIDEOGAME TO BE LICENSED BY A SOCCER CLUB FOR RECRUITING PURPOSES

Holder: FOOTBALL MANAGER 2009 (SEGA, 2008)
In November 2008, the English Premier League's Everton Football Club signed a deal with game developer Sports Interactive to make use of the *Football Manager 2009* database. Everton wanted to use the database to help with the scouting of new players, making the game the first to be officially used by a major soccer club for recruiting purposes.

LONGEST-RUNNING SOCCER SERIES

Holder: CHAMPIONSHIP MANAGER (Eidos, 1992 to present)
Management-focused soccer game *Championship Manager* has enjoyed an unbroken run of annual updates since its first release on 1 September 1992, a year before EA launched the *FIFA* series. Other rivals to the longest-running soccer series crown include Sensible Software's *Sensible Soccer*, a classic that was first released in 1992 but hasn't seen an update since 2007.

FIRST SOCCER GAME TO USE THE "STADIUM" VIEWPOINT

Holder: NASL SOCCER (Mattel Electronics, 1982)
The first soccer videogame to offer a side-on, or "stadium", viewpoint was Mattel's pioneering *NASL Soccer*, which arrived on the Atari 2600 in 1982. This viewpoint has since become the default perspective for many of the leading action-focused soccer games, including the two genre-leading series FIFA and Pro Evolution Soccer.

BEST-SELLING SOCCER FRANCHISE

Holder: FIFA (EA, 1993 to present)
Having shifted over 65 million copies since it was launched in 1993, EA's *FIFA* is the most successful soccer game franchise of all time. Following in second place is Konami's *PES*, which has shipped 48 million copies – a particularly impressive figure since it only debuted in 2001, eight years after *FIFA*.

* MOST REAL-LIFE PLAYERS TO APPEAR IN A SPORTS GAME

Holder: FOOTBALL MANAGER 2009 (SEGA, 2008)
When Sports Interactive and SEGA released *Football Manager 2009* in November 2008, it featured over 5,000 playable clubs from over 50 countries, and at least 370,000 players and staff from around the world. So comprehensive is the *Football Manager* database that Sports Interactive believes it has accurately predicted the rise of several world soccer stars, including Argentinian wonder-kid Lionel Messi, who top-scored in the 2008/09 UEFA Champions League playing for Barcelona.

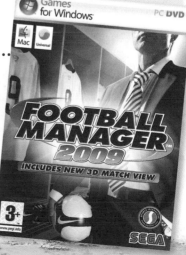

Games for Windows • PC DVD
FOOTBALL MANAGER 2009
INCLUDES NEW 3D MATCH VIEW
SEGA

AMERICAN SPORTS I

! IF COMBAT SPORTS ARE YOUR THING, CHECK OUT BOXING, WRESTLING AND MIXED MARTIAL ARTS ON P.116.

▣ NEW RECORD
▣ UPDATED RECORD

✱ LONGEST-RUNNING SPORTS GAME FRANCHISE

Holder: MADDEN NFL (EA, 1988 to present)
EA has released an incredible 20 games in the main *Madden* series, as well as several special editions. The series began in 1988 with *John Madden Football*, which came without a league option and featured fictional teams. The current game, *Madden NFL 10*, was released in August 2009 and marks an unbroken run of 19 annual updates.

« Critics are taking notice of the innovation we're delivering to capture our core audience and captivate the masses with more approachable gameplay.
Peter Moore, president of EA Sports »

TEN GAMES YOU SHOULD PLAY IN THIS GENRE

	GAME
1	*NFL Blitz 20-02* (2002)
2	*Tecmo Bowl* (1987)
3	*John Madden Football* (1988)
4	*John Madden Football '92* (1991)
5	*Madden NFL 99* (1998)
6	*R.B.I. Baseball* (1988)
7	*ESPN NFL 2K5* (2004)
8	*MLB 2K9* (2009)
9	*Madden NFL 09* (2008)
10	*NFL 2K1* (2000)

2 MILLION... the number of copies *Madden NFL 07* sold in the week after its release on 22 August 2006, making it the **fastest-selling NFL videogame of all time**.

✱ FIRST MLB PLAYER'S ASSOCIATION-LICENSED BASEBALL GAME

Holder: R.B.I. BASEBALL (Tengen, 1988)
R.B.I. Baseball stood out from the baseball game crowd of the 1980s by being the first to have the official licence of the MLB Player's Association. However, the Nintendo title did not have an MLB licence, so while it included eight official MLB teams listed by city name, it did not include the nicknames or logos of the teams.

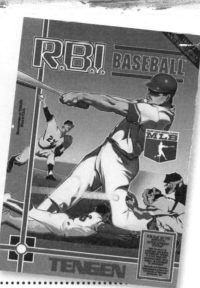

FIRST GAME TO FEATURE REAL NFL PLAYERS AND TEAMS

Holder: NFL FOOTBALL (LJN, 1989)
NFL Football, released for the NES in 1989, was intended to represent the 1988/89 NFL season, and used teams and play formations accurate to the era.

✱ LARGEST WINNING MARGIN IN MADDEN NFL 09

Holder: PATRICK SCOTT PATTERSON (USA)
The winning margin of 192 points, achieved by US gamer Patrick Scott Patterson in Texas, USA, on 24 June 2009, is the largest ever recorded on *Madden NFL 09*. Patrick's impressive blowout was clocked up on *Madden NFL All Play 09* on the Wii.

FACT

> Although legendary NFL commentator John Madden recently retired at the age of 73, the Madden NFL franchise will continue to use his name, and he'll carry on giving his advice to developer Tiburon.

TRIVIA

> *Madden NFL 10 is the first game in the series to feature two cover stars: Arizona's Larry Fitzgerald and Pittsburgh's Troy Polamalu.*

> *EA's decision not to release its games on the SEGA Dreamcast might have sealed the console's fate, but it also sparked SEGA into creating NFL 2K, a game some consider to be the best American football series ever made. NFL 2K1 even outsold Madden NFL 2001 by 49,000 units in its first two weeks of sale.*

OVERVIEW

> American sporting culture is very different to that of the rest of the world. The mainstays of the US sporting calendar are American football, baseball, basketball and ice hockey – everything else is secondary. The first two sports are covered in this section and, as you'd expect, the games are all about simulating the "razzamatazz" of the television experience. EA's phenomenally successful *Madden NFL* series is perhaps best at this, with thousands of lines of lively commentary and near photo-realistic graphics. Midway's *Blitz: The League* series (pictured right) has followed a different path, focusing on more over-the-top, brutal action, while 2K Sports' baseball franchise, *MLB 2K*, continues to hit home runs with each annual update.

TALKING TO...

PATRICK SCOTT PATTERSON (USA), HOLDER OF THE RECORD FOR THE LARGEST WINNING MARGIN IN MADDEN NFL 09

What key tactics did you use to achieve the high score?
I play very, very aggressive football against the computer. There's not time to play the percentages. I air out the ball on offence and blitz the living daylights out of the quarterback and running back on defence, and try to create turnovers constantly.

What team did you use, and why?
The Dallas Cowboys, of course. As a lifelong fan, I can't bring myself to choose another team. Great thing is, when I play *Madden*, the Cowboys always win big, and I like that.

What tips would you give to others who fancy their chances of beating your score?
Go at it head-on and manage the clock at all times. You don't have time to make long drives or allow the opponent to do so. Every second counts and you have to put the ball on the end zone as many times as you can.

AMERICAN SPORTS 2

! NOT KEEN ON HOCKEY, BUT LOVE HACK AND SLASH?, TURN TO P.114 TO ADD A BIT MORE GORE TO YOUR GAMING.

◘ LONGEST-RUNNING HOCKEY VIDEOGAME SERIES

Holder: NHL HOCKEY (EA, 1991 to present)

EA's *NHL* series began with *NHL Hockey*, which was released in August 1991 for the SEGA Genesis and was considered to be the most realistic hockey game of its time. The game's phenomenal success has sparked 19 annual iterations up to 2009's *NHL 10* and the series shows no sign of slowing down yet.

« *What! They don't have fighting anymore?... Why'd they get rid of the fighting? It was the best part of the old version.*

Mike, a character in the 1996 movie Swingers laments the removal of fighting from NHL Hockey 94

TEN GAMES YOU SHOULD PLAY IN THIS GENRE

	GAME
1	*NBA LIVE 06* (2005)
2	*NHL 2K6* (2005)
3	*Wayne Gretzky's 3D Hockey* (1996)
4	*NHL 2K9* (2008)
5	*NHLPA Hockey '93* (1992)
6	*Blades of Steel* (1987)
7	*NBA 2K9* (2008)
8	*NHL 94* (1993)
9	*NBA Jam* (1993)
10	*NHL 09* (2008)

✳ **NEW RECORD**
◘ **UPDATED RECORD**

[**$2,468 (£1,500)...** a week's takings for one lucky *NBA Jam* arcade cabinet in 1993, which is the **most income ever generated by a single arcade machine in one week**.]

OVERVIEW

> *Ice hockey and basketball complete the American sports sub-genre, with both having enjoyed their heyday during the 16-bit era. SEGA's Mega Drive and Nintendo's SNES consoles have played host to some classic virtual representations of the sports, with Midway's NBA Jam and EA's NHL series setting sales records. Nowadays, as is the trend across most sports games, realistic simulations are the order of the day. Each year, updates of EA's long-running NBA Live and NHL franchises go head to head with updates from 2K's own NBA and NHL titles, continuing a tradition of fierce rivalry that ensures the quality of all four franchises.*

NHL 09 OVERALL LEADERBOARD ON EA SPORTS WORLD AS AT AUG 2009

RANK	GAMER TAG/PSNID	POINTS	VERSION
1	Miso Sowwy	7,801	Xbox 360
2	Bone_Crusha	7,531	PS3
3	OoxSimPhan93xoO	7,385	PS3
4	Markquish	7,255	Xbox 360
5	BobRichards57	7,211	Xbox 360
6	UhH OoO	7,093	Xbox 360
7	S4NDR1CKA	7,066	Xbox 360
8	hbears93	6,884	PS3
9	Herms00	6,877	Xbox 360
10	o TAMU o	6,795	Xbox 360

※ BIGGEST BLOWOUT ON NHL 94

Holder: KYLE WATERS (USA)
On 20 March 2009, in Maryland, USA, Kyle Waters scored a record 34 goals without return in *NHL 94*. Kyle achieved the feat on the SEGA Genesis version in regular season mode with 10-minute periods.

※ MOST THREE-POINTERS SCORED ON NBA 2K9 IN ONE MINUTE

Holder: CHAD HEATHCOTE (USA)
Playing as Keith Nash, American Chad Heathcote scored a record 26 three-pointers in one minute on *NBA 2K9* (2K, 2008) at the NBA All-Star Jam Session in Phoenix, Arizona, USA, on 12 February 2009. At the same event, fellow US gamer Phil Ramirez took the record for highest number of free throws, making 13 in a minute from behind the stripe.

※ BIGGEST BLOWOUT ON NBA LIVE 06

Holder: ADAM DE ANDA (USA)
The most crushing blowout in *NBA Live 06* (EA, 2005) is 104-0, set by American Adam De Anda in Arizona, USA, on 7 November 2008. De Anda's score was achieved on the Xbox 360 on Starter difficulty and with 12-minute periods.

FIRST CONSOLE SPORTS MMO

Holder: NHL 09 (EA, 2008)
EA's *NHL 09* supports the EA Sports Hockey League, which allows players to create and level up virtual hockey avatars. Gamers can join teams made up of other real-world players and compete with each other in tournaments based on regular hockey seasons.

※※ MOST REVENUE GENERATED BY A COIN-OPERATED ARCADE GAME

Holder: NBA JAM (Midway, 1993)
The original *NBA Jam*, released in North American arcades in 1993, earned over $1 billion (£662 million) in its first year, "one quarter at a time", according to lead designer Mark Turmell. In an October 2008 interview with ESPN, Turmell said that one Chicago arcade was forced to shut down because of fights between players over whose turn it was to play. North American arcades frequently made over $2,000 (£1,216) per week from *NBA Jam* cabinets in 1993.

FACT

> *The PlayStation 3 version of NBA 2K7 introduced a unique free-throw control system that allowed players to fine-tune the accuracy of their shot by using the tilt-function of the Sixaxis controller.*

TRIVIA

> *Having started life in 1994, EA's NBA Live franchise is the **longest-running basketball series**.*

> *NHL 10 (EA, 2009) includes a new first-person fighting engine that enables players to throw and dodge punches with the opposing player.*

> *Hollywood director Kevin Smith has sneaked a number of hockey games into his films: NHL All-Star Hockey (SEGA, 1995) starred in 1995 movie Mallrats; NHLPA Hockey '93 (EA, 1992) was played in 1996 flick Swingers (see quote opposite); and 1997's Chasing Amy featured NHL 96 (EA, 1995).*

FELTON 5

NEW ORLEANS 23

GOLF & TENNIS

! FOR SOMETHING A LITTLE LESS SEDATE, TRY OUT COMBAT SPORTS ON P.116.

> *Golf is not that easy a sport to play, it's something you've got to master – but having All-Play controls allows someone who has never played the sport to have fun.*
> EA Sports Senior Product Manager Oliver Hughes on EA's new family-focused control system

* NEW RECORD
+ UPDATED RECORD

* LONGEST-RUNNING CONSOLE GOLF SERIES

Holder: EVERYBODY'S GOLF
(Sony, 1997 to present)
Everybody's Golf, known as *Hot Shots Golf* in the USA, has been running for 12 years. It is estimated that since the release of the first game in the series in 1997, the franchise has shifted 11 million units worldwide. EA's *Tiger Woods PGA Tour Golf* series began life a year later, hitting the stores in 1998.

TEN GAMES YOU SHOULD PLAY IN THIS GENRE

	GAME
1	*Everybody's Golf World Tour* (2007)
2	*SEGA Superstars Tennis* (2008)
3	*Virtua Tennis* (1999)
4	*Top Spin 3* (2008)
5	*Mario Power Tennis* (2004)
6	*Tiger Woods PGA Tour 09 (Wii)* (2008)
7	*Mario Golf* (1999)
8	*Super Tennis* (1991)
9	*Tiger Woods PGA Tour 09 (Xbox 360/PS3)* (2008)
10	*Virtua Tennis 3* (2006)

[**$600 MILLION (£364 MILLION)...** the estimated personal wealth of American golf legend Tiger Woods, which makes him the world's **wealthiest sports game cover star**.]

OVERVIEW

> Although soccer and some of the US sports have traditionally dominated the sports genre, gamers have enjoyed some truly incredible tennis and golf games down the years. For tennis fans, SEGA's *Virtua Tennis* has served up ace after ace of quality arcade-fuelled fun since the series began in 1999. Elsewhere, the more cartoon-styled *SEGA Superstars Tennis* has sold phenomenally well, while the more sim-focused *Top Spin* has impressed critics with its attention to detail. On the golf side, EA's *Tiger Woods PGA Tour* has provided serious golf fans with a unrivalled level of realism, while Sony's hugely successful *Everybody's Golf* series offers more light-hearted fun.

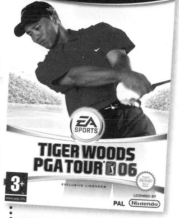

TIGER WOODS PGA TOUR 09 (PS3) ONLINE LEADERBOARD — AUGUST '09			
	ONLINE ID	**POINTS**	**LEVEL**
1	Hands_Ward	9,325	37
2	Hench_Boy	9,134	37
3	cheaptart	8,516	36
4	DarthVader56	8,429	36
5	Dr_Leo_Spaceman	7,919	35
6	MR__64	7,748	35
7	Ace_of_Clubs21	7,734	35
8	kevrfc1	6,613	33
9	PORTUGAL066	6,088	31
10	OASISDREAM	6,061	31

* FASTEST COMPLETION OF MARIO POWER TENNIS: ARTIST ON THE COURT

Holder: GUILLAUME "CPULL" BERTRAND (France)
It took Frenchman Guillaume "cpull" Bertrand just 14.1 seconds to complete the Artist on the Court mode in *Mario Power Tennis* (Nintendo, 2004). Guillaume achieved the impressive feat on 6 July 2006 using Nintendo poster boy Mario. Artist on the Court is a well-loved game mode in *Mario Power Tennis* that requires players to completely paint a wall by hitting tennis balls at it.

* LONGEST DRIVE IN TIGER WOODS PGA TOUR 06

Holder: MATT "PACKATTACK" FLEES (USA)
Measuring an enormous 543 yards, the longest drive on *Tiger Woods PGA Tour 06* (EA, 2005) was hit by American Matt "packattack" Flees on 3 September 2006. The Californian set the world record on the 12-hole Kapalua course using a custom-made character on the Nintendo GameCube version of the game.

FIRST TENNIS "VIDEOGAME"

Holder: TENNIS FOR TWO (William Higinbotham, 1958)
American physicist William Higinbotham's *Tennis for Two*, which simulates a game of tennis or ping pong on an oscilloscope, was unveiled at the Brookhaven National Laboratory in New York City, USA, on 18 October 1958. The game pre-dates the Magnavox Odyssey console's *Tennis* by 14 years.

FASTEST COMPLETION OF VIRTUA TENNIS

Holder: JAN-ERIK P SPANGBERG (Sweden)
On 14 February 2001, Jan-Erik P Spangberg completed SEGA's *Virtua Tennis* (1999) on the Dreamcast in a world-beating 44 seconds. To scoop the record, Jan-Erik played a singles Exhibition match on the Los Angeles court on the Very Hard setting.

FACTS

> Tiger Woods PGA Tour *is a spin-off of a series that began life 18 years ago. When EA Sports signed Tiger Woods in 1998, his name was added to an already long-running EA series called PGA Tour Golf, which began life back in 1990.*

> *While Mario has enjoyed plenty of his own golf games over the years, SEGA's Sonic the Hedgehog had to wait until 2008's SEGA Superstars Tennis to try his hand with a racquet.*

TRIVIA

> Wii Sports, *the Nintendo Wii launch title, featured both tennis and golf games. The Wii Remote and Nunchuck offered fans a more active way of playing these sports than on other consoles, though it also came with a certain degree of personal hazard – it wasn't unusual for players to lose their grip on the controls, throwing them across the room and either damaging their televisions or, occasionally, one another.*

> *The first game in the Mario Tennis series, Mario's Tennis, was released in 1995 on the Virtual Boy, Nintendo's short-lived shot at virtual-reality 3D gaming. The title has the infamous reputation of being one of the worst Mario games ever.*

! FROM EXTREME SPORTS, IT'S ONLY A SMALL STEP TO COMBAT SPORTS – CHECK THEM OUT ON P.116.

EXTREME SPORTS

OVERVIEW

> *Extreme sports games have traditionally opted for arcade action and points-scoring over the super-realism championed by their more conventional sports game cousins. The sub-genre hit the mainstream back in 1999 with Activision's sublime* Tony Hawk's Pro Skater, *but not before another game had smoothed the way a year earlier: designed for the N64 by Nintendo legend Shigeru Miyamoto, the beautifully crafted 1080° Snowboarding showed what could be done with the console and is considered one of the greatest extreme sports titles ever. While the sub-genre has since extended beyond board sports, skating and snowboarding remain the main events, though developers have begun to lean more towards simulation – EA's superb* skate *series being a fine example of the new breed.*

- ■ NEW RECORD
- ● UPDATED RECORD

TEN GAMES YOU SHOULD PLAY IN THIS GENRE

	GAME
1	720° (1986)
2	Skate or Die! (1987)
3	California Games (1987)
4	SSX (2000)
5	Shaun White Snowboarding (2008)
6	Pain (2007)
7	Tony Hawk's Pro Skater (1999)
8	1080° Snowboarding (1998)
9	Tony Hawk's Pro Skater 2 (2000)
10	skate (2007)

✱ BEST-SELLING EXTREME SPORTS SERIES

Holder: TONY HAWK'S PRO SKATER
(Activision, 1999 to present)
With 30 million units sold in a decade, the *Tony Hawk's* series is by far the most successful extreme sports franchise. In 2004 alone, the series fronted by the former pro skater generated roughly $150 million (£91.2 million) in revenue for publisher Activision. Since the game's launch in 1999, retail sales have hit $1 billion (£608 million).

$20 MILLION (£12.2 MILLION)... the sum for which Acclaim were sued by BMX star Dave Mirra for allegedly tarnishing his image by associating him with their controversial *BMX XXX* game.

PLAYER 1
400
CRSH $100

SKATE OR DIE

HURRY TO A PARK!

NEXT PARK TICKET AT 3,000 POINTS

« *Despite the fact we launched on three fewer platforms, skate outsold Tony Hawk's [Proving Ground] two to one.*
EA CFO Warren Jensen on the triumph of realism over arcade action in recent skate games »

Tholen achieved the score on 25 March 2001 on the PlayStation version without cheats enabled, and it is almost three times higher than the second-placed score of 10,703,896, set by fellow American Zabed Mahmood.

FIRST EXTREME SPORTS TITLE
Holder: 720°
(Atari, 1986)
Released in North American arcades in December 1986, Atari's pioneering skateboarding title *720°* was the first extreme sports game, pre-dating *Tony Hawk's Pro Skater* by some 13 years. The game, set both in the streets and at skateparks, is named after the "720" skateboarding trick: turning two full 360° rotations in the air after jumping off a ramp.

BEST-SELLING EXTREME SPORTS GAME
Holder: TONY HAWK'S PRO SKATER 2 (Activision, 2000)
With 4.58 million copies sold, *Tony Hawk's Pro Skater 2* is the top-selling extreme sports title. Widely considered to be the best game in the *Tony Hawk's* series, *Pro Skater 2*'s sales only just edged ahead of those of the first instalment, which managed to shift an impressive 4.42 million copies.

★ HIGHEST SCORE ON 720° DEGREES (ARCADE)
Holder: RON PERELMAN (USA)
The highest score ever achieved on *720°* (Atari, 1986) is 527,100 points, set by Ron Perelman on

17 June 1987. Perelman secured the world record at Camelot Arcade in Anaheim, California, USA, only six months after the game was released. The game's second highest score, 471,600, was recorded in 2008, over 20 years after Perelman's effort.

★ HIGHEST SCORE ON TONY HAWK'S PRO SKATER 2: HANGAR LEVEL
Holder: MATT THOLEN (USA)
The Hangar Level is one of the most popular stages on *Tony Hawk's Pro Skater 2* (Activision, 2000), and US gamer Matt Tholen holds the record high score of 30,887,653.

★ FASTEST TIME TRIAL IN 1080° AVALANCHE (GAMECUBE)
Holder: ANDREW "MRMIYAGI" NGUYEN (Australia)
The quickest run achieved in Time Trial mode on *1080° Avalanche* (Nintendo, 2003) is 40.38 seconds, set by Andrew "MrMiyagi" Nguyen (Australia) on 4 October 2006. Andrew beat the previous best of 40.48 seconds, set by Italian Andrea "Turtle7" Schiappacasse, using character Rob Haywood on the TenderFoot Pass course.

MOST CONTROVERSIAL EXTREME SPORTS TITLE
Holder: BMX XXX (Acclaim, 2002)
The most controversial extreme sports game is *BMX XXX*, which allows players to create topless female riders and unlock live action clips of strippers in action. While the Xbox and GameCube versions were released uncut, the PS2 version was censored in the USA and refused classification outright in Australia.

IMBORN

! LIKE A MORE URBAN FEEL TO YOUR RACING GAMES? CHECK OUT STREET RACING ON P.82.

SIMULATION RACING

* LARGEST PLAYABLE ENVIRONMENT IN A CONSOLE GAME

Holder: FUEL (Codemasters, 2009)

Codemaster's sim racer *FUEL* features a playable environment measuring a record 5,000 miles² (12,950 km²). The game's multi-terrain racing environment uses a cutting-edge engine that had been in development for four years. It contains 100,000 miles (160,000 km) of tracks and trails. According to executive producer David Brickley, *Burnout's* Paradise City only amounts to a "postage stamp" when placed on top of *FUEL*'s massive open world.

« *If you were to build it in a traditional manner it would fill about four [Blu-ray discs]. It's a gargantuan amount of data, just enormous.*
Codemasters' David Brickley on FUEL's racing environment »

	TEN GAMES YOU SHOULD PLAY IN THIS GENRE
	GAME
1	Gran Turismo (1997)
2	TOCA World Touring Cars (1997)
3	Metropolis Street Racer (2000)
4	FUEL (2009)
5	GTR 2 (2006)
6	Race Pro (2009)
7	Gran Turismo 4 (2004)
8	Race Driver: GRID (2008)
9	Project Gotham Racing 4 (2007)
10	Forza Motorsport 2 (2007)

36.07... the number of seconds it took Marc Cohen (USA) to complete his record run in *Gran Turismo 4 Driving Mission 01 – The Pass: Deep Forest* on 5 March 2009.

OVERVIEW

> Although arcade racers were the talk of the track during gaming's early years, it wasn't long before developers began creating realistic simulations for more discerning petrol heads. Winning races is still the aim, but thoughtful driving and racing know-how get you across the finishing line first. Sony's *Gran Turismo* series propelled the genre into the mainstream, but it has since been rivalled by Microsoft's *Forza* and *Project Gotham*, and Codemasters' *GRID*. And there's more to come, with *F1 2010*, *GRID 2* and new *Forza* and *Gran Turismo* games hurtling into view.

TALKING TO...

RALPH FULTON, DESIGN MANAGER, CODEMASTERS STUDIOS

What characteristics define the *Race Driver* series?

The series has always concentrated on the things that we find exciting about racing, so there has always been an emphasis on close, aggressive racing featuring large fields of cars. We also feel that crashes are a big part of motorsport, so we've always focused on a spectacular-looking damage modelling system. And, finally, the *Race Driver* series has always tried to inject some personality into the world of racing, either by telling a story or creating characters who bring the world to life.

Why has it been so successful?

I guess there are a lot of people who share our passion.

What were your primary goals with *GRID*?

Our goal with *GRID* was to take the key hooks of the *Race Driver* franchise to a much broader audience. We were still making a game with amazing race cars, large fields, world-class AI and spectacular damage, but we presented them in a much more exciting way. In doing so, we made a game which retained the feel of previous titles in the series, but which also had appeal in the US and Japan.

What can gamers expect from the next iteration?

There are lots of ideas for the future of the series being discussed, but right now the racing studio is focused on the creation of *Colin McRae: DiRT 2* and our forthcoming F1 titles.

In your opinion, what's the hardest achievement in *GRID*?

The toughest challenge in *GRID* has to be winning the full-length Le Mans 24-hour race – I don't know anybody who has managed it.

✳ MOST SUCCESSFUL PROJECT GOTHAM RACING 4 PLAYER OF 2008

Holder: WOUTER "HANDEWASSER" VAN SOMEREN (Netherlands)
The current World Cyber Games *Project Gotham Racing 4* (Microsoft, 2007) champion is Wouter "Handewasser" van Someren (Netherlands), who won the title in Cologne, Germany, on 8 November 2008.

✳ LONGEST DRAW DISTANCE IN A RACING GAME

Holder: FUEL (Codemasters, 2009)
Codemasters' *FUEL* boasts a draw distance of 40 km (24.8 miles), the longest in a simulation racing game. *FUEL*'s racing environment is inspired by the North American wilderness and allows gamers a view of recognizable landmarks including Death Valley and Mount Rushmore. The landscape, which is modelled from satellite data and rendered by the game engine, is battered by weather effects including blizzards, tsunamis and tornadoes.

✳ NEW RECORD
▣ UPDATED RECORD

TRIVIA

> Sony's record-breaking sim *Gran Turismo* has its own TV channel, *Gran Turismo TV*. The dedicated online channel, which is available to watch through the PlayStation Network, includes videos that go in-depth on the various cars that have featured in the series.

> *Gran Turismo 5 Prologue* became the first *Gran Turismo* game to feature online racing when it was released in Japan on 13 December 2007. Up to 16 players can drive against each other.

> The first simulation racing game is thought to be *REVS* (Acornsoft, 1986), which was a Formula 3 sim for the Commodore 64 and BBC Micro computers. It was designed by simulation racing-game legend Geoff Crammond, who went on to develop the *Formula One Grand Prix* (MicroProse, 1992) series that found success on the PC.

FIRST PS3 GAME TO REACH 1 MILLION PRE-ORDERS

Holder: GRAN TURISMO 5 PROLOGUE (Sony, 2007)
According to semi-official PlayStation blog Three Speech, Sony's *Gran Turismo 5 Prologue* became the PS3's first pre-release Platinum title when retailers across Europe received orders for 1 million copies of the game. *Gran Turismo 5 Prologue* has sold 3.31 million copies around the world to date.

✳ FIRST TRANSFER FROM VIRTUAL TO REAL-LIFE RACING DRIVER

Holder: LUCAS ORDOÑEZ (Spain)
The first person to successfully transfer his virtual-racing skills to a real racing track is Lucas Ordoñez, who, after winning the Nissan/PlayStation *Gran Turismo* Academy 2008, came third in his first GT4 European Cup race. Lucas was the first graduate of the GT Academy, an international driving competition from Nissan and PlayStation that invites *Gran Turismo* fans from across Europe to win the chance to compete in the real racing world. Ordoñez currently drives a (real) Nissan 350z for the RJN Motorsport team (UK).

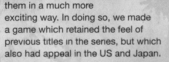

ARCADE RACING

! FOR MORE ARCADE GAMING FUN, TURN TO PP.178–81 FOR ALL THE HOT SLOT MACHINE ACTION YOU CAN HANDLE.

✳ MOST ADVANCED VEHICLE CREATION TOOL

◆ NEW RECORD
◼ UPDATED RECORD

Holder: PURE (Disney, 2008)

The bike creation editor in Disney's quad-bike racer *Pure* boasts an unprecedented number of customization options, including body styles, nose cones, decals, rear fenders, seats and even component colours. Developers Black Rock estimate that over 65,000 combinations are possible, making it unlikely that players will come across similarly designed ATVs online.

Hit the jump, launch yourself over the utterly gorgeous vista stretching out below.... Pull a Superman pose, grab the back of your ride, slip back into your seat, shift your weight and splatter down to earth before hammering the boost to leave your rivals in your muddy wake. »

Pure described by telegraph.co.uk

TEN GAMES YOU SHOULD PLAY IN THIS GENRE

	GAME
1	*Pole Position* (1982)
2	*Trackmania United* (2006)
3	*Blur* (2009)
4	*Pure* (2008)
5	*Super Mario Kart* (1992)
6	*Daytona USA* (1993)
7	*Ridge Racer* (1993)
8	*SEGA Rally* (1995)
9	*OutRun* (1986)
10	*Mario Kart Wii* (2008)

OVERVIEW

> *It could be argued that without arcade racers there would be no arcades. From* Gran Trak 10, *with its pioneering steering wheel, to SEGA classic* OutRun, *the focus has always been on speed, speed and even more speed. In arcades, huge screens, steering wheels and almost life-size car cockpit cabinets have lent a sense of spectacle other genres can't hope to match. At home, simulation and street racers have overtaken arcade-style racers in the popularity stakes, but the genre enjoys huge commercial success with the likes of Nintendo's* Mario Kart Wii, *and Bizarre Creation's much-anticipated, competitive, power-up filled racer* Blur.

TALKING TO...

BIZARRE CREATION'S COMMUNITY AND WEB LEAD, BEN WARD, ABOUT BLUR.

Why did you decide to do something so different to *PGR4*?
The *PGR* series was coming to the end of its life. We were feeling a little bit restricted in what we could do and what the next game would be. It was a combination of that and joining Activision about that same time.

What are your goals with *Blur*?
Hopefully this will be the start of something new, something more than just going round the track three times and whoever is first wins. It's not realism. Realism isn't key any more. It's Hollywood realism, that's what we call it internally.

Is the handling model quite different from *PGR4*?
Underneath the handling model, it's still *PGR4*. We've got more accessible, casual cars as well, the ones which have a lot more grip but go the same speed as the other cars.

If you want the added complexity, you can have it, and if you want the simple, easy-to-drive cars, you can have those as well.

How did you decide on what power-ups to include in the game?
Loads of usability tests. Originally they worked like *Call of Duty* perks in that you decided on them before the race, but it didn't work. It all depends on what's fun!

Are you finished with hardcore simulation racers now?
The hardcore sim is still in our game. We've got a lot of F1 fans at Bizarre who are really into hardcore racing. I think people still love simulation-style games but *Blur* is an attempt to try and do something different. Who knows what will happen in the future!

FACT

> *SEGA's prolific videogame soundtrack composer Takenobu Mitsuyoshi (Japan) is something of a racing game specialist, having composed the music for both the Daytona USA and SEGA Rally arcade racer series.*

TRIVIA

> *Among OutRun's many innovations was its laid-back beach music soundtrack. Three tracks were on offer, broadcast through fictional radio stations.*

> *While most people think Namco's Pole Position was the first racing game, Atari actually achieved that accolade with Gran Trak 10 eight years beforehand. The arcade game even had a steering wheel, a gear shifter and foot pedals.*

> *Four users can multiplay from a single game card on Mario Kart DS.*

> *As of September 2009, Ridge Racer 7 is the only console sports and racing game to consistently render graphics natively at 1080p resolution with a frame rate of 60 frames per second.*

> *The drivable vehicle in OutRun is a 12-cylinder Ferrari Testarossa convertible, but SEGA didn't obtain an official licence to feature the car in their game.*

⊙ FASTEST VICTORY ON SEGA RALLY CHAMPIONSHIP

Holder: JUSTIN TOWELL (UK)
Games journalist Justin Towell completed a three-lap race on *SEGA Rally Championship* on the Saturn in 2 min 30.73 sec. Towell played the game's desert circuit at the offices of Gamesradar in Bath, UK, on 29 January 2009. He saw the old record in the 2009 *Gamer's Edition* and just had to try beating it. His time was just 0.07 seconds faster than the previous record, held by Cristiano T Assumpção (Brazil).

✳ FASTEST LAP ON GHOST VALLEY 2 CIRCUIT ON MARIO KART WII

Holder: FRED BUGMANN (Brazil)
Mario Karter Fred Bugmann completed a time trial lap on the Ghost Valley 2 circuit on Nintendo's *Mario Kart Wii* in 19.777 seconds in Aruja, São Paulo, Brazil, on 11 June 2009. The Ghost Valley 2 circuit originally appeared in *Super Mario Kart*, the first game in the series, for SNES. By comparison, the **fastest time trial lap on the Ghost Valley 2 circuit in Super Mario Kart is a mere 12.93 seconds**, set by John Ohab (USA) in Washington, USA, on 9 August 2008. Ohab's speedy time made much use of power-sliding.

✳ FASTEST LAP ON RIDGE RACER (HIGH LEVEL)

Holder: ALEX T TRAMMELL (USA)
High-speed racer Alex T Trammell clocked a lap time of 1 min 0.757 sec on the High difficulty level of the PlayStation adaptation of Namco's classic arcade title *Ridge Racer* in Maple Valley, Washington, USA, on 21 June 2005.

⊙ BEST-SELLING RACING GAME

Holder: MARIO KART WII (Nintendo, 2008)
In May 2009, Nintendo revealed lifetime sales figures for a number of its Wii and DS games, including *Mario Kart Wii*. The game's 15.4 million copies sold beats the previous record held by Sony's *Gran Turismo 3 A-Spec*, which has sold 14.89 million copies. *Mario Kart DS* is the **best-selling racer on a handheld**, with 14.61 million copies sold.

STREET RACING

! FOR ANOTHER SPIN ON STREET RACING, CHECK OUT THE *GRAND THEFT AUTO* SERIES ON P.90.

* MOST POST-RELEASE DOWNLOADABLE PACKS FOR A RACING GAME

Holder: BURNOUT PARADISE (EA, 2008)

Since its launch in January 2008, EA's open-world street racer *Burnout Paradise* has seen the release of no fewer than seven downloadable content packs. These packs have tended to focus on adding new vehicles to the game, including police cars, toy cars, and others inspired by cars from film and television, such as the DeLorean from *Back to the Future* (1985), Kitt from *Knight Rider* (1982–86) and the Ecto 1 from *Ghostbusters* (1984).

« We knew that Burnout Paradise would be controversial to a very small number of gamers, but at Criterion we are always interested in looking forward, innovating and giving gamers a fresh new experience. »

Craig Sullivan, Lead Designer on Burnout Paradise

NEW RECORD
UPDATED RECORD

24 HOURS... the **longest racing game marathon**, achieved by UK gaming community Ready Up, who played *Burnout Paradise* without a break from 18 to 19 April 2009.

GUINNESS WORLD RECORDS

OVERVIEW

> Street racers are about souped-up cars and running red lights, which has helped distinguish the genre from the more serious thrills of circuit racing. Need for Speed *set the trend with a focus on "modded" rides,* Midnight Club *lends the genre some street cred, while* Burnout, *with its popular "Crash Mode" and eye-watering speeds, takes a more light-hearted approach. Open world is street racing* de rigueur, *but genre stalwarts* Need for Speed *and* Midnight Club *have dabbled with narrative in recent years.*

TEN GAMES YOU SHOULD PLAY IN THIS GENRE

	GAME
1	The Need for Speed (1994)
2	Midnight Club (2000)
3	Burnout (2001)
4	Burnout 2: Point of Impact (2002)
5	Need for Speed: Carbon (2006)
6	Burnout Revenge (2005)
7	Need for Speed: Most Wanted (2005)
8	Need for Speed: Shift (2009)
9	Burnout Paradise (2008)
10	Midnight Club: Los Angeles (2008)

✳ LARGEST LICENSED SOUNDTRACK IN A RACING GAME

Holder: MIDNIGHT CLUB: LOS ANGELES (Rockstar, 2008)
Featuring 97 licensed songs across seven music genres, *Midnight Club: Los Angeles* boasts the most impressive soundtrack of any racing game. Players can listen to an eclectic mix of hip-hop, rock and electronic tunes from artists such as Nas, Nine Inch Nails, The Chemical Brothers and many more.

✳ FIRST AMERICAN PRESIDENTIAL CANDIDATE TO USE IN-GAME CAMPAIGN ADVERTISING

Holder: BARACK OBAMA (USA)
Having run a billboard campaign in *Burnout Paradise* from 6 October to 3 November 2008, Barack Obama became the first candidate to use in-game advertising during a presidential campaign. The adverts that appeared in the game referenced Obama's own website, voteforchange.com.

✳ BEST-SELLING RACING GAME SERIES

Holder: NEED FOR SPEED (EA, 1994 to present)
In January 2009, when announcing three new *Need for Speed* titles for that year, the game's publisher, EA, revealed that their ever-popular street-racing series had sold "close to 100 million" copies over the course of the 15 years since its launch. Such stratospheric sales, achieved across 40 countries, have blown away the competitors and propelled the franchise to the forefront of the racing genre.

✳ MOST ADVANCED COCKPIT IN A RACING GAME

Holder: NEED FOR SPEED: SHIFT (EA, 2009)
Developer Slightly Mad Studios modelled the interiors in *Need for Speed: Shift* so that each cockpit features a functional dash as well as a realistic driver, whose head is affected by the g-forces created in cornering and accelerating.

FACT

> EA Games Europe Senior Vice President Patrick Soderlund, who collaborated on the development of Need for Speed: Shift (2009), is part of a real racing team that competed in the fourth edition of the TOYO TIRES 24H Dubai 2009. His team finished fifth in the high-profile race.

> Need for Speed: Undercover sold over 5.2 million units between its release on 18 November 2008 and the end of the year. The game's sales were down 7% compared to 2007's more successful Need for Speed: ProStreet.

TRIVIA

> Need for Speed: Undercover (2008) features live-action sequences starring Hollywood actress Maggie Q, who plays Agent Chase Linh in the game, a contact who helps players to infiltrate a crime syndicate.

> On 26 March 2008, Take-Two revealed that the Midnight Club series had sold 12 million units since its launch on 25 October 2000. Given that the figure did not include the sales of Midnight Club: Los Angeles or Midnight Club: L.A. Remix, both released in 2009, the actual lifetime sales figure for the franchise is certainly even more impressive.

ACTION-ADVENTURE GAMES

CONTENTS:

The **most detailed videogame character** is Lara Croft, the heroine of Eidos's 2009 release *Tomb Raider: Underworld*, with 32,816 rendered polygons used in gameplay.

INTRODUCTION

! SNEAK A PEEK AT STEALTH GAMES ON P.92.

* NEW RECORD
▶ UPDATED RECORD

AS GENRES GO, ACTION-ADVENTURE HAS IT ALL: GAMEPLAY CAN VARY, THE STORYLINE CAN BE COMPLEX OR SIMPLE, BUT THE PLAYER IS ALWAYS RIGHT IN THE THICK OF THE ACTION

KEY GAME ASSASSIN'S CREED II

Lauded for its lavish and evocative portrayal of Jerusalem, Acre and Damascus during the Third Crusade, Ubisoft's *Assassin's Creed* (2007) ushered in a new level of immersion in terms of interaction with the playing environment and the vast crowds that populate it. The game's sequel, *Assassin's Creed II*, transports the action to 15th-century Italy and the cities of Rome, Florence and Venice, while introducing the inventions of a young Leonardo da Vinci into the mix.

Tracing its history back to 1976 and the early text-only game *ADVENT* for the PDP-10, the richly diverse action-adventure genre really only hit the big time in 1981, with the release of the pioneering 2D platform game *Donkey Kong*.

At last, players were able to guide their characters through a richer game environment, using their skills and wits to negotiate a series of hazards – hazards that increased in fiendish complexity as more powerful computer processors opened up new possibilities for videogame programmers to explore.

The genre advanced again with the Apple Mac release of *Enchanted Scepters* in 1984. This title allowed players to interact with the game environment simply by clicking on objects with the mouse and selecting verbs from drop-down menus – it was the **first point n click game**.

Action-adventure took another bold leap two years later, when *The Legend of Zelda* launched on the Famicom in 1986. Massively influential, the game pioneered the concept of open-world exploration, with players directing their characters from an overhead perspective. This style of gameplay proved highly popular and was adopted the following year by the future smash-hit *Metal Gear*. The 2D platformer continued to proliferate on PCs and home consoles, long after *Super Mario 64* began to popularize a 3D take on the standard. Indeed, the multi-award-winning *LittleBigPlanet*, one of the PS3's biggest sellers in 2008, is itself a 2D platformer.

By the time the PlayStation was launched in 1995, console hardware was capable of producing even more complex gaming environments.

> « *Assassin's Creed is about someone who is going into a machine that lets him relive the life of an ancestor.*
> Patrice Désilets, creative director of Assassin's Creed II

TIMELINE

1976
ADVENT, the **first text adventure game**, is created on the PDP-10 computer. The game is later improved and retitled *Colossal Cave Adventure*.

1981
Donkey Kong, the **first true platform game**, is released in arcades. The game also marks the first appearance of "Jumpman", aka Mario.

The Legend of ZELDA
Includes invaluable maps and strategic playing tips.
Nintendo ENTERTAINMENT SYSTEM

1986
The Legend of Zelda (NES version, left) makes its debut, introducing gamers to the many action-packed adventures of a sword-toting Hylian named Link.

1987
Japanese videogame-designer Hideo Kojima's iconic stealth series *Metal Gear* launches on the ill-fated MSX2 platform – many sequels follow.

1990
Alpha Waves, the **first true 3D platformer**, is released, but it is Nintendo's *Super Mario 64* five years later that makes a success of 3D gaming.

207... the number of videogames published, including remakes and re-releases, that feature Shigeru Miyamoto's (Japan) intrepid mustachioed plumber Mario.

OVERVIEW

> Diversity is the key to the action-adventure genre, with no single style of gameplay dominating. Despite the name, the genre is rarely about brainless button-pounding, especially when it comes to stealth titles, which require a particularly high degree of tactical precision. Action-adventure games are usually built around a strong story and are often characterized by investigation, exploration and some kind of puzzle-solving that allows the narrative to develop. The action takes place on a 2D or 3D plane and can be as expansive as GTA IV's Liberty City sandbox or as restrictive as the detailed crime scenes of point n clicker Phoenix Wright, where the clues are often microscopic.

KEY GAME
PRINCE OF PERSIA

The initial instalment in Ubisoft's pioneering platform series, *Prince of Persia* (1989) became the **first game to use motion capture** when it employed the primitive rotoscoping technique whereby animators trace over film footage of real actors to produce more realistic movement. The series remains popular, with the most recent iteration, also titled *Prince of Persia*, released in 2008.

Several developers exploited this technology by pushing the definition of action-adventure games further, establishing many new sub-genres. *Resident Evil* shot the survival horror sub-genre to stardom upon its launch in 1996, while *Tomb Raider*, released in the same year, melded gameplay elements drawn from 2D platformers with 3D exploration and shooting.

Then in 2001, Rockstar's already-successful *Grand Theft Auto* franchise reinvented itself, taking full advantage of the improved processing power of the PS2 to produce the **first full sandbox**

KEY GAME
BATMAN: ARKHAM ASYLUM

Few games capture the variety of the action-adventure genre like Eidos' *Batman: Arkham Asylum* (2009). Set in Gotham City's infamous mental health facility, the game combines a tight narrative with strong elements of the 3D platform, stealth and beat-em-up sub-genres.

game in the guise of *GTA III*. Like all sandboxers, *GTA III* offered an open-ended and non-linear style of gameplay, enabling the player to dictate both the pace of the game and the order in which it progressed.

Today, as hardware continues to improve, videogame designers have to be increasingly creative in order to deliver engaging games that have it all, splicing genres to forge bold new worlds of gaming experience. At least for now, the action-adventure genre remains at the forefront of this exciting innovation.

EXPERT

> Gaz Deaves has been a gamer ever since he was seven years old. He has been a games publicist and commentator for five years and is currently the videogaming adjudicator for Guinness World Records. His apartment is filled with an assortment of games consoles and peripherals.

TRIVIA

> To mark the publication of rock fantasy action-adventure title *Brütal Legend*, the game's publisher, EA, organized an attempt on the world record for the **largest air guitar ensemble** at the Download music festival in Donington Park, UK, on 13 June 2009. Although the attempt was successful, with 440 participants showing off their best moves and rocking out with their air guitars, this immensely popular record has since been beaten three times, most recently by 1,436 participants at Brock University, Ontario, Canada, on 9 September 2009.

1996	1997	2001	2002	2009
Adventurous archeologist Lara Croft stars in *Tomb Raider*, her first videogame. Meanwhile, in Japan, *Resident Evil* hits stores under the moniker *Biohazard*.	The first game in the *Grand Theft Auto* franchise is unleashed. The controversial series goes on to popularize, and even dominate, the sandbox sub-genre.	*Jak and Daxter: The Precursor Legacy* is released and marks the **first seamless 3D world in a console game**. The pair later feature in various solo titles of their own.	Sam Fisher sneaks his way into the stealth game sub-genre with the release of *Tom Clancy's Splinter Cell* for Xbox.	Joined by new friend Keira, adventure buddies Jak and Daxter reunite in *Jak and Daxter: The Lost Frontier* (left) on PSP and PS2.

NARRATIVE ADVENTURE

IF YOU LIKE THESE GAMES, YOU'LL ALSO ENJOY 2D AND 3D PLATFORMERS, FROM P.96.

MOST CRITICALLY ACCLAIMED GAME OF ALL TIME

Holder: THE LEGEND OF ZELDA: OCARINA OF TIME (Nintendo, 1998)
The highest-rated videogame ever is *Ocarina of Time*, the fifth game in the *Zelda* series, which has an average online rating of 98%. Both *Ocarina of Time* and *Wind Waker* earned 40/40 from Japanese gaming magazine *Famitsu*, making *Zelda* the only series to achieve two perfect scores from the prestigious gaming publication.

■ NEW RECORD
□ UPDATED RECORD

> Ocarina of Time was the first title I worked on... I think this is the title I feel I impacted the most. I believe that experience made me what I am now.
>
> Eiji Aonuma, game designer

TEN GAMES YOU SHOULD PLAY IN THIS GENRE

	GAME
1	The Legend of Zelda: Ocarina of Time (1998)
2	Ico (2001)
3	The Legend of Zelda: A Link to the Past (1991)
4	Okami (2006)
5	The Legend of Zelda: Twilight Princess (2006)
6	Shadow of the Colossus (2005)
7	Psychonauts (2005)
8	Beyond Good & Evil (2003)
9	Brütal Legend (2009)
10	Kameo: Elements of Power (2005)

OVERVIEW

▷ Characterized by epic storylines and varied gameplay, narrative adventures usually feature a mixture of platforming, puzzle-solving and combat. They often also provide an open world that expands as the player progresses through the game, and an array of weapons and abilities that give access to new puzzles and allow the player to navigate through increasingly complex levels. The most obvious example of the genre is Nintendo's Zelda series, which has seen 2D and 3D entries while maintaining the same strong, varied gameplay throughout.

* MOST CRITICALLY ACCLAIMED SUPERHERO VIDEOGAME

Holder: BATMAN: ARKHAM ASYLUM (Eidos, 2009)
With an average online review score of 91%, *Batman: Arkham Asylum* is the most critically acclaimed superhero game ever released. The previous record holder was *Marvel vs. Capcom 2: New Age of Heroes* (2000) on Dreamcast, with an average review score of 90%. *Batman: Arkham Asylum*'s achievement is all the more impressive because superhero spin-off titles are typically reviled by games reviewers and often suffer from a lack of development time because their launch dates are timed to support the release schedule of a movie.

* MOST PLATFORM CHANGES DURING GAME DEVELOPMENT

Holder: KAMEO: ELEMENTS OF POWER (Microsoft, 2005)
While many games publishers are extremely secretive about the games they have in development, *Kameo: Elements of Power* is known to have been planned as a platform-exclusive for three different consoles. Starting life as a GameCube title, the game's developer, Rare, was bought by Microsoft in 2002 and production switched to Xbox. As the Xbox 360's release approached, the game's planned platform was switched again and it finally emerged as a launch title for Microsoft's seventh generation console in November 2005.

* HIGHEST SCORE ON BEYOND GOOD & EVIL

Holder: KENNETH RAY CRAIG JR (USA)
Ubisoft's *Beyond Good & Evil* (2003) features an innovative online score tracking system that allows gamers across all platforms to compare their progress with other players all over the world. This is done by visiting the "Darkroom" portion of the game's official website and entering a code that is generated each time the player saves the game. As of 23 March 2009, the lead score was held by Kenneth Ray Craig Jr, aka "maken90" (USA), with an overall score of 7,818,090 points.

TRIVIA

▷ The Legend of Zelda: Twilight Princess (2006) was released in left- and right-handed versions. In the GameCube edition, Link is left-handed, just as in all previous games. However, because of the Wii's motion-sensitive control and the fact that most players would be using the Wii Remote right handed, the Wii edition was released as an exact mirror image of the GameCube version – changing Link's dominant hand, but also swapping the East and West compass points in the game's world.

▷ Fumito Ueda's acclaimed Ico (2001) features a secret two-player mode that unlocks when the game has been completed for the first time. The second player takes control of the mysterious Princess Yorda.

* LEAST COMMERCIALLY SUCCESSFUL WINNER OF A GAME OF THE YEAR AWARD

Holder: OKAMI (Capcom, 2006)
While it garnered vast amounts of critical praise, even gaining several coveted Game of the Year awards from websites such as IGN and Game Revolution, *Okami* had sold just under 600,000 copies as of March 2009, almost three years after its release. This dismal performance qualifies *Okami* as the worst-performing winner of a Game of the Year accolade from a major gaming publication.

SANDBOX ADVENTURE

FOR MORE OPEN-WORLD ACTION, TRY MMORPGS FROM P.156.

> Grand Theft Auto is the worst assault on children since polio.
>
> Activist and former lawyer Jack Thompson, long-standing critic of the Grand Theft Auto series

■ **NEW RECORD**
■ **UPDATED RECORD**

✱ MOST CRITICALLY ACCLAIMED GAME ON THE NINTENDO DS

Holder: GRAND THEFT AUTO: CHINATOWN WARS (Rockstar Games, 2009)

With an average review score of 94%, *Grand Theft Auto: Chinatown Wars* is the highest-rated Nintendo DS game. However, less impressively, it is also the worst-selling *Grand Theft Auto* title since the series made the transition to 3D back in 2001.

TEN GAMES YOU SHOULD PLAY IN THIS GENRE

	GAME
1	Grand Theft Auto IV (2008)
2	Grand Theft Auto: Vice City (2002)
3	Grand Theft Auto: Chinatown Wars (2009)
4	Just Cause (2006)
5	Assassin's Creed (2007)
6	Crackdown (2007)
7	Grand Theft Auto: San Andreas (2004)
8	Grand Theft Auto III (2001)
9	PROTOTYPE (2009)
10	inFAMOUS (2009)

OVERVIEW

> Sandbox games are non-linear, free-roaming affairs where players are free to complete objectives in any order they choose, or to simply explore – or cause mayhem in – their open-world environment. If you've ever wanted complete freedom to do whatever you want in a game, this is the genre for you. While sandbox games have grown into an established genre with a rich vein of titles, there's no escaping the influence of the Grand Theft Auto series, which holds over 20 videogame records.

FIRST FREEFORM 3D VIDEOGAME
Holder: MERCENARY
(Novagen Software, 1985)
The first instalment in a series of three space-based games, *Mercenary* was the earliest title to offer players the chance to explore an open-ended 3D gameworld and find their own unique way to complete the game.

*LONGEST SURVIVAL ON A 6-STAR WANTED LEVEL ON GRAND THEFT AUTO IV
Holder: HENRIK LINDHOLM
(Denmark)
Defying police, federal agents and even a helicopter gunship complete with Gatling gun and sharpshooters,

LARGEST PLAYABLE ENVIRONMENT IN A SANDBOX VIDEOGAME
Holder: JUST CAUSE (Eidos/Valve Corporation, 2006)
The largest playable area in a sandbox action-adventure videogame can be found in *Just Cause*, published in 2006 for Xbox 360. The game, set on the fictional Caribbean Island of San Esperito, gives players freedom to explore over 250,000 virtual acres (1,012 km², 391 miles²) by land, sea and air.

Henrik Lindholm managed to survive *GTA IV*'s 6-star wanted level for an incredible 16 min 16 sec. Lindholm achieved the feat at the Copenhagen E-Sports Challenge, Copenhagen, Denmark, on 13 April 2009, by remaining on foot and avoiding cars, which present an easier target for the gunship's firepower.

*MOST CONSISTENT GAMES PUBLISHER
Holder: ROCKSTAR GAMES
According to research carried out by

GameQuarry.com, Rockstar Games is the videogame publisher with the most consistent record of game reviews, with 16 of its 23 games receiving average reviews of between 80 and 100%.

MOST SUCCESSFUL ENTERTAINMENT PRODUCT LAUNCH
Holder: GRAND THEFT AUTO IV
(Rockstar Games, 2008)
On 29 April 2008, the release of *Grand Theft Auto IV* generated $310 million (£159 million) of worldwide first-day sales, almost five times the $66.4 million (£33.2 million) generated by *Batman* film *The Dark Knight* in its opening 24 hours. *The Lost and the Damned* (right) is the first of the game's Xbox-exclusive expansions.

FACT

> When reviewing inFAMOUS and PROTOTYPE (both 2009), Ben "Yahtzee" Croshaw of online magazine The Escapist announced that he couldn't choose between them. As a tie-breaker, he decided the winner would be the game whose developer could produce the best picture of the other's protagonist wearing women's clothing. Both companies took part, but inFAMOUS developer Sucker Punch won out with a lovingly rendered picture of PROTOTYPE's hero Alex Mercer wearing a pink dress and riding a unicorn.

TRIVIA

> The cover art for Eidos's Just Cause (2006) is based on the famous Che Guevara image taken by Cuban photographer Alberto Korda. The game's developers explained that the lead character was in fact partly based on the Cuban revolutionary – as well as Jason Bourne, Rambo, James Bond and other famous action heroes.

IF YOU LIKE STEALTH, YOU'LL LOVE TACTICAL SHOOTERS ON P.52.

STEALTH

> Unfortunately, killing is just one of those things that gets easier the more you do it.
>
> Solid Snake, lead character from Konami's genre-defining Metal Gear series

✳ BEST-SELLING STEALTH SERIES

Holder: METAL GEAR
(Konami, 1987 to present)
Konami's *Metal Gear* is the top seller in the stealth genre, shifting 26.5 million copies to February 2009. The long-running series is one of a small number of videogames that successfully made the transition from 2D to 3D gameplay. Created by Hideo Kojima (Japan), the game also scooped the record for the **first game to fully utilise stealth**.

TEN GAMES YOU SHOULD PLAY IN THIS GENRE

	GAME
1	Metal Gear Solid 4: Guns of the Patriots (2008)
2	Thief Gold (1999)
3	The Chronicles of Riddick: Escape from Butcher Bay (2004)
4	Metal Gear Solid: The Twin Snakes (2004)
5	Thief II: The Metal Age (2000)
6	Tom Clancy's Splinter Cell: Chaos Theory (2005)
7	Metal Gear (1987)
8	Tenchu: Stealth Assassins (1998)
9	Hitman: Blood Money (2006)
10	Tom Clancy's Splinter Cell (2002)

1 MILLION... the number of registered users of *Metal Gear Online* as of 24 November 2008, making it the **most popular online stealth game ever**.

OVERVIEW

> A soft touch is needed for players of stealth games. Instead of all-out combat, this genre tasks gamers with silent infiltration – and the completion of objectives without ever being spotted is the Holy Grail. Stealth games are usually characterized by a highly demanding sudden-death gameplay style, where the slightest slip can alert the level's guards and result in player's having to restart sections several times to find that elusive perfect path. It's this seductive combination of high risk and even higher reward that attracts many speed runners to the genre and has ensured its continued popularity.

❋ MOST-DELAYED STEALTH GAME

Holder: STARCRAFT: GHOST (Blizzard Entertainment) Originally announced in 2002, *StarCraft: Ghost* was to be a third-person stealth game set in the universe of Blizzard's seminal real-time strategy game, *StarCraft*. Last heard of in 2006, when it was put on "indefinite hold", many gamers consider the game to have been cancelled. However, without any formal decision as to its fate from developer Blizzard, *StarCraft: Ghost* officially continues to exist, albeit in a bizarre state of development limbo.

NEW RECORD ❋
UPDATED RECORD ◆

FIRST 3D STEALTH GAME

Holder: DIMENSIONAL NINJA ACTION MOVIE: TENCHU (Sony/Activision, 1998) The first stealth game to adopt a 3D environment was *Tenchu*, released in Japan only on 26 February 1998 and preceding the better-known *Metal Gear Solid* by seven months. The game was remixed with additional content as well as significant plot and character upgrades for its Western release, as *Tenchu: Stealth Assassins*.

❋ MOST KILL ANIMATIONS FOR A CHARACTER

Holder: VELVET ASSASSIN (SouthPeak Interactive, 2009) A total of 50 distinct animation sequences were devised for the stealth kills carried out by protagonist Violette Summer in *Velvet Assassin*. Each unique and detailed sequence can be triggered by silently approaching enemies and dispatching them without being seen.

FASTEST TAG-TEAM COMPLETION OF THIEF: THE DARK PROJECT

Holder: HARRI "ROGSTON" VÄISÄNEN AND ESA "SAUNACHUM" KIVIRINTA (Finland) The team of "Rogston" and "SaunaChum" took just 34 min 50 sec to set the fastest segmented completion of *Thief: The Dark Project*. To achieve their impressive time, the gamers played alternate levels and spliced their runs together, while using some rather unorthodox strategies: "I noticed while speed-running [*Thief*] how broken the AI is when moving extremely fast," said Rogston. "In fact it is so broken that it is really easy to play the game just by running and jumping [instead of hiding in the shadows]."

TRIVIA

> The original *Metal Gear* for NES was followed in Europe and the USA by an unofficial sequel, *Snake's Revenge*, in 1990. It was only after the series' creator, Hideo Kojima (Japan), had a chance encounter with a member of the *Snake's Revenge* development team on a commuter train that he decided to produce the official sequel, *MGS2: Solid Snake*. While *Snake's Revenge* is now regarded as the black sheep of the *Metal Gear* family, Kojima has said of the game: "I thought it was very faithful to the *Metal Gear* concept. I enjoyed it."

❋ FASTEST COMPLETION OF METAL GEAR SOLID 3: SNAKE EATER

Holder: MERLIN "TAKE-CHAN" MEDAU (Germany) The fastest speed run through Konami's *Metal Gear Solid 3: Snake Eater* (2004) was completed in 1 hr 44 min 55 sec by Merlin "Take-Chan" Medau. On the toughest difficulty setting, Medau finished the run in a single segment on 21 May 2007. Even more impressive, he also achieved the hallowed rank of "Foxhound", by finishing the entire game without once alerting the guards or using special items and taking only minimal damage.

A FAN OF GORY GAMING? HEAD OVER TO HACK AND SLASH ON P.114.

SURVIVAL HORROR

✱ MOST CHARACTER DEATH ANIMATIONS IN A VIDEOGAME

Holder: DEAD SPACE (EA, 2008)

With over 30 different death animations, *Dead Space* boasts more unique ways for the main character to die than any other videogame. Because the game's enemies, Necromorphs, are a grotesque but extremely varied bunch of mutated and re-animated human corpses, the development team felt it had to come up with an equally creative range of ways for the game's protagonist, Isaac Clarke, to meet his end.

> The player takes on the role of a lone protagonist armed with just his or her wits and some high-calibre courage...
> *Survival horror in a nutshell by uk.gamespot.com*

■ **NEW RECORD**
◆ **UPDATED RECORD**

$379,552,748 (£225,421,318)... the revenue generated by the first three *Resident Evil* movies. A fourth, provisionally titled *Resident Evil: Afterlife,* is in production.

OVERVIEW

> A focus on fear is what separates survival horror from other action-adventure games. Usually set in dark, oppressive environments with relatively limited weapons and ammunition, survival horror games rely on a combination of unexpected attacks, atmospheric sound effects and gore to put the player on the edge of his seat. This relatively youthful genre was popularized by the PlayStation's *Resident Evil* in 1996, and has evolved from early efforts featuring confusing camera angles and unresponsive controls into the fast-paced shooter/survival hybrids seen today in the likes of *Dead Space* and *Resident Evil 4*.

TEN GAMES YOU SHOULD PLAY IN THIS GENRE

	GAME
1	Resident Evil 4 (2005)
2	Dead Space (2008)
3	Fatal Frame, aka Project Zero (2001)
4	Siren: Blood Curse (2008)
5	Resident Evil: Director's Cut (1997)
6	Silent Hill (1999)
7	Resident Evil 5 (2009)
8	Eternal Darkness: Sanity's Requiem (2002)
9	Alone in the Dark (1992)
10	Condemned 2: Bloodshot (2008)

☀ FIRST EPISODIC GAME FOR PLAYSTATION 3

Holder: SIREN: BLOOD CURSE (Sony, 2008)
Released on 13 July 2008, *Siren: Blood Curse* became the first episodic videogame to be released on PlayStation 3. The stealth/survival horror hybrid tells the story of an ill-fated American camera crew who travel to rural Japan to film a documentary on a lost village, only to find themselves under attack from a sect of undead nuns.

☀ FASTEST XBOX LIVE DEMO TO HIT 1 MILLION DOWNLOADS

Holder: RESIDENT EVIL 5 (Capcom, 2009)
The demo for Capcom's *Resident Evil 5* was downloaded an incredible 1.3 million times within three days of being made available to US and European gamers. The demo was released in Japan several months earlier, where it clocked up around 600,000 downloads. By the time the game was released, the demo had been downloaded over 5 million times worldwide.

TRIVIA

> The crowd of 1,000 virtual zombies in *Dead Rising 2* is actually significantly smaller than the current world record for most people dressed as zombies gathered together in a single location. The "Red White and Dead Zombie Party" attracted a crowd of 3,894 participants in Seattle, Washington, USA, on 3 July 2009.

> The name *Resident Evil* is the product of a naming competition held by developer Capcom when, owing to trademark issues, it decided to depart from the Japanese name for the game, *Biohazard*.

MOST SIMULTANEOUS ON-SCREEN ENEMIES IN A VIDEOGAME

Holder: DEAD RISING 2 (Capcom, 2009)
While many survival horror games focus on combat with small groups of powerful enemies, *Dead Rising 2* features up to 1,000 shambling zombies at the same time – more than any other commercially released game.

2D PLATFORMERS

IF YOU ENJOY PROBLEM-SOLVING, CHECK OUT PUZZLE GAMES, FROM P.134.

* NEW RECORD ■ UPDATED RECORD

TEN GAMES YOU SHOULD PLAY IN THIS GENRE

	GAME
1	Super Mario Bros. (1985)
2	Sonic the Hedgehog 2 (1992)
3	LittleBigPlanet (2008)
4	Doukutsu Monogatari (Cave Story) (2004)
5	Castlevania: Symphony of the Night (1997)
6	Super Mario Bros. 3 (1988)
7	Prince of Persia (1989)
8	Mega Man 3 (1990)
9	New Super Mario Bros. (2006)
10	Jet Set Willy (1984)

* MOST PLAYER-CREATED LEVELS IN A VIDEOGAME

Holder: LITTLEBIGPLANET
(Sony, 2008)
While some games use artificial intelligence (AI) to create millions of random computer-created levels, *LittleBigPlanet* boasts more unique levels created by humans than any other title. Due to its extremely powerful, yet simple, level-editing tools, Sony's *LittleBigPlanet* now features over 1 million playable levels, all designed by a highly creative community of players.

50 MILLION... the lifetime unit sales generated by SEGA's long-running and ever-popular *Sonic the Hedgehog* series, once the fierce rival of Nintendo's Mario.

OVERVIEW

> *The 2D platformer started with* Donkey Kong *in 1981, and went on to reign as the most popular game genre throughout the 1980s and much of the 1990s. These games require players to navigate a hazardous 2D environment by leaping between platforms, avoiding pitfalls and confronting enemies, often using little more than a "jump" button and the occasional mushroom. 2D platform titles have spawned some of gaming's biggest icons, including Super Mario and Sonic the Hedgehog, and the genre has enjoyed a recent revival through* New Super Mario Bros. *for Nintendo DS and the PS3 exclusive LittleBigPlanet.*

BEST-SELLING GAME ON ANY SEGA PLATFORM

Holder: SONIC THE HEDGEHOG 2 (SEGA, 1992)
Released on the Mega Drive in 1992, *Sonic the Hedgehog 2* went on to become the best-selling game across all SEGA platforms. Thanks to the character's US and European appeal, the title managed to sell 6 million units worldwide.

BEST-SELLING VIDEOGAME SERIES OF ALL TIME

Holder: SUPER MARIO BROS.
(Nintendo, 1985)
With over 201 million copies sold, the *Super Mario* series is the best-selling gaming franchise in history – across all genres. While the last 28 years have seen the intrepid Mario engaging in a wide variety of activities – including role-playing, medicine and several sports – the series remains firmly rooted in the 2D platforming that first brought it success with the original *Donkey Kong* in 1981.

MOST CRITICALLY ACCLAIMED FREE GAME

Holder: DOUKUTSU MONOGATARI
(Studio Pixel, 2004)
With an average review score of 95%, free-roaming 2D platformer *Doukutsu Monogatari* (*Cave Story* in English) is the most highly rated free computer game ever. Six years after its release, the game is still held in high regard by gamers as an example of bedroom coding done well.

FASTEST COMPLETION OF DESERT DEMOLITION

Holder: THIAGO TRUJILLO (Brazil)
The fastest speed run through the Genesis/Mega Drive platformer *Desert Demolition* (SEGA, 1995), which features Warner Bros. cartoon stars Road Runner and Wile E. Coyote, is 5 min 6 sec. The record was achieved by Thiago Trujillo at his home in Sorocaba, Brazil, on 10 October 2008.

Videogames are bad for you? That's what they said about rock 'n' roll.
Nintendo legend Shigeru Miyamoto

MOST ENTRIES IN AN ACTION-ADVENTURE SERIES

Holder: CASTLEVANIA
(Konami, 1986)
With 24 distinct and commercially released games, not including remakes or boxed compilations, there have been more titles in the *Castlevania* series than in any other action-adventure franchise – and with more games planned, the adventure looks set to continue.

TRIVIA

> *Nintendo's original* Super Mario Bros. *for NES (1985) features what is likely to be the first example of an accidental secret level, in the form of the Minus World. By using a glitch to pass through a wall at the end of level 1-2, the player can warp to level -1, which was never intended by the programmers to be accessible. The US and European Minus World versions feature a single level that loops infinitely, whereas the version found on Japanese cartridges has three – at the end of which the game returns to the title screen as if it had been completed.*

> *Named Bowser in the US and European Mario games, Mario's adversary is simply known as King Koopa in Japan.*

3D PLATFORMERS

FOR A MORE "OLD-SKOOL" FEEL, TURN BACK THE PAGE TO 2D PLATFORMERS.

OVERVIEW

> While developers had experimented with bringing the previously two-dimensional platform genre into 3D, it was left to Nintendo to live up to the promise with the release of *Super Mario 64* in 1996. Adding an extra dimension to gaming allowed players to explore more detailed open worlds than ever before, and while the genre saw its peak in the era of PlayStation and N64, it's still seeing innovation today in the form of first-person free-runner *Mirror's Edge* and Ubisoft's rhythm-platforming *Prince of Persia* reboot.

* MOST CRITICALLY ACCLAIMED 3D PLATFORMER

Holder: SUPER MARIO GALAXY
(Nintendo, 2007)
The record for best critical reception for a 3D platformer is held by *Super Mario Galaxy*, with an outstanding 97.26% and 97% from GameRankings and Metacritic, respectively. The game was praised for its gravity-bending level design and for staying true to the series' nostalgic roots.

✱ NEW RECORD
▣ UPDATED RECORD

TEN GAMES YOU SHOULD PLAY IN THIS GENRE

	GAME
1	Super Mario Galaxy (2007)
2	Ratchet & Clank 3: Up your Arsenal (2004)
3	Uncharted: Drake's Fortune (2007)
4	Super Mario 64 (1996)
5	Banjo-Kazooie (1998)
6	Prince of Persia: The Sands of Time (2003)
7	Jak & Daxter: The Precursor Legacy (2001)
8	Ape Escape (1999)
9	Tomb Raider: Underworld (2008)
10	Mirror's Edge (2008)

We gave [Mario] a hat rather than hair because that looked better, and he wears overalls because that shows the movement of his arms...
Shigeru Miyamoto on creating one of gaming's biggest icons

MOST OFFICIAL REAL-LIFE STAND-INS FOR A VIDEOGAME CHARACTER

Holder: LARA CROFT
Having been officially portrayed by 10 different models since 1996, *Tomb Raider*'s Lara Croft is the videogame character with the most real-life stand-ins. British actress Rhona Mitra and TV presenter Nell McAndrew are among the stars who became famous as the official face of Lara Croft. The current Lara is UK gymnast and model Alison Carroll (pictured), who took up the mantle from Karima Adebibe in 2008.

HIGHEST-RANKED PLAYER ON MIRROR'S EDGE TIME TRIALS

Holder: ADAM WOODCOCK (UK)
The most successful player on the *Mirror's Edge* (EA, 2008) Time Trial leaderboards is Adam "Oo Wo0dY oO" Woodcock, who has held the top spot on each of the game's 34 time trial levels as of May 2009.

FIRST CONSOLE GAME TO USE A DUAL ANALOG STICK CONTROLLER

Holder: APE ESCAPE (Sony, 1999)
Twin analog stick controllers such as the PlayStation's DualShock are now standard on most current-generation consoles (even the motion-sensing Wii offers one as an add-on), because they allow a level of precision that previous digital controllers simply couldn't live up to. The first console game to make exclusive use of a twin analog stick controller was the PlayStation 3D platformer *Ape Escape*, released by Sony on 31 May 1999. While earlier games supported both analog and digital controllers, *Ape Escape* was the first console title that would only function with the new and improved input method.

FASTEST COMPLETION OF PRINCE OF PERSIA: THE SANDS OF TIME

Holder: PAUL WAGENER (Netherlands)
Dutchman Paul Wagener completed the Nintendo GameCube version of *The Sands of Time* (2003) in 2 hr 6 min 3 sec on 1 October 2005. The game is the second 3D adventure in the *Prince of Persia* series after *Prince of Persia 3D*.

MOST SUCCESSFUL LIVE-ACTION TRANSFER

Holder: TOMB RAIDER
(Eidos, 1996 to present)
Released in 2001 and featuring Hollywood star Angelina Jolie in the lead role, *Lara Croft: Tomb Raider* became the highest-grossing film based on a videogame, earning over $274 million (£166 million). When combined with figures from 2003 sequel *The Cradle of Life*, the franchise has grossed $431 million (£261 million), making it the most successful live-action game-to-film transfer ever.

TRIVIA

After various solo adventures, the dynamic duo of Jak and Daxter were finally reunited in *Jak & Daxter: The Lost Frontier* for both PS2 and PSP.

From *Tomb Raider: Legend* onwards, the voice of Lara Croft in the videogames has been provided by British actress Keeley Hawes.

BEST-SELLING PLATFORMER FOR PS3

Holder: UNCHARTED: DRAKE'S FORTUNE (Sony, 2007)
With 2.49 million copies sold between its launch in 2007 and July 2009, the PS3-exclusive *Uncharted: Drake's Fortune* is the system's most successful platform game. The follow-up, *Uncharted 2: Among Thieves*, has attracted significant attention from games critics before its release, including a Best Overall Game of Show from the Games Critics Awards at E3 2009.

POINT N CLICK

FOR OTHER TITLES WITH STRONG NARRATIVES, TURN TO P.88.

* NEW RECORD
◼ UPDATED RECORD

* MOST ENTRIES IN A HANDHELD POINT N CLICK GAME SERIES

Holder: ACE ATTORNEY (Capcom, 2001 to present)
With five commercially released games for Nintendo DS and three Japan-only Game Boy Advance titles, the *Ace Attorney* franchise boasts more entries than any other handheld point n click adventure game series. However, the hugely successful *Professor Layton* series appears to be a likely contender for this record in the near future, with four releases over the last three years.

One of the best adventure games on the Nintendo DS to date, or any platform for that matter.
AdventureGamers.com reviews Phoenix Wright: Ace Attorney Trials and Tribulations

TEN GAMES YOU SHOULD PLAY IN THIS GENRE

	GAME
1	The Secret of Monkey Island (1990)
2	Sam & Max Hit the Road (1993)
3	Phoenix Wright: Ace Attorney (2001)
4	Tales of Monkey Island (2009)
5	Zack & Wiki: Quest for Barbaros' Treasure (2007)
6	Grim Fandango (1998)
7	Myst (1993)
8	Hotel Dusk: Room 215 (2007)
9	Day of the Tentacle (1993)
10	Full Throttle (1995)

OVERVIEW

> Dating back to the 1970s, point n click adventures focus on plot, dialogue and puzzle-solving, with the player using only a mouse (and now a stylus) to control the game. The sub-genre experienced a decline in the 1990s – as 3D graphics and action-based games dominated – but it is now enjoying something of a revival, thanks primarily to the Nintendo DS and its unique stylus, which picks up where the mouse left off. Current hits include the Sam & Max and Ace Attorney franchises.

✳ FASTEST-SELLING MUSICAL BASED ON A VIDEOGAME

Holder: TAKARAZUKA REVUE
The all-female Japanese theatre company Takarazuka Revue has so far produced two musical comedies based on Capcom's *Ace Attorney* series. Their second show, *Gyakuten Saiban 2*, ran for 26 nights between 20 August and 15 September 2009 in Tokyo, Japan, and sold out all 7,000 seats in under 4 hours.

BEST-SELLING POINT N CLICK SERIES

Holder: MYST
(Broderbund, 1993 to present)
With total sales of over 12 million copies across all titles in the franchise, Broderbund's classic *Myst* remains the best-selling point n click series of all time.

✳ FASTEST COMPLETION OF THE SECRET OF MONKEY ISLAND

Holder: "MIKE"
Released for the PC in 1990, *The Secret of Monkey Island* is the first game in the popular *Monkey Island* series of point n click games. One gamer, known only as "Mike", managed to run through the game in just 39 min 12 sec. Mike completed the game as a multi-segment, meaning that he saved his progress after each chapter. Fast though he was, Mike could have saved himself some time, as *The Secret of Monkey Island* can be completed without even playing the game. All the player needs to do is press CTRL-W on the keyboard to see the words "You Win" and the closing credit sequence, making it the **easiest point n click to complete**.

✳ LONGEST WAIT FOR A SEQUEL TO A POINT N CLICK ADVENTURE

Holder: TALES OF MONKEY ISLAND (LucasArts, 2009)
With a gap of 8 years and 242 days between *Escape from Monkey Island* in 2000 and *Tales of Monkey Island* in 2009, fans had a longer wait for a true *Monkey Island* sequel than any other series in the sub genre. The new episodic *Tales of Monkey Island* game was released alongside a graphically updated remake of the original *The Secret of Monkey Island* to widespread critical acclaim.

✳ MOST REGULAR EPISODIC GAME SERIES

Holder: SAM & MAX (Telltale Games, 2006 to present)
Several games publishers have experimented with releasing games in an episodic format by distributing smaller chunks of content at a lower price than a full release. However, to date only one has managed to deliver multiple episodes in a timely fashion: Telltale Games' *Sam & Max* series of point n click adventures has so far seen two series of six episodes, with an average gap between releases of just 35 days. By contrast, the average wait between releases for Valve's *Half-Life 2* episodes is a lengthy 529 days.

TRIVIA

> Ace Attorney Investigations: Miles Edgeworth (2009), the latest in the Ace Attorney series, was the most popular game at the Tokyo Game Show 2008, according to a survey of games companies conducted by Japanese games magazine Famitsu.

> Tim Schafer (USA), the creator of many well-loved point n click adventures such as Day of the Tentacle and Full Throttle, published online the full design document for his excellent Grim Fandango as a 72-page file that can be freely downloaded. The file provides a unique insight into the development process for adventure games. At the time of going to press, the document could be found at http://kotaku.com/5077780/tim-schafer-publishes-original-grim-fandango-design-doc.

! JUMP BACK TO P.28 TO CHECK OUT MIYAMOTO'S LATEST MARIO OUTING ON THE NINTENDO WII.

FEATURE/
SHIGERU MIYAMOTO

MIYAMOTO MAY NOT HAVE INVENTED THE VIDEOGAME, BUT PERHAPS MORE THAN ANYONE ELSE, HE HAS BEEN RESPONSIBLE FOR MAKING IT WHAT IT IS TODAY

N64

Launched in 1996, the N64 (short for Nintendo 64) was Nintendo's most powerful console to date – and the vehicle for Shigeru Miyamoto's Mario masterpiece *Super Mario 64*. Taking 3D to a new level, the game is the best-selling N64 title ever, with over 11 million sales.

* NEW RECORD
■ UPDATED RECORD

A delayed game is eventually good, but a rushed game is forever bad.

Miyamoto defends his reputation for delaying titles

Raised in the 1950s in the quiet, rural town of Sonobe, near Kyoto, Japan, the young Shigeru Miyamoto was, even then, well accustomed to creating his own entertainment. Growing up without a television, he relied instead on the natural world for kicks, spending his days exploring the woods, caves and riverbanks near his home. It was these childhood adventures that would foster Miyamoto's love of discovery and go on to inspire the games he created, perhaps most notably *The Legend of Zelda*, with his beloved caves and forests providing the series' enchanting backdrops.

Graduating in 1975 with a degree in industrial design, Miyamoto landed his first job two years later, after his

KEY GAME
NINTENDOGS

With sales of 22.5 million as of August 2009, Miyamoto's hugely popular pet sim is the best-selling game for the DS, surpassing even *Dr. Kawashima's Brain Training*. Infused with Miyamoto's characteristic charm and imagination, the 2005 title won the *PC World* Innovation Award in 2006.

KEY GAME
DONKEY KONG

Miyamoto's first ever title, *Donkey Kong* (or "Stubborn Gorilla") remains one of the most important videogames ever created, for without it, the likes of *Zelda and Mario* may never have seen the light of day. Released in 1981, the game was the young Nintendo employee's one big chance to break into game design – and Miyamoto seized it with both hands. Just as "Jumpman" climbs the scaffold to rescue his girlfriend in the game, the game itself saved the struggling Nintendo of America from the brink of bankruptcy – and from then on, Miyamoto's future was assured.

father called in a favour from an old friend – Hiroshi Yamauchi, the then president of Nintendo. Miyamoto started out designing panel art for arcade cabinets such as *Sheriff* and *Radar Scope*, but his big break came in 1979 when Yamauchi called him into his office and offered him a dream assignment: to design his own arcade game for the US market.

Released in 1981, Miyamoto's *Donkey Kong* was an instant success. To keep up with demand, 2,000 *Radar Scope* cabinets recently emblazoned with Miyamoto's artwork were refitted to play the more successful game. In the end, *Donkey Kong* sold 67,000 cabinets, turning Nintendo's handful of American staff, all of whom worked on commission, into millionaires overnight.

This was just the start of Miyamoto's career, and he was soon promoted to head of Nintendo's reseach and development studio, where he produced classics such as *Super Mario Bros.* and *The Legend of Zelda*. Unlike many of his contemporaries, Miyamoto managed to stay abreast of every generational leap in technology, and was the first to master the transition from 2D to 3D with his seminal titles *Super Mario 64* and the *Zelda* sequel *Ocarina of Time*.

Today, in his role as General Manager of Nintendo EAD, Miyamoto continues to redefine what games can and should be through the record-breaking success of his Wii console design. A pioneer of the use of the motion-sensing technology that defines the Wii, Miyamoto remains a prolific designer and producer, and despite having over 100 titles to his name, he continues to infuse new games with that same giddying sense of wonder that he himself enjoyed as a child.

KEY GAME
WII SPORTS

With *Super Mario Bros.* having held the **best-selling game** record for over 20 years, it was almost inevitable that the game's conqueror would be another Nintendo title from the Miyamoto stable – *Wii Sports* (2006), with 45.7 million copies sold as of May 2009.

FACT

▷ *Mario's bushy moustache was a forced design decision. As his character sprite in Donkey Kong was so small, it was difficult to display lips in a way that looked believable. The black blocky facial hair was an elegant solution to a tricky problem.*

▷ *In 2008, Miyamoto topped the "100 Most Influential People" list in* Time *magazine.*

TRIVIA

▷ *"When you draw a laughing face, your face should laugh. When you draw an angry face, your face should be angry. The character will capture your emotion. The emotions and fun in a game are not made while thinking about business."* Miyamoto on infusing game characters with emotion.

▷ *Miyamoto was honoured as the first inductee into the Academy of Interactive Arts and Sciences Hall of Fame in 1998.*

▷ *Miyamoto is ambidextrous but usually favours his left hand – as do his characters Mario, Link and Bowser Jr.*

▷ *Miyamoto is the only game designer to receive France's Order of Arts and Letters, which recognizes significant contributions to literature and the arts.*

FIGHTING GAMES

CONTENTS:

Since its release in November 2008, Midway's *Mortal Kombat vs DC Universe* has shifted over 1.9 million copies, enough to earn it a place in the developer's "Hall of Fame" of million-selling titles.

INTRODUCTION

! FROM FISTS TO FIREARMS: CHECK OUT THE BEST SHOOTING GAMES, FROM P.44.

KEY GAME TEKKEN

The first game to sell 1 million units on the PlayStation, *Tekken* was popular due to its intuitive control method, having one button per arm or leg. *Tekken 6* is one of the most hotly anticipated games of 2009.

WHEN PUSH COMES TO SHOVE, EVERY GAMER KNOWS THERE ARE FEW THINGS MORE SATISFYING THAN LANDING AN OPPONENT ON THE CANVAS WITH A PERFECTLY EXECUTED "COMBO"

The fighting genre can be traced back to SEGA's *Heavyweight Champ*, which punched its way to prominence in arcades in 1976. The **first fist-fighting game**, *Champ* also proved to be ahead of its time, featuring an ambitious boxing glove peripheral that players used to simulate punches and blocks.

Three years later, Vectorbeam unleashed the coin-op *Warrior*, in which two knights duelled it out in monochrome vector graphics. However, it was an unstable and volatile machine, and the fighting genre hit the ropes until the arrival of *Karate Champ* and *Kung-Fu Master* in the early 1980s. These games helped set the template for many of today's fighting games, but it was arcade classic *Kung-Fu Master* that had the greatest influence, spawning a sub-genre of its own, known as the "beat-em-up", which was characterized by side-scrolling action involving lots of AI-controlled enemies.

Fighters soon became a staple of the videogame world, and most major publishers invested in their own series in the late 1980s. The true watershed moment, though, came in 1991, when Capcom released *Street Fighter II* in arcades. Its perfect blend of colourful 2D characters, sublime animation and incredible playability single-handedly kick-started a fighting games boom.

> A clenched fist speaks louder than a hundred words.
>
> *Ryu, quoted in Street Fighter*

* **NEW RECORD**
■ **UPDATED RECORD**

TIMELINE

1976
SEGA pioneers the fighting game, with rudimentary boxing sim *Heavyweight Champ*, which is followed into the arcade three years later by *Warrior*, from Vectorbeam.

1984
The arcade launch of Irem's *Kung-Fu Master* marks the debut of the 2D side-scrolling fighter, and helps establish what becomes the beat-em-up sub-genre.

1991
With a strong cast of characters and moves, *Street Fighter II* sets the benchmark for 2D fighters and becomes the **best-selling coin-op fighting game**.

1992
Capitalizing on Capcom's *Street Fighter* success, Midway launches the first game in its *Mortal Kombat* series, which earns over $1 billion in just 12 months.

1993
SEGA takes fighters into a new dimension with the sensational *Virtua Fighter* (left), which is released to critical acclaim as the **first 3D fighting game**.

$1 BILLION (£660 MILLION)...
Midway's earnings from *Mortal Kombat* in its 1992 year of release, which is the **most successful launch of a fighting game**.

OVERVIEW

> The fighting game genre speaks for itself – usually with its fists doing the talking. In these games, players take control of a character and engage in close-quarters combat with one or more enemies. The first fighting games took place on a static, 2D plane, but it wasn't long before the beat-em-up introduced a side-scrolling, narrative element and multiple enemies for players to battle along the way. The games were incredibly popular in the 16-bit era of the late 1980s and early 1990s, until the advent of 3D fighting took things to a new level. Today, both 2D and 3D fighters happily co-exist, while beat-em-ups have largely been usurped by the hack-and-slash sub-genre.

2D fighters continued to flourish through the early 1990s, with *Mortal Kombat* and *Killer Instinct* proving popular both in the arcades and, later, on home consoles. The next defining moment came only two years later, in 1993, when SEGA released *Virtua Fighter* in arcades. The title was the **first fighting game to use polygon graphics** instead of sprites, and it set the stage for every 3D fighting series since, including *Tekken*, *SoulCalibur* and *Dead or Alive*.

The advent of 3D dealt a critical blow to the beat-em-up and helped define a new sub-genre called hack and slash, which added short-range weapons to the mix. These games are defined by over-the-top combat that rewards players for stylish play, and popular titles include *Devil May Cry* and *Ninja Gaiden*. For some time, it appeared that these 3D brawlers had in fact killed off the 2D format, yet the sub-genre hit back through 2008's phenomenally successful *Street Fighter IV*. Meanwhile, The Behemoth's Xbox 360-exclusive *Castle Crashers* gave the beat-em-up its own much-needed shot in the arm.

For now, then, it seems that while 3D looks set to dominate, there remains plenty of room within the genre for that rare, exceptional title that truly captures the imagination.

KEY GAME
PUNCHOUT!!

A fighting series that refused to die, the original *Punch-Out!!* arcade game was released by Nintendo back in 1984 and was followed by a number of iterations culminating in *Super Punch-Out!!* for SNES in 1994. Fans of the series then faced a wait of 15 years for the next instalment, *Punch-Out!!*, to be released on the Wii in May 2009.

EXPERT

> Guy Cocker is the features editor for GameSpot UK, where he writes and hosts the GameSpot UK Podcast and the weekly video show Start/Select. He has also written for The Telegraph newspaper, Hotdog magazine and CNET UK. Always up for a bit of videogame violence, Guy's favourite game is Virtua Fighter 5.

TRIVIA

> The late "King of Pop", Michael Jackson, had long been credited as an arcade collector, and was always a keen fan of fighting games. In April 2009, the US superstar was due to auction off much of his videogame collection, including over 110 arcade cabinets, pinball machines and other related items. To go under the hammer were such revered fighting titles as Mortal Kombat, Tekken 2, Super Street Fighter II and Marvel vs. Capcom. Unfortunately for collectors, Jacko pulled the plug on the sale at the last minute.

FRANCHISE VS FRANCHISE

The tradition of pitting fighters from one successful franchise against another began in 1996 when Capcom, publisher/developer of both the *X-Men* beat-em-ups and the genre-defining *Street Fighter* series, brought out the *X-Men vs. Street Fighter* arcade machine. The game, the first to feature tag-team fighting, was enough of a success to spawn a host of other "versus" titles, including Midway's *Mortal Kombat vs. DC Universe* (2008, pictured).

1994	1996	2001	2008	2008	2009
Tekken takes the arcades by storm and is later ported to the PlayStation in 1995, becoming one of the Sony console's most important titles in its fledgling days.	Overshadowed in the West by *Tekken*, Tecmo's arcade fighter *Dead or Alive* is well received in Japan, with its unique gameplay style focusing on speed and reaction.	*Devil May Cry* is released on the PlayStation 2, creating a sub-genre of "extreme combat" games that will inspire classics-to-be *Ninja Gaiden* and *God of War*.	*Castle Crashers*, from The Behemoth, breathes new life into the beat-em-up and, in just over four months, becomes the **best-selling Xbox Live Arcade title of 2008**.	After an 11-year gap in the series, *Street Fighter IV* arrives in arcades, achieving huge critical success – and the top spot in the charts when later released on PS3 and Xbox 360.	Produced by *Mario* creator Shigeru Miyamoto, *Punch-Out!!* hits the Wii, taking advantage of the console's motion-sensitive Remote, Nunchuk and Balance Board.

2D FIGHTERS

! IF YOU PREFER A MORE FREE-ROAMING AFFAIR, CHECK OUT SANDBOX TITLES ON P.90.

✱ MOST SUCCESSFUL CHARACTER IN STREET FIGHTER IV

Holder: SAGAT

According to figures released by Capcom that track the results of thousands of online matches, Sagat is statistically the strongest character in *Street Fighter IV* (2008). Sagat has a win-loss ratio of 49:31, meaning he wins around 61% of matches. By contrast, Rose is the weakest character, with a ratio of 53:67, equating to a measly 44% chance of victory.

« *Capcom had to make this game. We can't let the fans down. We can't let the company name down.* »
Yoshinori Ono, Street Fighter IV producer

OVERVIEW

▶ *The 2D fighting sub-genre is a relatively simple proposition – players engage in one-on-one combat with an opponent and battle it out until only one of them is left standing. These games take place on a flat plane, meaning characters can move back and forth across the screen and can jump in the air, but they cannot move between the foreground and background. Sometimes weapons are used, such as in Killer Instinct and Mortal Kombat, but the majority of 2D fighters focus on unarmed hand-to-hand combat based on martial arts. Characters are given various attributes such as power, speed and stamina, and players must maximize their strengths and avoid exposing their weaknesses.*

TEN GAMES YOU SHOULD PLAY IN THIS GENRE

	GAME
1	Super Street Fighter II Turbo HD Remix (2008)
2	Street Fighter IV (2008)
3	Killer Instinct Gold (1996)
4	Super Smash Bros. Brawl (2008)
5	The King of Fighters '98 (1998)
6	Marvel vs. Capcom 2 (2000)
7	X-Men: Children of the Atom (1994)
8	Street Fighter Alpha 3 Max (2006)
9	Guilty Gear XX (2002)
10	Mortal Kombat vs. DC Universe (2008)

LONGEST RUN OF WINS AGAINST HUMAN OPPONENTS IN STREET FIGHTER IV

Holder: ZAK BENNETT (UK)
In an event held to celebrate the European launch of *Street Fighter IV* on Xbox 360 and PlayStation 3, British gamer Zak Bennett beat 108 human opponents one after another, at HMV Oxford Street in London, UK, on 20 February 2009. Zak set the impressive record on his second attempt of the day, after his first had ended in defeat to fellow Brit Hatim Habashi (aka The Prince), who was previously crowned the Official UK *Virtua Fighter 2* Champion by SEGA Europe after an unbroken run of 28 victories.

BEST-SELLING FIGHTING GAME

Holder: SUPER SMASH BROS. BRAWL (Nintendo, 2008)
Nintendo's fun fighter *Super Smash Bros. Brawl* on the Wii has sold 8.43 million copies worldwide to date, more than any other fighting game in history. *Super Smash Bros. Brawl* also represents **Nintendo of America's most successful launch**, selling a staggering 874,000 copies on the day of release, 9 May 2008, alone. In fact, the game continued to fly off the shelves at an incredible rate during its entire first week on sale, with Nintendo reporting sales of 120 units every minute, or two units every second.

RAREST CONSOLE FIGHTING GAME

Holder: KIZUNA ENCOUNTER (SNK, 1996)
The rarest fighting game for a home console is the European PAL version of SNK's *Kizuna Encounter* on the Neo-Geo. It is uncertain whether the game was ever actually released in the PAL territories and only five copies of this version of the game cartridge are known to exist. If you are lucky enough to find one, a cartridge can fetch up to $12,500 (£7,740). Copies of the NTSC version are both cheaper and in more plentiful supply.

HIGHEST SCORE ON MARVEL VS. CAPCOM 2

Holder: ZACH ROBINSON (USA)
On 13 February 2008, Zach Robinson from Washington, USA, fought his way to an impressive score of 1,987,420,900 points on the arcade version of Capcom's *Marvel vs. Capcom 2* (2000). The attempt was made on the hardest difficulty setting and conducted under strict Twin Galaxies tournament rules.

MOST PLAYED WII GAME

Holder: SUPER SMASH BROS. BRAWL (Nintendo, 2008)
The Wii game that clocks up the most hours on average is Nintendo's *Super Smash Bros. Brawl*. According to statistics compiled by Gamer website Kotaku from data released on the Nintendo Channel (which tracks usage stats for the console's games), *Brawl* keeps the average gamer entertained for a marathon 66 hr 32 min.

FIRST FIGHTING GAME TURNED INTO A MOVIE

Holder: FATAL FURY (SNK, 1991 to present)
The first live-action movie based on a fighting game is 1994's *Double Dragon*. However, *Double Dragon* is actually pre-dated by an animated movie based on the fighting game series *Fatal Fury*. The movie, *Fatal Fury: The Motion Picture*, was released in Japan just weeks before *Street Fighter*, and though it does not follow the plot of the games, it does feature characters from the first two titles.

- ● **NEW RECORD**
- ● **UPDATED RECORD**

FACT

▶ *Street Fighter II's* (Capcom, 1991) Chun-Li was the **first playable female character in a fighting game**. She has since made appearances in *Marvel vs. Capcom* (1998) and *Capcom vs. SNK* (2000), while she's also the first fighting game character to have a movie based on her – *Street Fighter: The Legend of Chun-Li* (2009).

TRIVIA

▶ The PSP is the only Sony console to have launched in the UK without a fighting game in its software line-up.

▶ *Mortal Kombat vs. DC Universe* (2008) is not the first time the DC superheroes have had their own fighting game. No fewer than 14 years earlier, Batman, Superman and Wonder Woman all appeared in a little-known fighting game called *Justice League Task Force* (1995). The game was developed by Warcraft creator Blizzard.

▶ *Shaq-Fu*, a fighting game released by EA in 1994 and starring US basketball player Shaquille O'Neal, is widely considered to be one of the worst games ever made. Taking direct action against it, website Shaqfu.com is dedicated to buying up and destroying all remaining copies of the game.

3D FIGHTERS

! IF YOU PREFER FIGHTING WITH TOOLS, TURN TO P.114 FOR SOME HACK AND SLASH CARNAGE.

✱ MOST CRITICALLY ACCLAIMED FIGHTING GAME

Holder: SOULCALIBUR
(Namco, 1998)
The highest-rated fighting game is the SEGA Dreamcast version of Namco's *SoulCalibur*, which scored 98% on review aggregator website Metacritic, and 96.26% on GameRankings. The title is also the top-ranked Dreamcast game on both websites.

« *The greatest weapon-based fighting action game in the world...*
SoulCalibur, as described by its producer, Hiroaki Yotoriyama »

TEN GAMES YOU SHOULD PLAY IN THIS GENRE

	GAME
1	Tekken 5: Dark Resurrection (2005)
2	Virtua Fighter 5 (2006)
3	Dead or Alive 4 (2005)
4	SoulCalibur (1998)
5	SoulCalibur IV (2008)
6	Def Jam: Icon (2007)
7	Power Stone Collection (2006)
8	Mortal Kombat: Armageddon (2006)
9	Fighters Megamix (1996)
10	Dragon Ball Z: Budokai Tenkaichi 3 (2007)

✱ NEW RECORD
◼ UPDATED RECORD

1.7 MILLION... worldwide sales of the Saturn version of the spectacular *Virtua Fighter* (1993), making it the **best-selling game for the SEGA Saturn.**

OVERVIEW

> The 3D fighting game differs from its 2D counterpart by allowing players to move around the entire game environment, rather than just forwards and backwards on a 2D plane. The sub-genre was kick-started by SEGA's *Virtua Fighter* in 1993, which rendered its characters with polygons rather than traditional 2D sprites. The impact of this new technique on the games industry cannot be overstated – *Virtua Fighter* became the most popular game ever released on the SEGA Saturn, while the PlayStation's early success was largely down to Namco's 3D fighter *Tekken*. The genre enjoyed its peak popularity in the late 1990s, but it's still capable of producing big hits, especially from established franchises such as *SoulCalibur*, *Virtua Fighter* and *Tekken*.

FIRST FIGHTER TO USE 3D POLYGON GRAPHICS

Holder: **VIRTUA FIGHTER** (SEGA, 1993)
The first fully 3D fighting game was SEGA's *Virtua Fighter*, released in Japanese arcades in November 1993. The game employed polygon graphics to create its characters, as opposed to the animated sprites of 2D fighters. The game was also notable for its incorporation of a three-button layout (punch, kick and guard), when practically every other fighting game had four- or six-button configurations.

FASTEST COMPLETION OF MORTAL KOMBAT: ARMAGEDDON (ARCADE)

Holder: **MICHAEL J GIRARD** (USA)
American Michael J Girard completed the arcade version of *Mortal Kombat: Armageddon* (Midway, 2006) in just 13 min 16 sec in Grand Rapids, Minnesota, USA, on 9 May 2009. Michael played bouts lasting a maximum of 60 seconds, although the majority of his speedy slap-downs didn't go the distance.

HIGHEST SCORE ON SOULCALIBUR IV (XBOX 360)

Holder: **LANCE EUSTACHE** (USA)
On 18 June 2009, American Lance Eustache scored a record 395,480 on the Xbox 360 version of *SoulCalibur IV* (Namco, 2008), in Arverne, New York, USA.

FASTEST COMPLETION OF VIRTUA FIGHTER 2 (ARCADE)

Holder: **BRANDON SMITH** (USA)
It took Brandon Smith just 2 min 40.79 sec to complete the arcade version of *Virtua Fighter 2* (SEGA, 1994), on 6 November 2004. He did it all on the game's hardest setting.

FIRST 3D FIGHTING GAME FOR A HANDHELD CONSOLE

Holder: **TEKKEN ADVANCE** (Namco, 2001)
The first 3D fighting game on a portable console was *Tekken Advance*, released on the Game Boy Advance in 2001. While the game uses sprites for the characters, rather than polygons, it's still the first portable fighter that plays on a 3D plane.

FASTEST COMPLETION OF MORTAL KOMBAT 4 (N64)

Holder: **MICHAEL T VALENTI** (USA)
Michael Valenti fought his way through the US version of *Mortal Kombat 4* (Midway, 1997) in 7 min 33 sec, on his N64 at home in Indianapolis, Indiana, USA, on 9 December 2008.

FIRST 3D FIGHTING GAME TO OFFER ONLINE PLAY

Holder: **MORTAL KOMBAT: DECEPTION** (Midway, 2004)
Although online play is now a standard feature in all new fighting games, the first online-playable 3D fighter was *Mortal Kombat: Deception*, released in 2004. The game offered one-on-one fighting between two players over the Internet, in addition to two more sedate mini games – *Puzzle Kombat* and *Chess Kombat*.

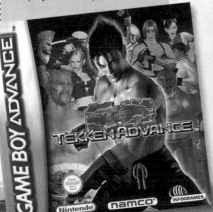

BEAT-EM-UPS

! FOR TITLES THAT PACK A LITTLE MORE FIREPOWER, CHECK OUT SHOOTING GAMES FROM P.44.

* BEST-SELLING XBOX LIVE ARCADE TITLE OF 2008

Holder: CASTLE CRASHERS (Microsoft, 2008)
Proving that a good beat-em-up never goes out of fashion, the best-selling Xbox Live Arcade title of 2008 was The Behemoth's *Castle Crashers*, which was the developer's follow-up to their 2007 release *Alien Hominid HD*. *Castle Crashers* managed to fend off *Geometry Wars: Retro Evolved[2]* and *Braid* to claim the top spot. Even more impressively, it did so with just over four months on the market, having only been released on 27 August 2008.

* NEW RECORD
* UPDATED RECORD

TEN GAMES YOU SHOULD PLAY IN THIS GENRE

	GAME
1	Castle Crashers (2008)
2	Streets of Rage II (1992)
3	Final Fight 3 (1995)
4	Double Dragon (1987)
5	Comix Zone (1995)
6	Golden Axe (1989)
7	The Simpsons Arcade Game (1991)
8	Teenage Mutant Ninja Turtles (1989)
9	Cadillacs and Dinosaurs (1992)
10	Viewtiful Joe (2003)

Thankfully, we have games like Castle Crashers to remind us how fun simplicity used to be.
thunderboltgames.com

2... the number of times the characters use swear words in Capcom's 1992 classic *Cadillacs and Dinosaurs* – which is twice more than was usual in those days.

OVERVIEW

> The beat-em-up sprung out of the fighting genre when Kung-Fu Master *broke into Japanese arcades in 1984. Instead of one-on-one fighting, the beat-em-up typically pits players against multiple on-screen enemies. The first mega-hits of the genre were 1987's* Double Dragon, *which was turned into a movie, and 1989's* Final Fight, *which originally began life as a* Street Fighter *sequel.* Streets of Rage II, *developed as SEGA's answer to* Final Fight, *is commonly considered to be the best example of the beat-em-up. Today, the genre is spearheaded by the highly acclaimed download title* Castle Crashers.

"I will get my revenge!"

✳ HIGHEST SCORE ON NINJA GAIDEN (NES)

Holder: KRISTIAN EMANUELSEN (Norway)
Norwegian Kristian Emanuelsen is Twin Galaxies' undisputed champion on the NES-era *Ninja Gaiden* (Tecmo, 1988), which is regarded as one of the toughest games of its time. Emanuelsen holds the records for highest score (1,226,800) and fastest completion (12 min 23 sec) of the US version of the game, as well as the fastest completion (13 min 26 sec) of the European version, known as *Shadow Warriors*.

✳ FIRST SIDE-SCROLLING BEAT-EM-UP

Holder: KUNG-FU MASTER
(Irem, 1984)
The first ever side-scrolling beat-em-up was *Kung-Fu Master*, released in Japanese arcades in 1984. Laying down the template for the genre, *Kung-Fu Master* featured multiple enemies, five side-scrolling floors and a clichéd storyline that revolved around saving a girlfriend. The game was ported to numerous home computers and consoles, and has been cited as the inspiration for a number of other series in the beat-em-up genre, including *Final Fight* and *Streets of Rage*.

✳ FASTEST 100% COMPLETION OF BATTLETOADS

Holder: PABLO "DJ MIKE HAGGAR" BERT (USA)
Battletoads (Nintendo, 1991) is revered by beat-em-up fans not only as one of the best-looking NES titles ever made, but also as one of the genre's most difficult games, which makes Pablo Bert's record completion time of 34 min 17 sec all the more impressive. Bert completed his record-breaking speed run through all 12 levels of the game on 13 May 2008.

✳ FIRST CEL-SHADED BEAT-EM-UP

Holder: VIEWTIFUL JOE (Capcom, 2003)
Released on the GameCube in Japan in June 2003, *Viewtiful Joe* was the first beat-em-up to feature cel-shading, a technique used to make videogame graphics appear hand drawn. Coming at the height of cel-shading mania (kicked off by *Jet Set Radio* in 2000), *Viewtiful Joe* combined traditional hand-to-hand combat with "VFX Powers", which allowed the player to slow down and speed up time.

FIRST BEAT-EM-UP VIDEOGAME ADAPTED TO FILM

Holder: DOUBLE DRAGON
(Taito, 1987)
The first movie based on a side-scrolling beat-em-up was *Double Dragon*, which was released in US cinemas on 4 November 1994. Incidentally, it's also considered to be one of the worst videogame movies ever made, ranking at number eight in *Time* magazine's "Top 10 Worst Video Game Movies" – go to www.time.com for the full list.

FACT

> *Makoto Uchida (Japan) was the first third-party game designer to have two games on the Nintendo Virtual Console in Europe. His beat-em-up titles* Altered Beast *and* Golden Axe *were released on 8 December 2006 to coincide with the launch of the online service.*

TRIVIA

> *SEGA classic* Golden Axe *(1989) sampled and digitized screams from the movies* First Blood *(1982) and* Conan the Barbarian *(1982) to create the blood-curdling death throes of the game's villains.*

> Fighting Force, *developed by Tomb Raider creators Core Design and released in 1997 by Eidos, was originally intended to be* Streets of Rage 4. *However, SEGA pulled the* Streets of Rage *name during development after a disagreement with Core, who wanted to port the game to rival formats such as the PlayStation and N64. In any case, by then the beat-em-up genre had stagnated, mainly thanks to a lack of innovation and the market's new obsession with 3D.*

NINTENDO GAMECUBE

VIEWTIFUL JOE

12+
CAPCOM
PAL Nintendo

HACK AND SLASH

! PREFER RUN AND GUN TO HACK AND SLASH? THEN CHECK OUT P.56.

* BEST-SELLING HACK AND SLASH SERIES

Holder: DEVIL MAY CRY (Capcom, 2001 to present)
Capcom's classic hack and slash series *Devil May Cry* has notched up a record 7.57 million games sold, as of June 2009. When the original *Devil May Cry* launched on the PlayStation 2 in 2001, it was an immediate hit and went on to sell 2 milion copies worldwide. The latest entry in the franchise, 2008's *Devil May Cry 4* (pictured), is the biggest-selling title in the series to date, shifting 2.4 million copies since its launch.

« A brilliant, gun-blasting, sword-swinging action-fest like you've never seen before. »

IGN.com's review of the original Devil May Cry

* **NEW RECORD**
■ **UPDATED RECORD**

TEN GAMES YOU SHOULD PLAY IN THIS GENRE

	GAME
1	Devil May Cry 4 (2008)
2	Ninja Gaiden Black (2005)
3	God of War II (2007)
4	Dynasty Warriors: Gundam (2007)
5	Onimusha: Dawn of Dreams (2006)
6	God of War: Chains of Olympus (2008)
7	Ninja Gaiden II (2008)
8	No More Heroes (2007)
9	Ninety-Nine Nights (2006)
10	Ninja Blade (2009)

93.44% AND 92.61%... the scores for PlayStation 2 versions of *God of War* and *God of War II* respectively on GameRankings, indicating exceptional critical acclaim.

OVERVIEW

> *The hack and slash genre as we know it today was defined by Devil May Cry on the PlayStation 2. The game laid the template for the stylish, fast-paced and visceral action that we've come to expect from a modern weapons-based action title. Japanese developers have tended to excel in the genre, especially with Ninja Gaiden on the Xbox and No More Heroes on the Wii, both of which rank as the finest hack and slash games on their formats. However, Western developers have also pushed the genre, notably with God of War on the PlayStation 2 and PSP, as well as the upcoming Dante's Inferno from EA.*

✴ FASTEST NINJA GAIDEN BLACK SPEED RUN

Holder: JOSH MANGINI (USA)
US gamer Josh Mangini completed Tecmo's 2005 release *Ninja Gaiden Black* on the Xbox 360 in a total time of 1 hr 55 min 5 sec. As well as being one of the best games ever to grace the original Xbox, *Ninja Gaiden* (with its remakes *Black* and *Sigma*) is also considered one of the hardest. Even on the default difficulty level, the powerful enemies and bosses mean that dying is a frequent occurrence. Not enough to stop Josh Mangini, though, who completed the game in an accumulated time of 1 hr 41 min 8 sec when he tackled the game in stages.

✴ FIRST PLAYSTATION 2 GAME TO SELL OVER 1 MILLION UNITS IN JAPAN

Holder: ONIMUSHA: WARLORDS (Capcom, 2001)
Capcom's *Onimusha: Warlords*, released on 25 January 2001, is the first PlayStation 2 game to sell over 1 million copies in Japan. Created by some of the same team behind *Resident Evil*, the *Warlords* title was a phenomenal success when it launched alongside the PlayStation 2 in Japan. The game, which was set in feudal Japan, surpassed the 1 million sales mark in that country in less than a month, and went on to sell over 2 million copies worldwide. The Xbox port of the game, *Genma: Onimusha*, also has the distinction of being the first game Capcom released for a Microsoft platform, as it hit the Xbox on 28 January 2002.

✴ BEST-SELLING HACK AND SLASH GAME

Holder: THE LORD OF THE RINGS: THE TWO TOWERS (EA, 2002)
In the hack and slash genre, the best-selling game of all time is *The Lord of the Rings: The Two Towers*, which has sold 4.28 million copies worldwide. This is more than any of the *Devil May Cry* or *Ninja Gaiden* games sold individually.

✴ MOST CRITICALLY ACCLAIMED PSP GAME

Holder: GOD OF WAR: CHAINS OF OLYMPUS (Sony, 2008)
God of War: Chains of Olympus has an aggregate score of 91.29% on GameRankings and 91% on Metacritic, making it the most highly acclaimed game on the PSP.

✴ FIRST GAME TO ALLOW SIMULTANEOUS FOUR-PLAYER CONTROL

Holder: GAUNTLET (Atari, 1985)
Launched in arcades in 1985, the first game to allow simultaneous four-player action was fantasy-themed *Gauntlet*. The game featured four sets of inputs, allowing cooperation through a number of unique play mechanics. It went on to have a huge influence on the arcades, with many of the big titles that followed also shipping in four-player cabinets.

TRIVIA

> *Games theorists Chris Bateman and Richard Boon cite Devil May Cry as the beginning of a new sub-genre of action games that they call "extreme combat". In their book 21st Century Game Design, the pair claim these games are characterized by powerful heroes fighting hordes of foes with a focus on stylish action. This idea has particularly influenced Japanese developers, especially former Tecmo developer Tomonobu Itagaki, who headed up Ninja Gaiden and Ninja Gaiden II on the Xbox and Xbox 360 respectively. Director Hideki Kamiya (Japan), creator of the Devil May Cry series, has returned to the genre he created with upcoming game Bayonetta. Now at Platinum Games, who recently developed MadWorld for the Wii, Kamiya-san has promised that Bayonetta "will blow the doors off the action genre".*

COMBAT SPORTS

! FOR A LESS PUNISHING PASTIME, HAVE A LOOK AT THE REST OF THE SPORTING WORLD, FROM P.64.

✳ MOST CRITICALLY ACCLAIMED BOXING FRANCHISE

Holder: FIGHT NIGHT (EA, 2004 to present)

With four titles under its belt since the series' 2004 debut, EA's *Fight Night* franchise has become the undisputed king of the ring. With an average rating of 85% on review aggregator website Metacritic, the series has managed to see off all challengers, only letting its guard down once, with the PSP version of *Round 3* achieving a below par average of 74%.

« UFC offers the fighting videogame genre a fresh and innovative look inside today's most exciting live sporting event in the world.

Dana White, UFC president

TEN GAMES YOU SHOULD PLAY IN THIS GENRE

	GAME
1	*Fight Night: Round 4* (2009)
2	*UFC 2009: Undisputed* (2009)
3	*Punch-Out!!* (1984)
4	*Fire Pro Wrestling Returns* (2005)
5	*WWE SmackDown! Here Comes The Pain* (2003)
6	*Rocky* (2002)
7	*Fire Pro Wrestling D* (2001)
8	*International Karate +* (1987)
9	*WWF Wrestlemania 2000* (1999)
10	*Victorious Boxers: Challenge* (2007)

2 SECONDS... all it takes for some gamers to win a bout in *UFC 2009: Undisputed* – with a perfectly executed "flash KO".

NEW RECORD UPDATED RECORD

OVERVIEW

> Sporting combat has been a staple of videogaming almost as long as the industry has existed. SEGA's basic boxing sim *Heavyweight Champ* arrived as early as 1976, but "the noble art" has since come a long way in gaming terms, with *Fight Night: Round 4* and Nintendo's *Punch-Out!!* remake for the Wii being the most notable recent releases. Away from boxing, it's wrestling that dominates the combat sports scene, with the *WWE* and *Fire Pro Wrestling* franchises proving particularly popular with fight fans. Martial arts, on the other hand, are less well represented, with these disciplines being more frequently incorporated into action-based fighting games. One exception, though, is Mixed Martial Arts, a controversial sport that is beginning to gain digital notoriety in its own right, in the form of titles such as *UFC 2009: Undisputed* and EA's hotly anticipated *MMA*.

BEST-SELLING WRESTLING FRANCHISE

Holder: **WWE SMACKDOWN!/ WWE SMACKDOWN! VS. RAW** (THQ, 1999 to present)
There have been well over 50 videogames based on the World Wrestling Entertainment (WWE) brand, but it's the *SmackDown!* series (known as *SmackDown! vs. RAW* since 2004) that has been the overwhelming success, selling over 47 million copies worldwide. The current developer of the franchise, Yuke's, is also responsible for the acclaimed Mixed Martial Arts title *UFC 2009: Undisputed* (THQ, 2009).

BEST-SELLING COMBAT SPORTS GAME

Holder: **WWE SMACKDOWN! VS. RAW 2008** (THQ, 2007)
With over 6.65 million copies sold across six console formats, *WWE SmackDown! vs. RAW 2008* is the best-selling combat sports game of all-time. The PlayStation 2 version, sometimes shortened to *WWE SvR 2008* or *SvR '08*, was the top performer, shifting an impressive 2.05 million units on its own. Meanwhile, the PlayStation 2 also plays host to the **best-selling combat sports game on a single format** – this record is held by 2000's *WWF SmackDown! 2: Know Your Role*, which was developed by Yuke's and published by THQ. It sold 3.2 million copies.

MOST RECORDED COMMENTARY IN A FIGHTING GAME

Holder: **UFC 2009: UNDISPUTED** (THQ, 2009)
With over 36 hours of voiceover work, the commentary accompanying each bout in *UFC 2009: Undisputed* is the most varied ever in a fighting game.

MOST PLAYABLE CHARACTERS IN A VIDEOGAME

Holder: **FIRE PRO WRESTLING RETURNS** (Spike, 2005)
With 327 fighters available to choose from, *Fire Pro Wrestling Returns* on the PS2 features the largest number of playable characters in a videogame. Hugely popular in Japan, the series remained a cult import for only the most dedicated of Western gamers until Japanese developer/ publisher Spike took over the series in 2001 and released *Fire Pro Wrestling* on the Game Boy Advance.

FIRST JUDO GAME

Holder: **UCHI MATA** (Martech, 1986)
Released on the Commodore 64 in 1986, *Uchi Mata* is the first videogame based on the combat sport of judo. The sport is generally under-represented in videogames, though certain fighting game characters do use judo moves, most notably Goh Hinogami from *Virtua Fighter 4: Evolution*.

TRIVIA

> In 1986, two games titled *Pro Wrestling* were released – one by SEGA for its Master System, and the other by Nintendo for the NES. Despite the SEGA game's memorable cover art – featuring a headless man cradling what appears to be his own head – it was the Nintendo game that proved the most successful and influential, becoming the **first combat sports videogame to sell over 1 million copies**.

> Sumo wrestling seldom makes the leap to videogame format, and even when it does, the games rarely see the light of day outside the sport's homeland, Japan. The only notable exceptions have been HESWare's *Sumo Wrestlers* (1985) for the Commodore 64, and DTMC's *Sumo Fighter* (1993) for the Nintendo Gameboy.

The **best-selling videogame of all time** is *Wii Sports*, which sold 45.7 million copies between its launch in 2006 and May 2009. Pictured is the game's sequel, *Wii Sports Resort,* launched July 2009.

CONTENTS:

INTRODUCTION

! IF YOU'RE INTERESTED IN MORE SIMULATION-STYLE GAMES, TURN TO P.170.

◆ NEW RECORD
◆ UPDATED RECORD

▣ BEST-SELLING RHYTHM GAME SERIES

Holder: GUITAR HERO (Red Octane, 2005; Activision, 2006 to present) Launched in 2005, the *Guitar Hero* series of games has seen total sales of over 32 million units between November 2005 and June 2009.

THANKS TO SOME SPECTACULAR INNOVATIONS IN MULTIPLAYER GAMING, IT HAS BEEN ONE BIG PARTY FOR VIDEOGAME FANS IN SEARCH OF THE ULTIMATE SHARED EXPERIENCE

Although early videogames such as *SpaceWar!* and *Pong* allowed two gamers to play together, and while the Nintendo Famicom (or "family computer") promoted videogames as a social experience, the party game genre is still relatively new.

It wasn't until the late 1980s, when the Amiga and its competitors began playing host to on-screen versions of board games such as *Trivial Pursuit* and *Hero Quest*, that the genre took off.

On consoles, technical limitations meant most games in the 8-bit and 16-bit eras supported a maximum of two players, until the PC Engine/TurboGrafx-16 became the **first console to support a multitap** – a peripheral that expanded the number of controller ports from one to five. Thereafter, expansions from two to four ports became

the norm, until the 1996 release of the Nintendo 64 (N64), which was the **first console to feature four controller ports**. The N64 soon became the party game console of choice for most gamers, with titles such as *Mario Kart 64* becoming multiplayer classics. The console also played host to the first incarnation of the *Mario Party* series, almost certainly the **most prolific party-game series on consoles**, with 11 games released to date.

Yet if Nintendo popularized the party game, it was Sony who revolutionized it. Former President of Sony Computer Entertainment Worldwide Studios Phil Harrison was a key champion of social gaming, helping to bring titles such as karaoke game *SingStar* and peripheral-enhanced quiz *Buzz!* to market.

« When we created the first Guitar Hero, we were advised that we should expect to sell around 150,000 copies.

Red Octane co-founder Charles Huang on the multi-million-selling Guitar Hero franchise »

TIMELINE

1961
The **first computerized two-player videogame**, *SpaceWar!*, is released for the PDP-1 computer and becomes an instant hit.

1972
Atari releases *Pong* – one of the most influential and important games in the history of the videogames industry, and a true two-player classic.

1983
Starpath releases *Party Mix* (right) for its Supercharger add-on to the Atari 2600 console. It is thought to be the **first ever four-player party videogame**.

1986
One of the most popular board games ever, *Trivial Pursuit* is released for home computers and consoles, supporting up to six players.

1995
Sierra releases the first instalment in comedy trivia series *You Don't Know Jack*. It is one of the only quiz/party games not suitable for younger players.

OVERVIEW

> Party games are multiplayer-centric experiences, created to encourage gamers to play together and targeted at a family audience. These games have quite simplistic controls and often feature a collection of straightforward, easily understandable tasks known as mini games. Nintendo's *Mario Party* series, starring Mario's nemesis Wario (right), is among the most popular of the genre's offerings, filled with dozens of games as part of a virtual board game. In recent years, the genre has expanded somewhat, with inclusive music-based experiences such as SingStar and Guitar Hero reinventing the party game, while quizzes such as Buzz! and Scene It? have encouraged families worldwide to gather around their consoles.

Neither game was the first of its kind, but each is the most successful within its sub-genre, with PlayStation 3 versions of both games also featuring online components.

Indeed, party games are no longer restricted to just one location, with music titles such as the wildly popular *Guitar Hero* and *Rock Band* franchises giving gamers the chance to party together while performing in different locations. *Guitar Hero*, in particular, has been a breakout success, becoming the **best-selling rhythm game series of all time**.

Meanwhile, Microsoft has launched rival titles of its own, with some success – karaoke game *Lips* was the **first karaoke game to feature wireless microphones**.

Yet it's Nintendo that has enjoyed the greatest success within the party-game genre, with its Wii console inviting a whole new audience to play games together. With its motion-sensing controller providing a more welcoming interface to less experienced players, it has proved a hit with consumers of all ages. Launch title *Wii Sports* has since gone on to become the **best-selling videogame of all time**, shifting more than 45 million copies

and even making an appearance at the 80th Academy Awards, such is its cultural significance.

As gaming expands its boundaries and becomes more inclusive, the party-game genre can only grow. The Wii has already played host to numerous mini-game compendiums and it's undeniable that such titles are making gaming far more socially acceptable than before. As games such as *Rock Band* and *SingStar* expand via downloadable content rather than yearly iterations, and Nintendo's Wii-branded titles bring new players into the fold, the party-game genre continues to be one of the most important recent developments in videogaming.

※ BEST-SELLING QUIZ SERIES

Holder: BUZZ! (Sony, 2005)
Finger-on-the-buzzer quiz franchise *Buzz!* passed the million mark for European sales as long ago as October 2008, and it continues to occupy the top sales spot in the Q&A genre.

EXPERT

> Chris Schilling has been gaming since the age of five. He is a prolific freelance writer, having contributed to a wide range of publications and websites, from The Daily Telegraph to the award-winning GamesTM.

TRIVIA

> Of the 15 launch titles for the original Xbox, the game reported to be Microsoft founder Bill Gates' (USA) favourite was not the incredibly popular sci-fi shooter Halo: Combat Evolved, nor acclaimed racer Project Gotham Racing. Gates' unlikely pick of the bunch was the simple yet addictive Fuzion Frenzy, a collection of 45 simple mini games.

> In November 2008, Microsoft's Scene It? box-office smash became the first game to support the user-created avatars of the format-holder's new Xbox Experience. The movie quiz title was also only the second game to be bundled with Microsoft's Big Button Pads.

1996	1998	2004	2005	2006
Nintendo launches the pioneering N64 (right), the **first home console to feature four controller ports**.	The first *Mario Party* collection of mini games is released for the N64.	Sony publishes the first instalment in its *SingStar* series – a hugely popular two-player home karaoke game that debuted on the PlayStation 2 platform.	Influenced by Konami arcade hit *GuitarFreaks*, developer Harmonix brings the rock star dream to the masses with the hugely successful *Guitar Hero*.	Nintendo launches its Wii console with *Wii Sports* – the most successful party game ever and one of the most important videogame releases of all time.

MINI GAMES

! IF YOU LIKE THESE, WHY NOT TAKE A LOOK AT SPORTS GAMES, STARTING ON P.64?

✱ FIRST GAME TO BE CONTROLLED BY THE PLAYER'S POSTERIOR

✱ NEW RECORD
▪ UPDATED RECORD

Holder: **RAYMAN RAVING RABBIDS TV PARTY** (Ubisoft, 2008)
Originally described by publisher Ubisoft as "the first video game you can play with your butt", *Rayman Raving Rabbids TV Party*, which was released in Europe on 18 November 2008, is the first game that can be controlled by the player's posterior. The "Beestie Boarding" mini game is controlled by sitting on the Wii Balance Board and shifting one's weight from cheek to cheek.

TEN GAMES YOU SHOULD PLAY IN THIS GENRE

	GAME
1	Wii Sports (2006)
2	WarioWare: Smooth Moves (2006)
3	Super Monkey Ball (2001)
4	Wii Play (2006)
5	Bishi Bashi Special (1998)
6	Mario & Sonic at the Olympic Games (2007)
7	Let's Tap (2008)
8	Rayman Raving Rabbids TV Party (2008)
9	Rhythm Paradise (2008)
10	WarioWare Inc.: Minigame Mania (2003)

91.366 M (299.75 FT)... the **farthest hammer throw** on *Mario & Sonic at the Olympic Games* by Andreas Danielsson (Sweden) in Stockholm, Sweden, on 26 March 2008.

GUINNESS WORLD RECORDS

OVERVIEW

Mini games are short challenges, often set against a time limit, which form part of a larger game. In multiplayer titles, such tasks are mostly competitive, requiring players to complete objectives, to collect certain items or to reach a specific points tally in order to triumph. Occasionally, players will have to team up, pitting two players against two others, or even three against one. Titles like *Mario Party* make use of mini games as a part of their central mechanic – in this case, to influence the outcome of a board game – whereas the *WarioWare* and *Rayman Raving Rabbids* games are comprised entirely of mini games.

Wii
WiiPlay
3+ PAL Nintendo

FACT

One of the funniest *Bishi Bashi Special* mini games didn't actually make it into the game itself – instead appearing as a Flash game on Konami's website to promote the title before its release. In the online-only mini game, you had to feed burgers and fries to Elvis Presley while keeping an eye on his weight.

* BEST-SELLING NON-BUNDLED GAME

Holder: WII PLAY
(Nintendo, 2006)
While *Wii Play* is the fourth all-time best-selling game, the top three were all sold as part of a bundle with the console on which they were released (for example, all-time best-seller *Wii Sports* was bundled with the Wii console). So, with sales of 22.98 million to date, *Wii Play* is the most successful game sold without a console.

TRIVIA

WarioWare Twisted! – regarded by many critics as the pinnacle of the series – was never released in Europe. The Game Boy Advance title came on a cartridge containing a gyroscopic sensor, which utilized the movement of the GBA itself, rather than button input, to control the mini games. The title's release was continually delayed, with some suggesting that the presence of mercury in the sensor meant it couldn't pass EU safety tests – though Nintendo refuted the suggestion. Ultimately, falling sales of the GBA in Europe made a late release a non-starter.

* BEST-SELLING GAMING CHARACTER CROSS-OVER

Holder: MARIO & SONIC AT THE OLYMPIC GAMES
(Nintendo/Sega, 2007)
Mario & Sonic at the Olympic Games has sold over 7.09 million copies on Wii and 4.22 million on DS since its launch in 2007, making it the most popular game to feature characters that originally starred in their own games. It was the first videogame to feature both iconic characters, who had been rivals for many years as mascots for Nintendo and Sega.

World first – the game even penguins can play!
Yuji Naka, describing his creation Let's Tap

MOST CRITICALLY ACCLAIMED MINI GAMES COMPILATION

Holder: WARIOWARE INC.: MINIGAME MANIA (Nintendo, 2003)
Nintendo's *WarioWare Inc.: Minigame Mania* received average review scores of 89% and 89.08% on review aggregator websites Metacritic and GameRankings respectively. The game is closely followed in the rankings by its sequel, *WarioWare: Twisted!*, which scored just one percentage point lower.

* MOST MINI GAMES IN A SINGLE VIDEOGAME

Holder: WARIOWARE: TWISTED (Nintendo, 2005)
WarioWare: Twisted boasts 223 mini games – more than any other release. However, the (currently) Japan-only *WarioWare: Myself* has the potential to outdo it via user-generated content – with players able to create and share their own mini games.

* FIRST THIRD-PARTY GAME TO SUPPORT THE WII BALANCE BOARD

Holder: FAMILY SKI (Namco-Bandai, 2008)
Namco-Bandai's *Family Ski* is the first third-party game to support the Wii Balance Board. In the game, the Wii Remote and Wii Nunchuck simulate ski poles, while the Wii Board enables players to simulate turning as they ski.

LIFESTYLE GAMES

⚠ IF YOU LIKE LIFESTYLE GAMES, CHECK OUT P.28 FOR THE BEST OF WII.

✳ BEST-SELLING PC GAME SERIES OF ALL TIME

Holder: THE SIMS (Maxis, 2000 to present)
Since its launch in 2000, *The Sims* series has sold over 100 million units, including expansions, making it the most successful PC game franchise ever. *The Sims* and its sequel *The Sims 2* are first and second respectively in the chart of the best-selling PC games of all time.

TEN GAMES YOU SHOULD PLAY IN THIS GENRE

	GAME
1	*Wii Fit* (2007)
2	*The Sims 3* (2009)
3	*Animal Crossing: Wild World* (2005)
4	*The Sims 2* (2004)
5	*Kudos 2* (2008)
6	*EA Sports Active* (2009)
7	*EyeToy: Kinetic* (2005)
8	*Cooking Mama* (2006)
9	*Imagine: Teacher* (2008)
10	*Let's Pilates* (2008)

NEW RECORD ✳
UPDATED RECORD ◆

« *The Sims was one of those games that you just didn't see coming. It smacked the gaming world upside the head with its quirky nature and long reaching appeal.*
IGN.com »

77... the total number of releases in *The Sims* series, including expansion packs and console spin-offs.

OVERVIEW

▶ *Lifestyle games are a relatively recent development in videogames, becoming more and more popular as developers and publishers look to expand the boundaries of what a game can be, or what experiences a console or computer can provide. Some titles, such as* My Health Coach: Stop Smoking with Allen Carr, *could hardly be described as games, though they do contain game-like elements. Ultimately, lifestyle games tend to fall into two categories – the first recreating everyday activities in game form (*Cooking Mama, The Sims*) and the second offering real-world benefits such as improving mental or physical skills (*Wii Fit, English Training: Have Fun Improving Your Skills!*).*

MOST POPULAR PHYSICAL FITNESS GAME

Holder: WII FIT
(Nintendo, 2007)
With over 19.24 million copies sold since its launch in Japan In December 2007, *Wii Fit* is the most successful physical fitness videogame ever. As of July 2009, there are more copies of *Wii Fit* in circulation than there are PlayStation 3 consoles. The title also holds the record for **most weeks at No.1 in the UK games charts**, with 16 weeks.

MOST TITLES IN A LIFESTYLE SERIES

Holder: IMAGINE
(Ubisoft, 2007 to present)
The largest number of titles in a single lifestyle brand is 27, held by Ubisoft's *Imagine* series. The franchise has captured the hearts and minds of young girls across the USA and Europe, its games offering its youthful audience the chance to take on their dream career – whether that's looking after pets in *Imagine: Animal Doctor* or becoming a virtual Vivienne Westwood in the popular *Imagine: Fashion Designer*. The most successful game in the series to date is *Imagine: Babyz*, which launched in 2007. The game, which offers players the opportunity to look after young children and qualify as a nanny, has sold over 2.67 million copies across all territories.

BEST-SELLING LANGUAGE TRAINING GAME

Holder: ENGLISH TRAINING: HAVE FUN IMPROVING YOUR SKILLS!
(Nintendo, 2006)
With sales of over 3 million copies, the Nintendo DS game *English Training: Have Fun Improving Your Skills!* is the world's best-selling language trainer. First released in Japan, the game was part of the craze for educational DS games that began with the *Brain Training* titles.

HIGHEST SCORE ON WII FIT HULA HOOPING

Holder: ANDY FULWOOD (UK)
Andy Fulwood (far right) acheived a score of 325 on Wii Fit Hula Hooping at ASDA Supermarket in Derby, UK, on 16 April 2009.

BEST-SELLING COOKING GAME SERIES

Holder: COOKING MAMA
(Taito, 2006 to present)
The most successful culinary franchise is the *Cooking Mama* series, which has sold over 7.85 million copies since its launch in 2006. The first game was something of a surprise success – after very modest sales in Japan, Majesco and 505 Games picked up the title for publishing in the USA and Europe respectively, and the game's popularity soared. Tellingly, the sequel, *Cooking Mama 2: Dinner With Friends*, was released in the USA before Japan – though only two days earlier. The *Cooking Mama* series has also spawned two less successful Wii titles.

FACT

▶ The Sims creator Will Wright's Oakland home was destroyed in a fire in 1991, and his experiences moving house with his family and rebuilding his life are said to have inspired the creation of the popular series. One of his research sources was the 1977 architecture book A Pattern Language: Towns, Buildings, Construction, which suggests a series of rules for designing everything from rooms to cities.

TRIVIA

▶ Many pop musicians have had their hit tunes featured in The Sims series, though their songs have been reworked into the franchise's fictional language of Simlish. Artists such as The Black-Eyed Peas and The Pussycat Dolls have re-recorded songs in Simlish, while Lily Allen's hit "Smile", remixed for The Sims 2, has had over 5.2 million views on YouTube.

GUINNESSWORLDREC

RHYTHM GAMES: KARAOKE

IF YOU'D RATHER DANCE THAN SING, TURN TO P.130 FOR DANCE MAT GAMES.

■ NEW RECORD
■ UPDATED RECORD

✳ MOST SUCCESSFUL SINGING VIDEOGAME SERIES

Holder: SINGSTAR (SCEE, 2004 to present)
The first *SingStar* game was published in May 2004 and went straight to the top of the charts in most territories. Since then, it has had 55 instalments, including editions in Turkish, Norwegian and Italian, as well as band-specific releases. More than 16 million *SingStar* units have now been sold and the games are available in over 67 countries worldwide.

Finnish developer SoittoPeli released a pitch-based music game titled PlaySingMusic in Finland in 2000. Pre-dating Karaoke Revolution by three years, it is thought to have been the first game of its kind.

TEN GAMES YOU SHOULD PLAY IN THIS GENRE

	GAME
1	SingStar (2004)
2	Lips (2008)
3	Karaoke Revolution (2003)
4	Karaoke Joysound Wii (2008)
5	SingStar: Pop (2005)
6	Boogie Superstar (2008)
7	Daigasso! Band Brothers DX (2008)
8	High School Musical: Sing It! (2007)
9	Karaoke Revolution Presents: American Idol (2007)
10	Get On Da Mic (2004)

00:41

8,680 POINTS... the highest *SingStar* score for "Take On Me", achieved by Bert Bauwens (Belgium) playing on Hard mode. Aha's 1985 hit is considered to be the hardest song on SingStar.

OVERVIEW

> Given that the pastime originated in Japan, and that it only gained popularity in the West during the 1990s, it's no surprise that the first karaoke videogame is Japanese. More surprising is that it arrived as early as 1987, in the form of Karaoke Studio for the Nintendo Famicom. Successors were rare until disc-based media arrived on the scene, so it wasn't until 2003's Karaoke Revolution that the genre had its first real hit. Shortly afterwards came Sony's popular SingStar and, in 2008, Microsoft brought us Lips from Japanese developer iNiS, better known for esoteric rhythm games such as Ouendan and Gitaroo Man.

MOST CRITICALLY ACCLAIMED KARAOKE GAME
Holder: KARAOKE REVOLUTION (Konami, 2003)
According to review aggregator sites Gamerankings and Metacritic, the most critically acclaimed karaoke title is Konami's 2003 hit *Karaoke Revolution*, with an average of 84% and 83% respectively. The game was created by Harmonix and was incorporated by Konami into its popular Bemani line of music titles.

★ MOST SUCCESSFUL KARAOKE GAME ON THE WII
Holder: HIGH SCHOOL MUSICAL: SING IT! (Disney Interactive Studios, 2007)
High School Musical: Sing It! is the most successful karaoke game on the Wii. The game, which is based on the incredibly successful Disney movie franchise, has sold over 1.41 million copies since its launch in 2007 and has easily outperformed its closest rivals in the karaoke games sector, *Boogie Superstar* and *Karaoke Revolution Presents: American Idol Encore*.

FIRST KARAOKE GAME TO SUPPORT DOWNLOADABLE CONTENT
Holder: KARAOKE REVOLUTION (XBOX) (Konami, 2004)
The Xbox version of *Karaoke Revolution*, released in 2004, is the first karaoke game to offer downloadable content to its players. The additional songs were available for purchase via Xbox Live, though they were actually featured on the disc itself, with the $4.99 (£2.60) fee for each track pack of five or six songs used to unlock them. In total, the two games had 20 track packs, including one free bonus pack.

★ FIRST KARAOKE GAME WITH WIRELESS MICROPHONE SUPPORT
Holder: LIPS (Microsoft, 2008)
Released on 18 November 2008, the first karaoke game to support wireless microphones was *Lips* on the Xbox 360. The game comes bundled with two microphones as standard, which are not only wireless but also motion-sensing. This feature allows players to join in by shaking their mic, as well as to perform gestures in the various mini games included.

LARGEST SELECTION OF SONGS IN A KARAOKE VIDEOGAME
Holder: KARAOKE JOYSOUND WII (Hudson Soft, 2008)
Karaoke Joysound Wii has the largest selection of songs in a karaoke videogame, with around 30,000 tracks available for Japanese players to sing along to. The game utilizes an innovative system that allows players to stream songs from a massive library to their Wii console, as the internal flash memory is too small to store them locally. All songs are available to choose from when the player purchases one of several "passes" – ranging from a one-day pass costing 300¥ ($3.17; £1.90) to a 90-day pass available for 2,000¥ ($21.12; £12.64).

★ FIRST KARAOKE GAME
Holder: KARAOKE STUDIO (Bandai, 1987)
Arriving in the form of a subsystem that plugged into the Nintendo Famicom's cartridge slot, Bandai's *Karaoke Studio*, released in 1987, is the first karaoke videogame ever. It was shortly followed by two expansion cartridges.

ふじさんのうえで おにぎりを
ぱっくん ぱっくん

RHYTHM GAMES: INSTRUMENT

! WANT TO SWAP YOUR GUITAR FOR A REAL AXE? TRY HACK AND SLASH ON P.114.

✱ MOST CRITICALLY ACCLAIMED RHYTHM GAME SERIES

Holder: ROCK BAND
(EA, 2007 to present)
With an average online review score of 91.5% for its two main series entries, the *Rock Band* franchise is the most critically acclaimed rhythm game series, beating rival *Guitar Hero*, which scores 88.25%, into second place.

The most unusual music peripheral came with SEGA's Shakka To Tambourine – a Japan-only arcade game that used a tambourine as a controller. The game cabinet tracked its motion in 3D space as it was tapped and whirled in time to the music.

✱ NEW RECORD
▯ UPDATED RECORD

TEN GAMES YOU SHOULD PLAY IN THIS GENRE

	GAME
1	Rock Band 2 (2008)
2	Guitar Hero: Metallica (2009)
3	BeatMania IIDX (1999)
4	Samba de Amigo (1999)
5	Wii Music (2008)
6	Donkey Konga (2003)
7	GuitarFreaks (1998)
8	Shakka To Tambourine (2000)
9	KeyboardMania (2000)
10	Mad Maestro (2001)

[**16...** the number of music-themed games created between 2001 and 2009 by prolific US-based developer Harmonix.]

OVERVIEW

▸ *Developers have explored the idea of player action causing a musical reaction for over 20 years, in games such as Toshio Iwai's Otocky. However, it wasn't until 1996's PaRappa The Rapper that the rhythm genre had its first real breakout title. Shortly afterwards, Konami's Bemani music division produced a series of titles reliant on devices that emulated musical instruments – games like 1997's Beatmania, which used a simplified turntable and keys to allow gamers to play as a virtual DJ. Then came GuitarFreaks and DrumMania, but it was Guitar Hero from Harmonix that gave the West its first big instrument game. Since then, the genre has become hugely popular, with Rock Band sparking a trend for group-based musical titles with more of a focus on multiplayer action.*

FACT

▸ Donkey Konga's "DK Bongos" were used for two GameCube sequels, though the third game never made it outside Japan.
The drums were also used for a non-music game, Donkey Kong: Jungle Beat, which is the first and only platform game to be controlled with this input method. Quirky pinball strategy game Odama was originally intended to support the DK Bongos, with the second player able to beat out a rhythm to motivate the first player's army – however, the feature was dropped prior to the game's release.

TRIVIA

▸ PlayStation 2 rhythm game Mad Maestro is one of very few games to use the pressure sensitivity of the console's DualShock 2 controller to let the player control the volume of the notes. It is rare for music games to utilize volume control, though Wii Music allows players to vary volume with certain instruments by tilting the Wii Remote, while the volume of Guitar Hero: World Tour's drums are affected by how hard the player hits the drum pads. The Rhythm Tap mode in Sega's Let's Tap also features volume control – the Wii Remote registering light and strong taps of the player's fingers.

✴ FIRST DRUM CONTROLLER FOR A HOME CONSOLE

Holder: TAIKO NO TATSUJIN: TATAKON DE DODON GA DON (Namco, 2002)
First appearing in Japanese arcades in 2001 as Taiko no Tatsujin (pictured above), the first drum peripheral to make it into gamer's homes was a version for the PS2 entitled Taiko no Tatsujin: Tatakon de Dodon ga Don. Like the arcade original, Tatakon de Dodon ga Don required players to strike the skin or the rim of a drum peripheral in time to scrolling notes on the screen,

✴ MOST MUSICAL INSTRUMENTS SIMULATED IN ONE INSTRUMENT GAME

Holder: WII MUSIC (Nintendo, 2008)
The largest number of musical instruments simulated in one instrument game is 66, achieved in 2008's Wii Music by Nintendo. The game sees players use the Wii Remote and Nunchuk to simulate the actions of playing each of the huge array of instruments. Ranging from cowbell to clarinet, dulcimer to djembe drum, and banjo to human beatbox, Wii Music offers a truly eclectic mix.

MOST CRITICALLY ACCLAIMED INSTRUMENT GAME

Holder: GUITAR HERO II (Harmonix, 2005)
The second of three Guitar Hero titles developed by Harmonix prior to their Rock Band series, Guitar Hero II remains the most critically acclaimed instrument game, with a rating of 92% and 92.38% on game review aggregator sites Metacritic and GameRankings respectively. In its year of release, it picked up five key awards in website IGN's Best Of 2006 list, including Best Music Game, Best Licensed Soundtrack and Best PlayStation 2 Offline Multiplayer Game.

✴ SINGLE TRACK HIGH SCORE ON GUITAR HERO III

Holder: DANNY JOHNSON (USA)
The highest score ever achieved on Guitar Hero III: Legends of Rock is 985,206 on "Through the Fire and Flames", by Danny Johnson (left) at Book Expo America in New York City, USA, on 30 May 2009. Danny also holds the record for the first player to achieve a "full combo" (or FC) on "Through the Fire and Flames" at a public event.

RHYTHM GAMES: DANCE MAT

LIKE TO SEE MORE ACTIVE GAMING? TURN TO P.28 FOR THE BEST OF WII.

NEW RECORD
UPDATED RECORD

⁜ HOTTEST VIDEOGAME

Holder: DANCE DANCE IMMOLATION (Interpretive Arson, 2005)

The highest temperature experienced in a videogame is 1,200°C (2,192°F), held by *Dance Dance Immolation*, which debuted at The Crucible's Fire Arts Festival in Oakland, California, USA, in June 2005. Using a hybrid of the PC game engine *StepMania* and developed to emulate *Dance Dance Revolution*, the *Immolation* version is the brainchild of performance art group Interpretive Arson.

The hardest *Dance Dance Revolution* track is thought to be Pluto Relinquish *from* Dance Dance Revolution X. *It has a difficulty ranking of 18, though the new difficulty scale brought in for DDRX goes up to 20.*

TEN GAMES YOU SHOULD PLAY IN THIS GENRE

	GAME
1	Dance Dance Revolution (Arcade) (1998)
2	DDRMAX: Dance Dance Revolution (2002)
3	ParaParaParadise (2000)
4	StepMania (2005)
5	Family Trainer: Aerobics Studio (1987)
6	Dance Factory (2006)
7	Dance Dance Revolution Konamix (2002)
8	Dance With Intensity (2000)
9	In The Groove (2004)
10	Dance Dance Revolution: Mario Mix (2005)

640... the number of calories per hour a person weighing 68 kg (150 lb) would burn playing *Dance Dance Revolution*, making it the **healthiest videogame ever**.

OVERVIEW

Anyone who has been to London's Trocadero Centre (UK) will be familiar with the dance mat genre. Here, audiences regularly gather around expert players, as their feet move at a furious pace on Konami's *Dance Dance Revolution* and other, similar games. Konami's series dominates the genre, though other titles that have dared to try and wrest the mantle from this ever-popular franchise include *In The Groove*, *StepMania* and *Dance Factory*. Konami innovated further within the genre with 2000's *ParaParaParadise*, which uses motion sensors rather than foot-activated pads, but it's DDR that continues to reign supreme.

HIGHEST KEYBOARD SCORE ON STEPMANIA

Holder: FREDRICK LID MONSLAUP (Norway)
The record high score for *StepMania*, using a keyboard as the controller, is held by Fredrik Lid Monslaup, who reached 99,061,121 at The Gathering, Vikingskipet Olympic Arena, Hamar, Norway, on 9 April 2009.

FIRST DANCE MAT GAME TO GENERATE MOVES FROM ANY MUSIC CD

Holder: DANCE FACTORY (Codemasters, 2006)
The first dance mat game ever to allow players to dance to their own music CDs was Codemasters' *Dance Factory*, which was developed for the PlayStation 2 and generates dance routines for any song. Not only does the game software create its own moves based on the beats and rhythms of any inserted track, but players can also manually input their own moves if they're unsatisfied with the results provided.

MOST SUCCESSFUL DANCE MAT SERIES

Holder: DANCE DANCE REVOLUTION (Konami, 1998)
Having sold over 10 million copies to date, Konami's *Dance Dance Revolution* is, unsurprisingly, the world's most successful dance mat series. Although primarily considered to be an arcade experience, there have been over 100 home console versions of the game worldwide.

FIRST RHYTHM GAME

Holder: FAMILY TRAINER: AEROBICS STUDIO (Bandai, 1987)
Launched in Japan on 26 February 1987, *Family Trainer: Aerobics Studio* for the Nintendo Famicom was the first rhythm videogame ever released. The series, which pioneered the dance mat controller, was originally called *Family Trainer*, but later renamed *Family Fun Fitness* and then the *Power Pad* in the West. *Aerobics Studio* was the third in the series of *Family Trainer* games on the Famicom console.

HIGHEST "STEALTH" SCORE ON DANCE DANCE REVOLUTION SUPERNOVA 2

Holder: KRIS PEARMAN (UK)
The highest score set on Stealth mode on *DDR Supernova 2* is 996,670 (out of a possible 1 million), achieved by Kris Pearman (near right) on the song *Jet World* at Insert Coin '09, Northampton, UK, on 18 July 2009. Stealth mode requires the player to complete the song without any visual clues as to where to step.

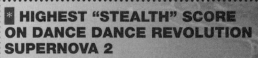

COUCH CASUALTY

FROM "SPACE INVADERS WRIST" TO TORN CARTILAGE, PLAYING VIDEOGAMES CAN BE STRESSFUL FOR YOUR BODY. HERE ARE OUR TIPS FOR INJURY-FREE GAMING...

! SEARCHING FOR LIFESTYLE GAMING? LOOK NO FURTHER THAN P.124.

21 MILLION... worldwide sales of *Wii Fit*, Nintendo's premier fitness game, as of August 2009.

EYES /

PROBLEM: Eye strain; risk of photosensitive seizures, which can be caused by flashing or flickering light from the screen.

HOW TO AVOID IT: Play in a well-lit room away from direct light sources. Avoid playing when tired or drowsy and, ideally, save your progress and take a 15-minute break after every hour of gameplay.

NECK /

PROBLEM: Neck ache; poor posture.

HOW TO AVOID IT: Make sure your seat offers good support, and position monitors in such a way as to minimize any bending and twisting of the head and shoulders. Clear the space around you, too, so that you are not restricted in your movements.

WRIST /

PROBLEM: *"Space Invaders* wrist" – wrist problems for videogame players were first identified back in 1981, when the condition was described as painful stiffness resulting from "repeated, prolonged playing of *Space Invaders*". Nowadays, "*Halo* wrist" might be more appropriate.

HOW TO AVOID IT: During long gaming sessions, take regular breaks and increase the range of your wrist movements.

SHOULDERS /

PROBLEM: Inflammation of the shoulder, dubbed "Wiiitis" by family GP Dr Julio Bonis (Spain) in the *New England Journal of Medicine* in June 2007, is often caused by the repetitive strain placed on it during games involving movement of the upper body, such as those played on the Wii.

HOW TO AVOID IT: Vary your playing style to avoid falling into a set pattern of movement.

HANDS /

PROBLEM: Tendon strain.

HOW TO AVOID IT: Hold the controller in a relaxed grip. Press the buttons and manipulate the control sticks with a light touch. Another tip is to take advantage of cutscenes to put down the controller and stretch your fingers.

SKIN?

PROBLEM: In February 2009, the *British Journal of Dermatology* identified a new videogame-specific skin disorder known as *palmar hidradenitis*.

The condition arises through prolonged gripping of a controller, which causes excessive sweating and trauma to the hands and results in painful lesions on the palms and fingers.

HOW TO AVOID IT: Wash your hands regularly. If you notice red lumps or sores developing, you should see your doctor and take a few days' break from gaming.

JOINTS/

PROBLEM: An article in the *British Medical Journal Case Reports* published in June 2009 identified a patient who had suffered a torn cartilage, a common sports injury, from playing a vigorous sports simulation game.

HOW TO AVOID IT: It might sound unlikely, but videogame players could follow the lead of professional athletes and take some time to stretch and warm up properly before beginning a gaming session that is likely to involve significant movement of the body.

* YOUNGEST PERSON TO HAVE A STUDY ON GAMERS' HEALTH PUBLISHED
Holder: SAFURA ABDOOL KARIM

In June 2005, 13-year-old Safura Abdool Karim (South Africa) conducted a survey of 120 of her schoolmates for a science project on the physical effects of frequent videogame use. Her study showed that of her sample, 45 children played games regularly, of which 15 suffered from blisters on their hands. Safura's findings were later published in the *South African Medical Journal*.

* NEW RECORD
◆ UPDATED RECORD

AS THE NUMBER OF PEOPLE PLAYING VIDEOGAMES CONTINUES TO GROW, DOCTORS ARE ASKING WHAT EFFECT ALL THIS GAMING IS HAVING ON OUR BODIES

PERCEPTION
Following on from their 2003 experiment, which showed gamers performed better at visual tasks than non-gamers, a team of researchers led by Daphne Bavelier, Assistant Professor at the University of Rochester, New York, USA, reported findings in March 2009 that playing videogames improved users' ability to perceive contrast in images (i.e. they were more aware of colour change and movement within on-screen images). The findings were based on a small sample of 13 non-gamers who were assigned either a first-person shooter or a more sedate simulation game to play for 50 hours over nine weeks. Those who played shooters saw the greatest benefits, with 43% registering an improvement in their contrast perception.

BRAIN STRUCTURE
In September 2009, the journal *BMC Research Notes* published a study on the effects of regular *Tetris* use on the brains of adolescent girls. The study, conducted by a team of researchers from the Mind Research Network in Albuquerque, New Mexico, USA, showed that the brains of girls playing *Tetris* exhibited structural changes in the thickness of the cortex in areas associated with critical thinking, language and reasoning. This evidence led the team to believe that playing the game boosts the amount of grey matter in the brain, a possible explanation as to why previous studies have shown that mental practice increases brain efficiency.

WRIST INJURIES
Shortly after he joined the US Major League Baseball team Detroit Tigers in the 2006 season, professional baseball pitcher Joel Zumaya (USA, pictured) began complaining of pain and inflammation in the wrist and forearm of his throwing arm. At first, the team's training staff were puzzled – the player's injuries were not the type usually associated with pitching. The injury was more consistent with the kind of grip required for *Guitar Hero*, a rhythm game that Joel had been playing avidly. Luckily for Joel, he recovered fully once he stopped playing the game, but with a salary of around $325,000 (£165,000), his gaming habit could have proved extremely costly.

PUZZLE GAMES

CONTENTS:

Based on online reviews, *Braid* is the **most critically acclaimed downloadable game for Xbox 360**, averaging 93%. It was praised for its time-bending puzzle mechanics and abstract storyline.

INTRODUCTION

! PUZZLED WHERE TO FIND TURN-BASED STRATEGY GAMES? THE ANSWER IS ON P.166.

WHEN CHARTING THE HISTORY OF PUZZLE GAMES, ONE TITLE ECLIPSES ALL OTHERS – TETRIS, CREATED BY ALEXEY PAJITNOV IN THE EARLY 1980s

KEY GAME
TETRIS
For many years it was thought that Alexey Pajitnov hadn't received any money for creating *Tetris* due to copyright issues in the USSR in the 1980s. However, in 2007 Alexey revealed that "Originally, I granted my rights to *Tetris* to my Computer Centre, to my organization, for 10 years. And when those 10 years expired, I got my rights back. And since 1996, I've been receiving some royalties [for *Tetris*]."

Created by Alexey Pajitnov (USSR) and inspired by Russian "pentomino" puzzles, *Tetris* is one of the most popular puzzle games ever, with more than 177 million people having played the game since its first arrival 25 years ago.

Tetris is the original block-dropping puzzle game and the one by which all others are judged. Such is its popularity that it has become more than just a game or a brand. Indeed, scientists have used *Tetris* to study dream activity; players have sought help for *Tetris* addiction; and there's even an online Church of Tetris, which is founded on the belief that all people should receive the glory of the game. However, despite the fact that the "church" doesn't recognize any events that occurred before the coming of *Tetris* in 1984, puzzle games did exist before that time.

The first computer puzzle game was created in 1952 by Alexander S. Douglas (UK), who programmed Cambridge University's EDSAC analogue computer to play a game of noughts and crosses. Following this breakthrough, bored computer boffins everywhere began tinkering with these huge valve-driven machines, producing simple programs that were often based around board or number games. In 1973, a number of puzzle-style games were designed for the PDP-11 minicomputer, including a title called *Cube*, which is the earliest known computer version of the puzzle game *Minesweeper* (which later found popularity as one of the games that came as part of the Windows operating system in the early 1990s).

During the 1970s, the burgeoning arcade scene began to dominate videogaming, with fast-paced sports and shooting titles becoming the gaming mainstream. Fierce competition among rival arcade cabinet manufacturers looking for the next big hit and, in later years, in the home console and computer markets, meant that game-makers strove to produce more and more sophisticated offerings. The humble and plain puzzle game was often severely overlooked in this push towards better graphics, so it is ironic that *Tetris* – a simple, yet incredibly addictive, console game about tesselating falling shapes – should become such a massive commercial success and a huge driver to purchase for Nintendo's fledgling handheld, the Gameboy.

« *I never thought that Tetris would become so big, but later on in the Computer Centre I didn't see anybody who wasn't addicted.*
Alexey Pajitnov, Tetris creator »

* **NEW RECORD**
■ **UPDATED RECORD**

TIMELINE

1952	1973	1985	1988	1990
The **first puzzle game**, a noughts and crosses game known as *OXO*, is produced for the EDSAC analogue computer by Alexander S. Douglas.	*Cube*, the precursor to *Minesweeper*, is created for the PDP-11 and further developed by American programmer David Ahl.	Originally designed and programmed on the Elektronika 60 computer by Alexey Pajitnov in June 1984, *Tetris* is released internationally.	*Tetris* becomes a worldwide phenomenon. **1989** *Klax* is released, and introduces match-the-colours gameplay.	Bizarre *Tetris* clone with a medical theme, *Dr. Mario* is launched on Nintendo's NES and Gameboy platforms.

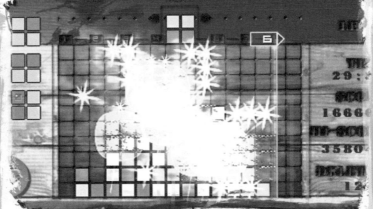

OVERVIEW

▶ *Due to the massive popularity of titles like Tetris and Bejeweled, when someone talks or writes about puzzle games they're usually referring to falling block or match-the-colours games. Yet the genre is much wider than that and definitions can vary. Traditionally, a puzzle game is one where the player engages the brain to discover solutions and solve problems, but some puzzle games rely as much on quick reflexes as cerebral skill. The general rule for a successful puzzle game is that it's easy to pick up but difficult to put down, and takes minutes to grasp but years to master.*

Tetris went on to become the **most ported videogame** ever, with versions released for 55 different computer and console formats. When publishers such as Atari and Nintendo weren't wrangling over the official rights to the game, they were devising their own *Tetris*-inspired titles. The most important of these was Atari's *Klax*, which was released in 1989 and was the first to introduce the concept of arranging falling blocks by colour. Popular variations on this theme arrived in the shape of *Columns* (1990), *Dr. Mario* (1990) and *Dr. Robotnik's Mean Bean Machine* (1992), starring the villain from the *Sonic the Hedgehog* games.

The graphical symplicity and time-sapping, addictive qualities of many puzzle games make them particularly suited to handheld devices such as the Apple iPhone and the Nintendo DS, a fact underlined by the success of *Dr. Kawashima's Brain Training* series, which has sold more than 31 million copies since its launch. But the next generation consoles are far from bereft of puzzle games – most Xbox 360s come with a copy of Alexey Pajitnov's *Hexic HD* pre-installed on the hard drive, while an increasing number of graphically sophisticated games also feature puzzle game elements. One such example is the atmospheric first-person shooter *Bioshock*, which contains a puzzle mini game similar to *Pipe Mania*, in which players must use random pipes to guide the flow of a fluid from one place to another.

Looking to the future, many of today's quirkiest, most imaginative and addictive videogames are puzzles – such as *Eets*, *Braid* and *World of Goo* (pictured right) – so for pure, unadulterated innovation, the genre is certainly one to watch.

MOST CRITICALLY ACCLAIMED PUZZLE GAME FOR PSP

Holder: LUMINES (Ubisoft, 2005) Created by Japanese game designer Tetsuya Mizuguchi, the PSP launch title *Lumines* is an addictive block-dropping puzzle game with mesmerizing graphics and sound effects. With an average online review score of 90%, *Lumines* is both the top-rated puzzle game for the PSP and the platform's overall second best-reviewed game (after *God of War: Chains of Olympus*).

EXPERT

▶ *Martyn Carroll's first article on videogaming was published in 1997, and since then he's contributed features and reviews to many publications, including* Retro Gamer, GamesTM, Micro Mart *and* Eurogamer.net. *Martyn was launch editor of* Retro Gamer *in 2003 and still contributes regularly to the magazine.*

TRIVIA

▶ *The success of the Gameboy is often attributed to the shrewd decision by Nintendo to bundle its handheld system with the game* Tetris. *With sales of 32 million,* Tetris *is the* **best-selling Gameboy title** *and the* **best-selling handheld puzzle game**.

▶ *Peggle was listed as one of the most addictive games ever in a feature on msnbc.com. The article claimed that PopCap's spin on pachinko was "downright insidious" and included the game alongside such time drains as* EverQuest *and* World of Warcraft.

1995	2001	2006	2007	2008	2009
Colour-matching game *Bust-a-Move* (aka *Puzzle Bobble*) appears in arcades, featuring 2D platformer *Bubble Bobble*'s diminutive dino characters Bub and Bob.	*Bejeweled* hits PCs as a browser-based puzzle game. **2005** Addictive match-the-colours game *Meteos* is released for the Nintendo DS.	*Dr. Kawashima's Brain Training* (aka *Brain Age*) is unleashed on the world, sparking the growth of a whole sub-genre of brain training-style games.	Inspired by the Japanese pinball game pachinko, *Peggle* debuts on PC. Physics puzzler *Portal* is also released as part of Valve Corporation's *The Orange Box*.	Independent game *Braid*, which plays with the conventions of 2D platform games, hits Xbox Live. *Professor Layton and the Curious Village* is also released.	The *Art-Style* puzzle series, designed as downloadable games for the Wii console, are released for DSi via the Nintendo DSi shop.

BLOCK PUZZLES

IF LOGIC PUZZLES ARE YOUR THING, THEN THE LOGICAL PLACE TO GO WOULD BE P.144.

MOST POPULAR PUZZLE GAME SERIES OF THE CENTURY

Holder: BEJEWELED
(PopCap, 2001 to present)
The *Bejeweled* series has been downloaded more than 350 million times since its release in May 2001, making it the most popular puzzle game of this century. *Bejeweled* and its sequel, *Bejeweled 2*, account for nearly one third of the 1 billion-plus downloads of all PopCap's games. In addition, the games have clocked up sales of more than 25 million units, and these unprecedented figures are still rising thanks to the November 2008 release of *Bejeweled Twist*.

TEN GAMES YOU SHOULD PLAY IN THIS GENRE

	GAME
1	*Tetris* (1984)
2	*Bejeweled* (2001)
3	*Meteos* (2005)
4	*Super Puzzle Fighter II Turbo* (1996)
5	*Klax* (1989)
6	*Tetris Attack* (1996)
7	*Columns* (1990)
8	*Hexic* (2003)
9	*Lumines* (2004)
10	*Roogoo* (2008)

It's certainly surprising that Bejeweled has taken on such a life of its own.
Bejeweled designer, Jason Kapalka

OVERVIEW

> *Block puzzle games generally see the player arranging or aligning shapes so that they match and disappear from the playing field. The classic example is* Tetris, *where falling blocks must be quickly rotated and positioned so that they tessellate and create solid horizontal lines, which then disappear and give the player temporary breathing space before more blocks appear. The rate at which the blocks fall increases as more lines are completed, and, as such,* Tetris *becomes more of a reflex test than a cerebral workout. The game has inspired numerous clones and imitations, as well as match-em-up games such as* Bejeweled *and* Zoo Keeper, *where the aim is to match up three or more similar shapes by flipping the position of two shapes.*

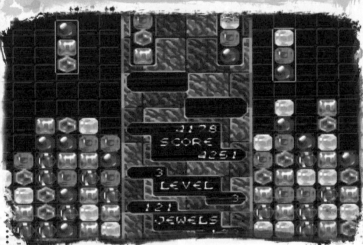

＊ FASTEST PERFECT SCORE ON TETRIS DS

Holder: ISAIAH JOHNSON (USA)
The fastest time to achieve a perfect score on *Tetris DS* is 18 hr 10 min 22 sec, and was set by Isaiah "TriForce" Johnson on 19 August 2008 in New York City, USA. TriForce also holds the score record for both of the game's marathon modes and is part of the "League of Legendary Gamers" along with *Donkey Kong* supremo Billy Mitchell and FPS record holder Johnathan "Fatal1ty" Wendel.

counter at the 999,999 mark: "It was such an adrenaline rush to say the least… I only had a small number of lines left to get the maximum score and I was fortunate enough to get the right pieces to get the job done."

＊ HIGHEST POINTS TOTAL ON COLUMNS (MEGA DRIVE VERSION)

Holder: KEITH DANFORTH (USA)
The highest score ever recorded on the Mega Drive/Genesis version of *Columns* is 99,999,989, by Keith Danforth on 11 June 2006. At first glance it would appear that Keith's luck cruelly ran out when he was just a few points shy of 100 million, but in truth the counter freezes at 99,999,989. As such, he has earned the honour of being the **first person to earn a perfect score** on this game.

＊ MOST EXPENSIVE PUZZLE GAME

Holder: TETRIS (NINTENDO WORLD CHAMPIONSHIPS GOLD EDITION) (Nintendo, 1990)
A special version of *Tetris* included as part of the ultra-rare *1990 Nintendo World Championships Gold Edition* cartridge for NES, became the most expensive puzzle game after James Baker of New York, USA, paid $15,000 for a copy in April 2008.

＊ FIRST PERFECT SCORE ON TETRIS (NES VERSION)

Holder: HARRY HONG (USA)
Harry Hong of Los Angeles, California, USA, became the first person to earn the maximum score of 999,999 on the NES version of *Tetris*. The record was achieved on 19 April 2009 and took Harry an astounding four years of practice to amass the perfect score. Speaking to Twin Galaxies, he reflected on the moment when he finally froze the points

＊ FIRST MASH-UP OF PUZZLE AND RPG GENRES

Holder: PUZZLE QUEST: CHALLENGE OF THE WARLORDS
(Infinite Interactive, 2007)
The first game to mix puzzle game elements with traditional RPG gameplay was *Puzzle Quest: Challenge of the Warlords*, released for the Nintendo DS and PlayStation Portable in 2007. It has since been published on several home console and mobile platforms including the iPhone. An expansion to the original game, *Revenge of the Plague Lord*, was released in 2008.

FACT

> An expert panel of gamers voted Tetris as the second best console game ever in last year's Guinness World Records Gamer's Edition. It was pipped to the number one spot by the revered SNES racing game Super Mario Kart.

TRIVIA

> The largest game of Tetris ever was played on the side of a 96 m (314 ft 11 in) high building at the Delft University of Technology in Delft, the Netherlands. The impressive feat was engineered by students in November 1005, and required 400 lights linked together by 3.5 km (2.1 miles) of cable.

> Released in 1990, the Atari 2600 version of puzzle game Klax was the last officially licensed arcade game conversion to be released for the ageing console.

> Tengen, Atari's home console division, released a version of Tetris in 1989 but was forced to stop selling its version after a legal dispute with Nintendo over the rights to distribute the game.

＊ NEW RECORD
● UPDATED RECORD

SPATIAL PUZZLES

! IF YOU LIKE TO PUZZLE IT OUT, HAVE A LOOK AT 2D AND 3D PLATFORMERS, FROM P.96.

✳ FASTEST UNAIDED COMPLETION OF PORTAL

Holder: CODY MILLER (USA)

Cody Miller of Los Angeles, California, USA, completed the Xbox 360 version of *Portal* in 24 min 37 sec on 7 November 2007. Completion times as fast as 13 min 6 sec have been achieved on the PC version of *Portal*, but unlike Cody's unaided run, those attempts rely on glitches in the game as well as keyboard scripts to save large chunks of time.

TEN GAMES YOU SHOULD PLAY IN THIS GENRE

	GAME
1	*Braid* (2008)
2	*Portal* (2007)
3	*Eets* (2006)
4	*LostWinds* (2008)
5	*Lemmings* (1991)
6	*Katamari Damacy* (2004)
7	*Echochrome* (2008)
8	*Toki Tori* (2001)
9	*The Incredible Machine* (1992)
10	*Noby Noby Boy* (2009)

> I wanted to make a game that cannot be expressed by words.
> *Keita Takahashi, creator of Noby Noby Boy*

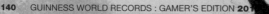

$200,000 (£121,600)... the development cost of spatial puzzler *Braid*. To put that in perspective, if developer Jonathan Blow had had the budget of *GTA IV*, he could have created *Braid* 500 times over.

OVERVIEW

▶ Spatial puzzle games are all about using the brain to explore and solve an on-screen problem, usually to guide a character to a certain position using the objects or skills at its disposal. Such titles often rely on trial and error, with the solution to the problem becoming clearer with each successive – and increasingly frustrating – failed attempt. An excellent example of a game that draws on spatial intelligence is Valve's *Portal* (2007), which requires the player to progress through a series of fiendishly designed chambers by manipulating objects and creating entrances and exits with a "portal gun". Understandably, records in spatial puzzle games generally involve completing challenges in the fastest possible time.

✱ FASTEST COMPLETION OF LOSTWINDS

Holder: JUSTIN SALAMON (USA)
● The fastest single-segment completion of Square Enix's *LostWinds* (2008) is 22 minutes, registered by Justin Salamon of Midland, Michigan, USA, on 17 March 2009. However, by tackling the game in 18 individual segments, his cumulative completion time is actually slightly faster, at 21 minutes.

✱ FASTEST COMPLETION OF KATAMARI DAMACY

Holder: TOM BATCHELOR (USA)
After the "King of All Cosmos" accidentally destroys the stars, he tasks his son with the unenviable job of recreating them – so goes the story behind Namco's *Katamari Damacy*, one of the surprise hits of 2004. The game requires players to roll a magical sticky ball, or "Katamari", around various locations to collect material with which to rebuild the sky. With a single-segment completion time of 30 min 26 sec, American Tom "slowbro" Batchelor became the game's undisputed champion on 3 August 2006.

FIRST GAME TO USE INDIRECT CONTROL

Holder: LEMMINGS (Psygnosis, 1991)
Lemmings, the 1990s classic from developer DMA Design, was the first major title to introduce the concept of "indirect control". As the hapless creatures march to their doom, players must guide them to safety using only the geography of the level.

HIGH SCORES ON EETS — AUG '09		
RANK	**USERNAME**	**SCORE**
1	x Sinistar x	2,242,829
2	Superfly777	2,072,790
3	AC Venom	2,057,137
4	CookieSnarf	2,020,804
5	Smashing Drive	1,875,597

✱ LONGEST LENGTH CONTRIBUTED BY A PLAYER ON NOBY NOBY BOY

Holder: SSSS7960 (USA)
By the time the *Noby Noby Boy* (Namco Bandai, 2009) character "Noby Noby Girl" had stretched her way to the planet Mars on 23 May 2009, player SSSS7960 had contributed 2,744,536,547 metres to Girl's total length, more than any other player. As gamers continue to play, Girl will eventually stretch to other planets in the solar system, making new levels available.

✱ **NEW RECORD**   ● **UPDATED RECORD**

FACT

▶ *Portal* was originally included as part of Valve Corporation's *The Orange Box*, a 2007 compilation package also featuring *Half-Life 2* and *Team Fortress 2*. On its release, *Portal* quickly garnered critical praise – as well as several Game of the Year awards – and was reissued in 2008 as a standalone title for the PC and, later, for the Xbox 360, as *Portal: Still Alive*.

TRIVIA

▶ *Eets* (Klei Entertainment, 2006) was the first game to officially feature a character from the Penny Arcade webcomic, with "The Merch" making a cameo appearance on several levels.

▶ *Toki Tori*, the egg-collecting puzzle game released as a downloadable Nintendo Wii title in 2008, has a little-known history that stretches back almost 15 years. The WiiWare title is an update of the Game Boy Color version that was released in 2001, which itself was based on a game called Eggbert, released for the MSX-2 home computer in 1994.

PHYSICS-BASED PUZZLES

! IF YOU LIKE EXERCISING THE GREY MATTER, TURN TO STRATEGY RPG ON P.172.

✴ MOST DOWNLOADED PHYSICS PUZZLE GAME

Holder: PEGGLE (PopCap, 2007)

With over 50 million downloads since its release in 2007, *Peggle* is the most downloaded physics puzzler. Although the highly addictive game first appeared in early 2007, it wasn't until a themed demo was included with Valve's *The Orange Box* that it started to gain the fanbase it enjoys today.

« *Peggle* has become a cult gaming phenomenon, becoming as big a hit with hardcore gamers as it has with casual players. »

Greg Canessa, former Vice President of PopCap

TEN GAMES YOU SHOULD PLAY IN THIS GENRE

	GAME
1	Boom Blox (2008)
2	Peggle (2007)
3	Bust-a-Move (1994)
4	World of Goo (2008)
5	Armadillo Run (2006)
6	Crayon Physics Deluxe (2009)
7	Zuma (2003)
8	Plotting (1989)
9	Puzz Loop (1998)
10	Elebits (2006)

✴ NEW RECORD
▪ UPDATED RECORD

OVERVIEW

Physics-based puzzles, unsurprisingly, revolve around the basic laws of physics and are all about calculating or anticipating motion and trajectory. In most cases, an object is fired into the playing field with the aim of connecting to or destroying other objects and triggering chain reactions. The player's skill comes in selecting the angle and force of the initial shot, as once the projectile is released he or she often has no further control over it. This is particularly true of Peggle and Boom Blox, two of the most popular physics-based puzzle games of the past few years, and, strictly speaking, the sub-genre has more in common with pinball than traditional puzzle titles.

FIRST EUROPEAN PEGGLE CHAMPION

Holder: CHERISE SELLERS (UK)
British gamer Cherise Sellers from Hull, UK, was crowned the first European Grand Champion of *Peggle* (PopCap, 2007) at i36, the i-Series event held in Coventry, UK, during April 2009. Having topped the *Peggle Deluxe* leaderboard with an incredible score of 1,111,920, amassed from playing three pre-selected levels (Das Bucket, Birdy's Crib and The Last Flower), Cherise went on to beat contestant and championship organizer Vini Holden of Preston, UK, in a *Peggle* head-to-head. Her reward for winning the competition was a special trophy plus PopCap games and goodies.

TALLEST TOWER BUILT IN WORLD OF GOO

Holder: KAMAL HASSIBA
On 8 January 2009, after playing 2D Boy's *World of Goo* (2008) for 21 hours over a five-day period, Kamal Hassiba completed a goo-ball tower measuring 50.82 metres. Kamal also built the second tallest tower of 48.61 metres, but even though he is his own closest rival, he's not taking any chances: "If someone made a higher tower, then I would definitely challenge them," he said.

MOST CRITICALLY ACLAIMED WII PUZZLER

Holder: WORLD OF GOO
(2D Boy, 2008)
According to GameRankings and Metacritic, *World of Goo* is the most critically acclaimed puzzler on the Wii, with scores of 93.95% and 94% respectively, overtaking previous holder *Boom Blox* (2008). It is also the third "best" Wii title, behind *Super Mario Galaxy* (97%) and *The Legend of Zelda: Twilight Princess* (95%).

MOST POPULAR PUZZLE GAME ON FACEBOOK

Holder: BUBBLE TOWN
(I-Play, 2007)
According to figures released by Facebook in July 2008, the most addictive puzzle game on the popular social networking site is *Bubble Town*. The figures showed that the game had been installed by almost 1 million Facebook users and, of those, 150,000 people played it every day.

FIRST PHYSICS-BASED PUZZLE GAME FOR THE NINTENDO WII

Holder: ELEBITS (Konami, 2006)
Released in Japan on 2 December 2006 and in the USA the following week, *Elebits* was the first physics-based puzzle game released for the Nintendo Wii console. The game, which sees players manipulating the Wii Remote to uncover and capture small creatures, was released in Europe and Australia in May 2007 under the title *Eledees*. It was Konami's first game release for the Wii.

FACT

The 2D puzzle game Crayon Physics Deluxe, designed by Petri Purho, won the prestigious Seumas McNally Grand Prize at the 2008 Independent Games Festival. It was finally released to great critical acclaim in 2009, on both PC and the Apple iPhone.

TRIVIA

During the first month of its US release in July 2008, Boom Blox for the Nintendo Wii sold just 60,000 copies and was quickly branded a failure. But thanks to high-scoring reviews and positive word of mouth, the game gathered momentum and its first-year worldwide sales eventually reached 930,000. The figures were good enough to earn the game a sequel, Boom Blox Bash Party, which was released in May 2009.

Since the original Bust-a-Move (aka Puzzle Bobble) arcade game debuted in 1994, a total of 20 follow-ups have been released to date, across a wide variety of formats – on average, that's more than one per year. The most recent, Puzzle Bobble Plus!, was released in Japan as a downloadable WiiWare game on 7 April 2009.

LOGIC PUZZLES

! IF YOU LIKE A CHALLENGE, TURN TO P.162 AND CHECK OUT SOME OF THE BEST STRATEGY TITLES.

✱ MOST UNIQUE OBJECTS IN A PUZZLE GAME

Holder: SCRIBBLENAUTS
(Warner, 2009)
Featuring over 10,000 unique useable items, *Scribblenauts* boasts more in-game objects than any other puzzler in history. In the game, players are tasked with using their imagination to conjure up a range of objects that will help them to solve the game's puzzles – whether they be chainsaws, bears, hot-air balloons, dinosaurs or even Albert Einstein!

TEN GAMES YOU SHOULD PLAY IN THIS GENRE

	GAME
1	*Dr. Kawashima's Brain Training* (2005)
2	*Picross DS* (2007)
3	*Professor Layton and the Curious Village* (2007)
4	*Buku Sudoku* (2006)
5	*Scribblenauts* (2009)
6	*Big Brain Academy* (2005)
7	*Mystery Case Files: MillionHeir* (2008)
8	*Art Style: Code* (2008)
9	*The Sun Crossword Challenge* (2008)
10	*42 All-Time Classics* (2006)

✱ NEW RECORD
▪ UPDATED RECORD

« I love the concept that Nintendo is reaching out to new audiences with their self-improvement products like Brain Training. I've quickly found that training my brain is a great way to keep my mind feeling young.
Oscar®-winning actress Nicole Kidman

IOO MILLION... the number of people who have played a *Mystery Case Files* game since the first title in the series, *Huntsville*, was released as a PC download on 18 November 2005.

OVERVIEW

> *Lateral thinking is the key to success with a logic puzzle. The player is usually presented with an arrangement of numbers, words or shapes, and the aim is to find a pattern or complete a sequence. In its purest form, there are no time limits or evolving conditions – just a problem that the player absorbs and picks away at until discovering the solution. The Sudoku number-placement puzzle is a classic logic game that has been translated to many videogame platforms, most notably as part of the multi-million-selling* Dr. Kawashima's Brain Training *for the Nintendo DS. Although logic puzzles do not require fancy graphics, titles such as* Professor Layton and the Curious Village *have successfully managed to marry brain-teasing puzzles with a strong visual style.*

FASTEST COMPLETIONS OF MINESWEEPER

Holder: VARIOUS

The top *Minesweeper* players are listed at minesweepers.org, which records the best times achieved on *MSO Minesweeper*, a special version of *Windows Minesweeper* that allows times to be submitted to the website. D. Jockser (UK) achieved 11.738 seconds on Intermediate difficulty, el Jefe (USA) recorded 53.445 seconds on Expert, while theflyingtad (USA) completed Expert Plus in a barnstorming 75.177 seconds.

※ FIRST PUZZLE GAME TO WIN A BAFTA AWARD

Holder: DR. KAWASHIMA'S BRAIN TRAINING (Nintendo, 2005)

Dr. Kawashima's Brain Training was the first puzzle game to win a prestigious BAFTA award. The Nintendo DS brain-booster won the Innovation category at the 2006 British Academy Video Games Awards event, beating off competition from *LocoRoco* (Sony, 2006) and *We Love Katamari* (Namco/EA, 2005). Since then, two more puzzle games have been honoured, at the 2008 event – *Boom Blox* (EA, 2008) won in the Casual category, while *Professor Layton and the Curious Village* (Level-5, 2007) took home the Handheld award.

※ FASTEST COMPLETION OF PICROSS DS: NORMAL MODE – CATCH

Holder: MICHELE MAGNATERRA (Italy)

Italian Michele Magnaterra has achieved the fastest times in all 10 Normal Mode – Catch challenges on *Picross DS* (Nintendo, 2007), including 7.99 seconds on Catch 02.

▣ BEST-SELLING BRAIN-TRAINING VIDEOGAME

Holder: DR. KAWASHIMA'S BRAIN TRAINING (Nintendo, 2005)

As of May 2009, the Nintendo handheld's *Dr. Kawashima's Brain Training* (*Brain Age* in the USA) is the best-selling brain-workout game, with worldwide sales of 17.4 million copies. The follow-up, *More Brain Training from Dr. Kawashima*, has proved almost as popular, selling 13.7 million copies, meaning that total series sales have topped 31 million. In Japan, demand for the sequel was so huge that retailers received 850,000 pre-orders prior to the game's release in late 2005.

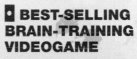

> Perennial time-waster Minesweeper has been included in every version of Microsoft Windows going back to Windows 3.1, which was released in 1992. The Windows Vista version of the game introduces a new "pacifist" option in which the mines can be replaced with flowers.

HINT

> There are 120 standard puzzles in Professor Layton and the Curious Village, plus a further 15 bonus puzzles you can unlock by completing various objectives. If you need a clue to unlocking the bonus puzzles, try the following: gather up all of the gizmo pieces in The Inventor's House; position all of the furniture in its correct place in The Decorator's House; and solve the portrait jigsaw puzzle in The Art Lover's House.

※ RAREST VIDEOGAME FOR THE NEOGEO POCKET COLOR

Holder: POCKET REVERSI (SNK, 2000)

Puzzle game *Pocket Reversi* is the most sought-after release for the NeoGeo Pocket Color handheld console. Released by publisher SNK in 2000, it is estimated that only 1,000 copies of the game were manufactured for the European market and, of these, fewer than 100 copies were actually sold. As such, a complete copy of the game with packaging and instructions is a highly desirable collector's item and is likely to fetch in excess of £100 ($162) in today's market.

ROLE-PLAYING GAMES

The **fastest-selling multi-platform role-playing game** is Bethesda Softworks' *Fallout 3*, which sold over 644,000 copies in its first week on sale from 28 October to 4 November 2008.

CONTENTS:

INTRODUCTION

FOR MORE ESCAPISM, TURN TO P.84 FOR THE BEST ACTION-ADVENTURE GAMES.

KEY GAME
DRAGON AGE: ORIGINS

Described as a "dark, heroic fantasy" by its creators, *Dragon Age: Origins* (EA, 2009) is an epic single-player RPG. With six different starting points, or Origins, the player's experience of the story is shaped by the unique background and perspective of his chosen character. The game also features a "developer-grade" tool-set that allows players to create and customize content.

FEATURING VAST VIRTUAL LANDSCAPES, MASSIVE BATTLE SCENES AND RICHLY IMAGINED STORYLINES, ROLE-PLAYING GAMES OFFER THE VIDEOGAMER ESCAPISM ON AN EPIC SCALE

The role-playing game's (RPG) history stretches back towards the dawn of videogaming. In 1974, Gary Wisenhunt and Ray Wood, students at Southern Illinois University, USA, created *dnd*, the very **first computer-based RPG**, in which characters venture into the Wisenwood dungeon in search of treasure. Based on *Dungeons & Dragons*, the wildly popular tabletop gaming series, *dnd* became the blueprint for many RPGs to come.

The **first RPG to appear on a personal computer** was 1979's *Space*, designed for the Apple II. Set in a futuristic interstellar society that drew influence from popular science-fiction movies of the era, it paved the way for today's sci-fi RPGs, such as *Mass Effect*.

The rise of the home PC brought with it a flurry of new RPG releases – from the Commodore PET's *Dunjonquest*, which would become the **first RPG game trilogy**, to 1980's *Ultima*, created by the charismatic Richard Garriot, or "Lord British" as he's better known to his fans. Garriot's third *Ultima* title, released in 1983, was the **first RPG to feature animated graphics**. The most recent title in the series, *Ultima Online: Kingdom Reborn*, was released in November 2007, making *Ultima* the **longest-running RPG franchise**, at 27 years.

The early 1980s saw the rise of the videogame console, thanks to the successes of arcade legend Atari. In 1982, the Atari 2600 enjoyed the **first console RPG**, *Dragon Stomper*, a game described boldly by *Forbes* magazine in 2005 as "the best title ever made in the history of US videogaming".

It wasn't until 1984 that the RPG arrived in Japan, courtesy of Bulletproof Software's Henk Rogers, a US citizen living in Tokyo, who used an NEC-8801 to design the **first Japanese RPG**, *Black Onyx*.

A fantastic story, combat, gameplay...

Bioware Project Director Dan Tudge on the key ingredients of a successful RPG

■ **NEW RECORD**
■ **UPDATED RECORD**

TIMELINE

1974
dnd becomes the **first computer-based RPG**, created for the PLATO computer by a group of students at Southern Illinois University, USA.

1984
Visionary designer Henk Rogers walks into the offices of a Japanese videogames magazine to show the writers the **first ever Japanese RPG**, *Black Onyx*.

1995
Chrono Trigger, the first collaboration between *Dragon Quest* creator Yuji Horii and *Final Fantasy*'s Hironobu Sakaguchi, launches on the Super Famicom.

1996
Pokémon Red and *Blue* are released for Nintendo's Gameboy platform, establishing what would later become the **best-selling RPG series**.

1997
Final Fantasy VII breaks records on its debut on the PlayStation, and goes on to become one of the most influential role-playing games of all time.

OVERVIEW

Role-playing games (RPGs) are videogaming's true epics. Inspired by the fantasy works of British author JRR Tolkien, players usually take control of a small band of heroes on a long, winding adventure to save the world from some great evil. While Western and Japanese RPGs share many similarities, the former often take a free-roaming approach to combat and exploration, whereas the latter often follow a linear storyline and feature turn-based combat. The RPG genre saw a huge explosion in popularity with the advent of Massively Multiplayer Online Role-Playing Games (MMORPGs) – RPGs that potentially hundreds or thousands of people can play together in shared games online.

KEY GAME
DUNGEONS & DRAGONS

Released in 1974 as a book of intricate rules for pencil-and-paper wargames, *D&D* effectively invented the RPG. Since then, the game has been enjoyed by over 20 million players, brought in over $1 billion (£630 million) in book and equipment sales and inspired a generation of computer RPGs.

KEY GAME
WORLD OF WARCRAFT

The fourth game set in developer Blizzard's fantasy universe, *World of Warcraft* is by far the **most popular paid-for MMORPG**, with over 11.6 million monthly subscribers. Players create a character, such as an elf or mage, and then set off into the vast virtual realm, collecting gold and enhancing their character along the way through the game's almost limitless number of quests.

Although the RPG genre moved into another dimension in 1985 when EA released *The Bard's Tale*, the **first RPG with 3D environments**, it was *Black Onyx* that secured the RPG's future in Japan. In 1986, Japanese developer Enix released *Dragon Quest*, while Sega launched *Phantasy Star*. A year later, Square (who later merged with Enix to become Square Enix) released *Final Fantasy*, the game that would save the young company from bankruptcy.

In 1991, AOL and Stormfront Studios released *Neverwinter Nights*, which became the **first graphical Massively Multiplayer Online** Role-Playing Game before the term MMORPG was even coined (by *Ultima's* Richard Garriot in 1997). *Neverwinter Nights'* servers were switched off in 1997 and it wasn't until 2000 that gamers saw the **first console MMORPG**, in the form of Sonic Team's *Phantasy Star Online* on the ill-fated Dreamcast.

Today, the RPG genre continues to flourish. *Dragon Age: Origins*, a new series from veterans Bioware, offers a new take on linear storytelling, while *Final Fantasy* and *Dragon Quest* both have new releases, each more spectacular and grandiose than ever. Online, the most popular paid-for MMORPG, *World of Warcraft*, now has over 11.6 million subscribers – which is mightily impressive for a genre that began with a dice roll.

EXPERT

Simon Parkin has been writing about videogames professionally for seven years, first for Edge magazine and later for websites Eurogamer, Yahoo, Gamasutra and many others. A Japanese RPG expert, Simon has travelled to Tokyo and interviewed the genre's key creators on many occasions. He also runs the popular gaming blog Chewing Pixels.

TRIVIA

In 2008, RPG designer Richard Garriot joined the Russian space mission Soyuz TMA-13 as a self-funded tourist, launching for the International Space Station on 12 October. The trip cost him $30 million (£18.2 million) and made Garriot the only videogame creator to have visited space.

Secret of Mana, released in 1993 for the Super Famicom, allowed two players to quest together at the same time in what proved to be the system's first and only fully multiplayer RPG.

1998	1999	2002	2004	2006	2009
Panzer Dragoon Saga is released for the Sega Saturn. With a mere 10,000 copies produced, it quickly becomes the **rarest and most valuable RPG** ever sold at retail.	*Final Fantasy VIII* establishes itself as the **biggest launch-week hit in RPG history**, shipping a truly staggering 2.5 million copies in the seven days from 11 February.	The **first cross-platform MMORPG** ever created, *Final Fantasy XI*, debuts on the PlayStation 2 in Japan on 16 May and, six months later, is released for the PC.	Blizzard release the MMORPG *World of Warcraft*, a game that wows audiences worldwide and goes on to take a stranglehold on the online market.	Bethesda's *The Elder Scrolls IV: Oblivion*, the **first RPG to be released for Xbox 360**, awes gamers with its previously unimaginable sense of size and scope.	Square Enix's *Dragon Quest IX* and *Final Fantasy XIII*, the **biggest JRPG series** in the world, are released on both Nintendo's DS and Sony's PlayStation 2.

JAPANESE RPG

! IF YOU ENJOY STRATEGY GAMES, CHECK OUT P.162 FOR MORE TITLES.

✳ LARGEST DEVELOPMENT TEAM ON A JAPANESE RPG

Holder: FINAL FANTASY XIII (Square Enix, 2010)

Boasting the largest development team of any Japanese RPG (JRPG) in history, *Final Fantasy XIII* employed a crew of 100 to create the game's extensive CGI cutscenes, while a further 200 staff were involved in designing and coding the rest of the game. Producer Yoshinori Kitase claims that almost every member of the Japanese staff at Square Enix was invited to have input on the game's development to one extent or another.

> There are no explicit rules for how a Final Fantasy game should be, and so every version is that design team's interpretation of certain themes.
>
> Final Fantasy XIII *designer Tetsuya Nomura*

✳ **NEW RECORD**
▪ **UPDATED RECORD**

OVERVIEW

> The computer-based RPG was pioneered in Japan by American ex-pat Henk Rogers (right) back in the early 1980s. His groundbreaking game, *Black Onyx*, wowed the Japanese gaming press, going on to sell 150,000 copies in 1984 and establishing the template that would later be adopted by best-selling Japanese series *Dragon Quest* and *Final Fantasy*. Distinguished from Western RPGs by their linear stories, random, turn-based combat and protagonists with improbably large swords and spiky hair, the JRPG continues to be one of the most popular genres in gaming. Its current zenith, *Final Fantasy XIII*, has taken a team of 300 coders, artists and designers no fewer than five years to create.

FACT

> *Final Fantasy: The Spirits Within* (2001) was both the **most expensive videogame-inspired movie of all time**, as well as the one that lost the most money at the box office. Costing its creator $137 million (£83.4 million) including marketing costs, the film only recouped $32 million (£19.5 million). The substantial loss threatened to derail the proposed merger between Final Fantasy creator Square and Dragon Quest maker Enix, though the deal did eventually go ahead.

TEN GAMES YOU SHOULD PLAY IN THIS GENRE

	GAME
1	*Final Fantasy VII* (1997)
2	*Chrono Trigger* (1995)
3	*Dragon Quest VIII* (2004)
4	*Final Fantasy XII* (2006)
5	*Secret of Mana* (1993)
6	*Persona 4* (2008)
7	*Final Fantasy VI* (1994)
8	*Tales of Vesperia* (2008)
9	*White Knight Chronicles* (2008)
10	*Lost Odyssey* (2007)

TRIVIA

> The Final Fantasy franchise was exclusive to Nintendo hardware until 1997, when the seventh game in the series became the flagship RPG for Sony's new PlayStation platform.

> Nobuo Uematsu (Japan), composer of many Square Enix game soundtracks, also performs in a rock band called The Black Mages with two other Square Enix composers: Kenichiro Fukui and Tsuyoshi Sekito (both Japan).

> In its day, Final Fantasy VII broke numerous records: it was delivered across three discs – a first for a PlayStation game – and featured no fewer than 330 CG maps and 40 minutes of video.

MOST EXPENSIVE VIDEOGAME SOUNDTRACK

Holder: SAGA (Square Enix, 1989)
With an asking price of ¥21,000 ($216, £130), the most expensive commercially available videogame sountrack is the *SaGa Series 20th Anniversary Original Soundtrack Premium Box*. The compilation features 20 CDs with remastered recordings of songs from each of the nine games in the *SaGa* series.

FIRST VIDEOGAME CONCERT BASED ON MUSIC FROM AN RPG

Holder: DRAGON QUEST (Square Enix, 1986)
The first live concert featuring music from a videogame was the "Family Classic Concert", held on 20 August 1987 at Suntory Hall in Tokyo, Japan. The concert featured music from *Dragon Quest I* and *Dragon Quest II*, performed by the Tokyo String Music Combination Playing Group.

BEST-SELLING JAPANESE RPG TITLE

Holder: POKÉMON RED/BLUE/ GREEN (Nintendo, 1996)
With sales of 31.38 million copies, the best-selling Japanese RPG is *Pokémon Red/Blue/ Green*. First released in Japan on 27 February 1996, the game came in three different colour variants, each one featuring some *Pokémon* exclusive to that edition.

✳ BEST-SELLING JAPANESE RPG SERIES

Holder: POKÉMON (Nintendo, 1996 to present)
At the top of the JRPG pile is the ever-popular *Pokémon* franchise. With sales of the mainline series tipping 130 million worldwide, it is by far the best-selling RPG series ever created – though much of its success comes from Nintendo's habit of selling multiple versions of the game. Hot on its heels is the *Final Fantasy* franchise, whose numerous incarnations have generated over 85 million recorded sales worldwide.

WESTERN RPG

! FINISHED WITH RPG AND WANT TO SEE SOME FPS? THEN TURN TO P.48.

✴ BEST-SELLING WESTERN RPG

Holder: THE ELDER SCROLLS IV: OBLIVION (Bethesda Softworks/ 2K Games, 2006)

Since its release on Xbox 360 on 20 March 2006, *The Elder Scrolls IV: Oblivion* has sold 2.67 million copies, making it the best-selling Western RPG of all time. Of that figure, a staggering 1.86 million copies (nearly 70%) were sold in the USA. Second place goes to offline RPG *Fable 2*, with 2.60 million sales on Xbox and PC.

This is a rare and remarkable achievement – a huge, open-ended, complex, detailed role-playing game that's fun to play and a pleasure to behold.

uk.gamespot.com discussing The Elder Scrolls: Oblivion

✴ NEW RECORD
◻ UPDATED RECORD

TEN GAMES YOU SHOULD PLAY IN THIS GENRE

	GAME
1	*Fallout 3* (2008)
2	*The Elder Scrolls IV: Oblivion* (2006)
3	*Mass Effect* (2007)
4	*Star Wars: Knights of the Old Republic* (2003)
5	*Planescape Torment* (1999)
6	*Baldur's Gate II: Shadows of Amn* (2000)
7	*Dragon Age: Origins* (2009)
8	*Ultima III: Exodus* (1983)
9	*Neverwinter Nights* (2002)
10	*Ultima Underworld II: Labyrinth of Worlds* (1993)

15,000... the number of towns, cities, villages and dungeons in *The Elder Scrolls II: Daggerfall*, which boasts the **largest ever land-based game world**, at 161,600 km² (62,394 miles²).

OVERVIEW

The Western RPG is a direct descendant of classic tabletop role-playing games such as Dungeons and Dragons. For 10 years, from PLATO's dnd to Ultima III, videogame RPGs very closely mimicked the form and function of their pen-and-paper predecessors. They only began to explore new ways of presenting the epic adventure in titles such as Wasteland, The Elder Scrolls: Arena and Fallout. Today, the Western RPG is exemplified by games such as Oblivion, Fallout 3, Mass Effect and Star Wars: Knights of the Old Republic. It is usually a free-roaming affair featuring a core storyline with hundreds of optional off-shoots and real-time combat.

* MOST ADVANCED CHARACTER FACE GENERATOR

Holder: MASS EFFECT (Microsoft, 2007)
The videogame with the most advanced character face generator is the Bioware creation *Mass Effect*. Blending together over 150 different facial features, the system offers over 1 billion permutations for the face of lead character Commander Shepherd. Most impressive is the software that animates the full range of face options, turning a lifeless doll into an expressive personality, a character that acts her lines rather than simply reading them aloud.

MOST CRITICALLY ACCLAIMED WESTERN RPG

Holder: BALDUR'S GATE II: SHADOWS OF AMN (Black Isle Studios, 2000)
The Western RPG with the highest critical rating is *Baldur's Gate II*, which scored an average of 95% over 30 reviews on score aggregator Metacritic. The game is closely followed by *The Elder Scrolls IV: Oblivion* with 94%.

LONGEST-RUNNING RPG FRANCHISE

Holder: ULTIMA (Origin Systems, EA, 1980 to present)
The *Ultima* franchise is the longest-running RPG series, at 29 years. *Ultima I: The First Age of Darkness* was released in 1980 while the most recent entry to the series, *Ultima Online: The Stygian Abyss*, came out in 2009. It is beaten to the record of overall longest-running videogame franchise by *Space Invaders*, which was first released in 1978 and most recently updated with *Space Invaders Extreme 2* in 2009.

* MOST CRITICALLY DIVISIVE ROLE-PLAYING GAME

Holder: TWO WORLDS (SouthPeak Interactive, 2007)
With an enormous 61% between its best and worst reviews, *Two Worlds* is the most critically divisive RPG ever. *PC Gamer USA* called it "a huge, open-ended role-playing world with a ton of depth and a rousing storyline" and awarded it 81%, while UK magazine *GamesTM* gave the game a less flattering 2 out of 10.

FIRST FULLY 3D RPG

Holder: ULTIMA UNDERWORLD: THE STYGIAN ABYSS (Origin Systems, 1992)
The first RPG to make use of a fully three-dimensional environment was *Ultima Underworld*, developed by Looking Glass Technologies and acclaimed designer Warren Spector, who also produced *Deus Ex*.

FACT

The Elder Scrolls IV: Oblivion *features 94,013 trees and fallen logs, 35,544 shrubs and bushes, 67,730 plants and mushrooms and 395,696 rocks.*

TRIVIA

Fallout 3 *is loosely based on Cormac McCarthy's post-apocalyptic novel The Road.*

The collector's edition of The Elder Scrolls IV: Oblivion, which features a documentary, a guide to the empire and a Septim gold coin, is the best-selling collector's edition of any game ever made.

"If there is a cannon and there's a door and I fire the cannon... it sure as heck should break that door. If I'm going to stop that I better find a steel door to try and resist it, if you know what I mean. I tried to make sure that world was very completely and realistically simulated." Ultima creator Richard Garriot talking to The Escapist about creating virtual worlds.

While it's possible to kill any adult in Fallout 3, the designers decided to remove the ability to murder children, a decision that sparked controversy among gamers as an act of censorship.

ACTION RPG

! FOR MORE ACTION, LESS ROLE-PLAY, FLIP BACK TO P.84.

✱ BEST-SELLING RPG SERIES ON THE PSP

Holder: MONSTER HUNTER FREEDOM (Capcom, 2005 to present) With 7.52 million copies sold to date, *Monster Hunter Freedom* is the best-selling RPG series for the PSP. The most recent game in the franchise is *Monster Hunter Freedom Unite*, which, since release on 27 March 2008, has sold 3.14 million copies in Japan, while its predecessor sold 3.8 million copies globally. The title is now a sensation in Japan, where strangers frequently gather in public to play in multiplayer.

OVERVIEW

> Unlike more traditional role-playing games, action RPGs are less about character interaction and more about hack-and-slash, real-time combat with large numbers of enemies. However, what roots them firmly within the RPG genre, and sets them apart from standard action games, is their retention of traditional RPG features, such as gathering loot, gaining experience points and leveling. Nintendo's *Legend of Zelda* is one example of a game that falls just outside the sub-genre for lack of the key role-play characteristics, though it did go on to influence later action RPGs. Modern examples include Blizzard's genre-defining *Diablo* series, and the more recent *The Witcher*, which re-established the emphasis on traditional RPG dialogue and interaction.

This is the great conundrum: how can a game so frustrating be so addictive?
Wesley Yin-Poole struggling to get to grips with Monster Hunter Freedom Unite for eurogamer.net

TEN GAMES YOU SHOULD PLAY IN THIS GENRE

	GAME
1	*Fable II* (2008)
2	*Diablo II* (2000)
3	*Kingdom Hearts* (2002)
4	*Pokémon Mystery Dungeon* (2005)
5	*Monster Hunter Freedom Unite* (2008)
6	*Sacred 2: Fallen Angel* (2008)
7	*The Witcher* (2007)
8	*Sudeki* (2004)
9	*Brave Fencer Musashi* (1998)
10	*Diablo* (1996)

* FIRST ACTION RPG

Holder: DUNGEONS OF DAGGORATH
(Tandy Corporation, 1982)
Developed by DynaMicro for the TRS-80 Colour Computer, *Dungeons of Daggorath* combined real-time combat with rudimentary RPG features such as object collecting and character building. In the game, players progress through a series of five dungeons, battling increasingly powerful foes in first-person perspective. The black-and-white game is also one of the smallest in programming terms – at only 8k!

Capcom's Monster Hunter Freedom Unite (2008), the third instalment in the Monster Hunter Freedom series for the PSP, features over 1,400 different weapons and 2,000 armour items.

Blizzard's Matt Uelmen (USA) is credited with working on the soundtracks of all three of the Diablo games.

Every creature in Diablo III boasts 35 unique death animations.

■ FASTEST-SELLING RPG ON XBOX 360

Holder: FABLE II (Microsoft, 2008)
The Xbox 360's fastest-selling role-playing game is *Fable II*, the 360-exclusive from developer Lionhead Software. The game shifted 1.5 million copies in the month following its launch on 21 October 2008, overtaking previous record-holder *Mass Effect* (2007). However, the record falls some way short of other fastest-selling titles on the system: *Halo 3* sold a staggering 3.3 million copies in its first month. Lionhead had intended to release an expansion pack a few weeks after release, but the team was so exhausted after the rush to get the game finished that it had to be delayed into 2009.

* FIRST ACTION RPG TO OFFER IN-GAME PRIZES VIA ITS OFFICIAL WEBSITE

Holder: FABLE II (Microsoft, 2008)
The official *Fable II* website features two browser-based games that reward players with prizes that can be transferred to their in-game characters. *Chicken Kickin'* is a simple but amusing game requiring the player to boot a chicken around in return for bonus gold. *The Hero's Tale*, on the other hand, is a more charming, interactive story, which is presented as a puppet show and narrated by British actress Zoë Wanamaker. It offers players who finish it one of five unique prizes, including a three-piece chicken suit that players need in order to earn one of the game's achievements.

■ **NEW RECORD**
● **UPDATED RECORD**

* FASTEST COMPLETION OF DIABLO

Holder: MACIEJ "GROOBO" MASELEWSKI (Poland)
The fastest segmented speed run through Blizzard's *Diablo* (1996) was achieved on 16 January 2009 by Maciej Maselewski of Poland, who played as the sorceror character and took only 3 min 12 sec to finish the game. This is a particularly impressive feat as the game normally takes most gamers between 10 and 20 hours to complete. Maselewski played each of the 27 segments over and over to produce a near-perfect speed run that exploited *Diablo*'s dungeon design and allowed him to move quickly to the exit of each randomized level without wasting time on unnecessary combat.

In August 2009, a petition signed by over 61,000 Diablo fans was handed to developer Blizzard Entertainment, complaining about the art style of the new Diablo III game. The petition, "Renewed Artistic Direction for Diablo 3", was created in protest at some fans' perception that the game was "influenced by the Warcraft universe" with "vivid colors, beautiful forests with colorful vegetation". Instead, the fans called for "gothic and obscure scenarios" and "cryptic, dark and shadowy dungeons" more in tune with the game's previous instalments. In response, Blizzard produced T-shirts with a new "Diablo III" logo that features smiling unicorns and a rainbow.

* FIRST RPG TO RECEIVE AN AWARD FOR ITS ETHICAL TREATMENT OF ANIMALS

Holder: FABLE II (Microsoft, 2008)
Fable II was the first RPG to be rewarded for its kindness to animals. In December 2008, animal rights group PETA (People for the Ethical Treatment of Animals) handed the game a Proggy Award for being "the most animal-friendly game of the year". PETA said they believed the game to be pro-vegetarian for awarding the player "purity" points for eating non-meat products and "corruption" points for eating meat. *Fable II* was only the second videogame to receive the award, the first being *Nintendogs* (2005).

MMORPG: FANTASY

! FOR RECORD-BREAKING RPGs WITH A STRATEGY ELEMENT, WHY NOT TURN TO P.172

* NEW RECORD
◻ UPDATED RECORD

FIRST CROSS-PLATFORM MMORPG

Holder: FINAL FANTASY XI
(Square Enix, 2002)
Final Fantasy XI was the first inter-console and PC-based MMORPG, allowing gamers across multiple platforms – Xbox 360, PlayStation 2 and PC – to play together. It was first released in Japan on PS2 on 16 May 2002, before hitting PCs in November 2002. An Xbox 360 version was released worldwide in April 2006, becoming the Microsoft system's first ever MMORPG.

> « *I hate gold sellers with every fibre of my being...*
> Warhammer Online's CEO Mark Jacobs on the illicit trade in fantasy-game currency »

OVERVIEW

> While it was Richard Garriott who first coined the term "Massively Multiplayer Online Role Playing Game" to describe his game *Ultima Online* in the late 1990s, the multi-user RPG has existed for a lot longer. The first graphical MMORPG was *Neverwinter Nights,* which was playable on AOL between 1991 and 1997. Contemporary fantasy MMORPGs, however, are overwhelmingly defined by the most popular entry to the genre, *World of Warcraft,* with its richly imagined land of dwarves, orcs and epic quests. But the genre also takes many other forms, from the cutesy side-scrolling anime look of the Korean *Dragonica* to the squat cartoon style of the French-made *Dofus.*

II.6 MILLION... the number of subscribers to Blizzard's *World of Warcraft* as of January 2009, making it the world's **most popular subscription MMORPG**.

LARGEST FREE MMORPG

Holder: RUNESCAPE
(Jagex, 2001)
With over 150 million registered users to its name, the browser-based fantasy title *RuneScape* is the largest free MMORPG by userbase. The game has been running since 2001 and, in addition to the free option, offers a subscription service that provides access to additional game content.

✱ TOUGHEST 1,000 ACHIEVEMENT POINTS TO EARN ON XBOX 360

Holder: FINAL FANTASY XI
(Square Enix, 2002)
The set of 1,000 achievement points in *Final Fantasy XI* are the Xbox 360's most difficult to earn. They can only be achieved by, among other things, levelling every job class in the game to a dizzying level 75. There are 18 job classes in total and it takes the average player anywhere between 12 and 18 months to progress a single job to that level – doing so for all the jobs in the game could take around two decades. Other tasks include completing the various missions, obtaining items and reaching certain ranks. Nobody in the world has legitimately earned the game's 1,000 achievement points to date.

	TEN GAMES YOU SHOULD PLAY IN THIS GENRE	
		GAME
1	World of Warcraft	(2004)
2	Maple Story	(2003)
3	Guild Wars	(2005)
4	Warhammer Online	(2008)
5	The Lord of the Rings Online	(2007)
6	Dragonica	(2009)
7	Final Fantasy XI	(2002)
8	Runescape	(2001)
9	EverQuest	(1999)
10	Dofus	(2005)

✱ LONGEST TOTAL TIME SPENT PLAYING AN MMORPG

Holder: SARA LHADI (Netherlands)
Law student and *RuneScape* fanatic Sara Lhadi has spent an amazing 16,799 hours in-game between November 2004, when she created her character, and September 2009. This averages out to an incredible 9 hours 30 minutes of play every day since she started on the game.

✱ HIGHEST-GROSSING VIDEOGAME

Holder: WORLD OF WARCRAFT
(Blizzard Entertainment, 2004)
In 2008, a combination of game sales and subscriptions brought in a total of $1.34 billion (£797 million) for *World of Warcraft* creator Blizzard Entertainment, making the game the highest-grossing ever made. On its release in November 2009, the game's second expansion pack, *Wrath of the Lich King*, sold 2.8 million copies in 24 hours, and 4 million in its first month, making it the **fastest-selling PC game ever**.

✱ FANTASY MMORPG WITH THE MOST EXPANSION PACKS

Holder: EVERQUEST (Sony, 1999)
Since its release in 1999, *EverQuest* has spawned 16 expansion packs, more than any other fantasy MMORPG. Expansion packs are purchased separately from the main game and provide additional content such as new races, equipment and quests. EverQuest's first expansion was March 2000's *The Ruins of Kunark*.

✱ LARGEST STUDY INTO ONLINE GAMING HABITS

Holder: UNIVERSITY OF MINNESOTA (USA)
Researchers from the University of Minnesota who were looking into online gaming habits were supplied with almost 60 terabytes of information in the world's largest study of its kind. The data came from the MMORPG *EverQuest 2* (2004) and consisted of every player action over a four-year period – nearly 400,000 individuals playing, chatting, trading and questing. The study provides a detailed profile of the average MMORPG gamer as well as insight into the triggers that provoke certain gaming responses.

MMORPG: SCI FI

! ARE YOU AIMING FOR MORE SCI-FI GAMING ACTION? TURN TO P.54 FOR THE BEST THIRD-PERSON SHOOTERS.

* SHORTEST-LIVED MAJOR MMORPG

Holder: TABULA RASA (NCsoft, 2007) MMORPGs are usually designed so players can develop their characters over years. *Tabula Rasa*, the sci-fi MMORPG from *Ultima Online* creator Richard Garriott, is one of the exceptions. It was supported by live servers for just 1 year 3 months 26 days before it was finally shut down on 28 February 2009.

> It was a game that was hitting its stride enough where it could keep what I'll call a critical fan base, and had the opportunity to continue to be grown.
>
> Richard Garriott telling GameDaily why he though Tabula Rasa should have continued

TEN GAMES YOU SHOULD PLAY IN THIS GENRE

	GAME
1	EVE Online (2003)
2	City of Heroes (2004)
3	Star Wars Galaxies (2003)
4	Anarchy Online (2001)
5	Star Wars: The Old Republic (2009)
6	Phantasy Star Universe (2006)
7	Shin Megami Tensei: Imagine (2007)
8	PlanetSide (2003)
9	The Matrix Online (2005)
10	Earth and Beyond (2002)

NEW RECORD
UPDATED RECORD

■ * NEW RECORD ■ ✳ UPDATED RECORD

GUINNESS WORLD RECORDS

OVERVIEW

> *For those MMORPG fans who have no interest in orcs and elves and all of the other sword and sorcery trappings of the fantasy genre, where better to find solace than in the stars? The sci-fi MMORPG is designed to appeal to those players who are more interested in a mythical future than a mythical past. They allow users to pilot spaceships through distant star systems, to colonize lonely planets or, in the case of* City of Heroes, *to assume the role of costumed heroes and villains in a comic book world. Sci-fi MMORPGs also offer extremely varied gameplay, from the MMORPG shooter* PlanetSide *to the demon wrangling of* Shin Megami Tensei: Imagine *in post-apocalyptic Tokyo.*

✱ LARGEST VIRTUAL THEFT IN AN MMORPG

Holder: EVE ONLINE
(CCP Games, 2003)
In *Eve Online*, players accumulate resources and ISK, the game's currency, by fair means or foul. The largest haul for an in-game fraudster goes to a character called Cally, who set up the Eve Intergalactic Bank. To start with, it operated like a normal bank, taking deposits, loaning money and charging interest, until Cally stole an estimated 790 billion ISK from its coffers and posted a video confession online. Since such actions are allowed under the game's licence, Cally got away with his "crime".

LONGEST-LASTING PLAYER CORPSE

Holder: STAR WARS GALAXIES
(LucasArts, 2003)
An early feature of *Star Wars Galaxies* demanded that players return to their corpses after being killed in-game to retrieve their loot and equipment. However one player, Icir, never returned to fetch his belongings. His corpse was left lying at the Talus Imperial Base on the Bloodfin server for no less than three years, untouched, before being cleared away by a gamesmaster.

✱ LARGEST NUMBER OF ACCESSIBLE SOLAR SYSTEMS IN AN MMORPG

Holder: EVE ONLINE
(CCP Games, 2003)
As of June 2009, the Icelandic MMORPG *Eve Online* boasts 5,201 accessible solar systems, more than any other sci-fi MMORPG. While there are actually 5,431 solar systems currently referenced in the *EVE* database, 230 of them are yet to be made open to the public.

✱ MMORPG WITH THE MOST EXPANSION PACKS

Holder: CITY OF HEROES
(NCsoft, 2004)
The popular superhero MMORPG *City of Heroes* can boast an impressive 17 updates or "issues", which add new content, customizations, play areas and storylines to the game. This is more than any rival MMORPG, beating even *EverQuest*, the big daddy of MMORPGs, which has 16 updates to its name. However, *City of Heroes* might soon have some stiff competition in the super power stakes with the release of both *Champions Online*, designed by Cryptic Studios, the same people who developed the original *City of Heroes*, and the much-anticipated *DC Universe Online*.

✱ FIRST SCI-FI MMORPG

Holder: PHANTASY STAR ONLINE (SEGA, 2000)
The first sci-fi MMORPG was SEGA's *Phantasy Star Online*, released in Japan for the SEGA Dreamcast on 21 November 2000. Prior to this release, MMOs had been set exclusively in fantasy realms, from *Neverwinter Nights* (1991), the **first graphical MMO**, through to *Meridian 59* (1996), the first **MMO to feature first-person 3D graphics**. *Phantasy Star Online* was soon followed by two other sci-fi MMOs, *Anarchy Online* in June 2001 and *DarkSpace* in December 2001.

MMORPG: SOCIAL

! FOR MORE SOCIAL GAMING, TURN TO P.124 AND CHECK OUT ALL THE BEST LIFESTYLE GAMES.

+ NEW RECORD
◇ UPDATED RECORD

✱ MOST-DEDICATED MMORPG PLAYERS

Holder: SECOND LIFE
(Linden Lab, 2003)
Players of *Second Life* are officially the most dedicated of all MMORPG gamers, committing, on average, 760 minutes per week to the online game. A Nielsen report produced in March 2009 placed *Second Life* well ahead of its rivals, beating into second place Blizzard's MMORPG heavyweight *World of Warcraft*, whose players devote a "paltry" 653 minutes per week to the fantasy role-player.

« *Second Life is a virtual real-estate business but it is a little less abstract than a lot of people suggest...*
Philip Rosedale, founder of Second Life »

TEN GAMES YOU SHOULD PLAY IN THIS GENRE

	GAME
1	*Habbo* (2000)
2	*Club Penguin* (2005)
3	*Entropia Universe* (2003)
4	*Second Life* (2003)
5	*Free Realms* (2009)
6	*Monster and Me* (2002)
7	*PlayStation Home* (2008)
8	*Oz World* (2006)
9	*Disney's Virtual Magic Kingdom* (2005)
10	*Mini Friday* (2006)

$350 MILLION (£243 MILLION)... the amount paid by the Walt Disney Company for *Club Penguin*, which was the **highest sum ever paid for an MMORPG**.

OVERVIEW

> For some players, the "game" element of the MMORPG experience is less important than the social aspect. For these gamers, an entire sub-industry has sprung up, offering virtual spaces in which meeting others and customizing Avatars and in-game residences are top priority. While fantasy and sci-fi MMORPGs often encourage players to act in-character, role-playing an assumed personality, social MMORPGs encourage them to be themselves, recreating their looks and tastes in a virtual space. As a result, many real-life relationships have blossomed in social MMORPGs, in some cases even leading to marriage, both in-game and out.

❊ FIRST SOCIAL MMORPG TO OPEN VIRTUAL BRANCHES OF REAL-LIFE BANKS

Holder: ENTROPIA UNIVERSE (MindArk, 2003)
On 8 May 2007, MindArk announced the results of the world's first virtual-world banking licence auction. Five licences were sold for a total of $404,000 (£238,000), snapped up by a mix of real-world banks, entrepreneurs and *Entropia* participants, all of whom wanted to invest in and profit from the virtual realm.

❊ MOST FINANCIALLY REWARDING MMORPG FOR PLAYERS

Holder: SECOND LIFE (Linden Lab, 2003)
The virtual world where players are most likely to make a real-world profit is *Second Life*. In February 2009, 64,000 users made a profit in the virtual world. Over half made less than $10 (£5.90), but 233 earned more than $5,000 (£2,940). *Second Life* allows its users to build virtual objects and add simple functionality to enable the creation of clothing, household items and so on. Users retain copyright for any content they create, which they can then sell on to others.

❊ MOST VALUABLE VIRTUAL ITEM IN AN MMORPG

Holder: ENTROPIA UNIVERSE (MindArk, 2003)
Club Neverdie, an asteroid space resort in *Entropia Universe*, ranks as the most expensive virtual item

legitimately sold in an MMORPG. It was bought for $100,000 (£59,000) in 2005 by British gamer Jon "Neverdie" Jacobs, who mortgaged his real-world house to fund the purchase. The gamble proved to be a shrewd investment that paid off when he made his money back within a year. The vast resort includes a nightclub, sports stadium, shopping mall, bio dome, space dock and over 1,000 apartments. It is now estimated to be worth a cool $1 million (£590,000) and generates a healthy monthly income for its entrepreneurial owner.

❊ FIRST CONCERT HELD IN A REAL AND A VIRTUAL SPACE SIMULTANEOUSLY

Holder: THE DARES (USA)
On 2 June 2009, US pop-punk band The Dares (pictured with GWR's Gaz Deaves) performed the first music concert to take place in both the real world and in a virtual space. The gig was held at E3 2009 in Los Angeles, USA, and online in *Free Realms* (Sony, 2009).

STRATEGY & SIMULATION GAMES

With total sales exceeding 11 million copies, *StarCraft* (Blizzard, 1998) is the **best-selling strategy game** in history. Pictured is the game's sequel, *StarCraft II*, which is due for release in early 2010.

CONTENTS:

INTRODUCTION

FOR MORE STRATEGIC GAMEPLAY, MAKE A TACTICAL SWITCH TO RPGs FROM P.146.

HIGHEST PERCENTAGE OF ILLEGAL PLAYERS ONLINE

Holder: DEMIGOD (Stardock, 2009) When Stardock investigated reports that *Demigod*'s online servers were becoming unresponsive, they discovered that 102,000 of the 120,000 people connected to the servers (85%) were using illegal copies.

A FAR CRY FROM THE FRANTIC ACTION OF MANY VIDEOGAMES, THE STRATEGY AND SIMULATION GENRE IS ALL ABOUT TACTICS, PLANNING AND THE TRIUMPH OF MIND OVER (BUTTON) MASHING

For many years, strategy combat games were confined to the table-top, being too complicated to convert in a meaningful way to videogame format. However, when what could be coded caught up with what could be imagined, it was only a matter of time before the genre made the leap.

That moment came in 1977, when California Institute of Technology (USA) student Walter Bright (USA) applied his programming know-how to create *Empire*, a turn-based war simulator that he had originally mapped out on a sheet of plywood as a child.

By the 1980s, the graphics capability of games hardware had developed to the point where titles such as *Strategic Conquest* (1984) could visualize geography, cities and units. Developments in processing technology also paved the way for the creation of the real-time strategy (RTS) game – at last, opponent players could operate their factions simultaneously rather than in consecutive turns, with titles such as *Stonkers* (1983) and *Herzog Zwei* (1989) emphasizing the importance of immediacy and time management in controlling each unit.

In 1985, Activision released *Little Computer People*, which took the innovative step of removing the combat context from strategy games and effectively created the social simulation sub-genre. In the absence of combat and any obvious win conditions, the player instead interacts with and controls aspects of a household occupied by a lone character.

＊ NEW RECORD
● UPDATED RECORD

TIMELINE

1977	1982	1983	1989	1991	1992
Walter Bright, a mechanical engineering student at Caltech, writes the code that becomes *Empire*, the **first strategy videogame**.	Originally created as a military-style board game, *Ambush!* is translated to the screen to become the **first widely released strategy videogame**.	Imagine Software's *Stonkers*, a military title generally recognized as the **first real-time strategy game**, is released in the UK on the ZX Spectrum.	*SimCity*, the original city-building simulator designed by the legendary Will Wright, is released by Maxis across numerous platforms.	Epic in scope and richly imagined, Sid Meier's strategy-sim *Civilization* is the first instalment in what becomes a genre-defining franchise.	Westwood Studios' *Dune II* pioneers the term "real-time strategy" (RTS) and introduces the concept of gathering, refining and spending resources.

[**IOO MILLION...** worldwide sales of US game designer
Will Wright's life-simulation franchise *The Sims*, making it the
best-selling PC series of all time.]

OVERVIEW

> Harvest. Build. Win. With these concepts in mind, and armies, cities and sometimes life itself at a player's command, the scope of the strategy and simulation genre is vast. While strategy titles tend to have a military conquest theme and revolve around planning and executing battlefield victories, simulation games are more about civilization building – though there is plenty of overlap between the two, as expertly demonstrated by Sid Meier's epic *Civilization*. For over 25 years now, the genre has been a videogames mainstay, and it is a testament to its influence that its most innovative masters, such as Will Wright and Sid Meier, have become giants of the industry as a whole.

In spite of your warning, several members of our staff did become addicted to the game while they were testing it.
Extract from letter sent to Empire's Walter Bright by games publisher Epyx »

Inspired by this, designer Will Wright (USA) came up with his now legendary *SimCity*. Released to great acclaim by Maxis in 1989, it is the quintessential government simulation game, relying on effective resource and time management to guide a city to economic and social success.

The real explosion of strategy and simulation games, though, came in 1991, when game designer Sid Meier (USA) created *Civilization* for the PC. Based on ideas from a board game of the same name, the genius of the title is its huge scope: developing and guiding an entire civilization over the course of millennia. Combining classic strategy gameplay with an unprecedented level of random play elements, *Civilization* spawned several sequels, won many Game of the Year awards and was selected in

1996 as the best game of all time by *Computer Gaming World* magazine.

The 1990s continued to see new RTS franchises competing for the top spot within the strategy hierarchy. Although played in very different story settings, *Warcraft*, *Command & Conquer* and *StarCraft* were all hugely successful series, inspiring numerous sequels and spin-offs on the way to becoming benchmarks in strategy gaming.

The success of these titles was ultimately overshadowed, though, by another Will Wright classic, *The Sims*. Released in 2000, *The Sims*, which allows players to create and

then live out rich and expansive simulated lives, quickly became a sales behemoth. Follow-ups, spin-offs and multiple releases soon followed, ensuring that *The Sims* would become the **best-selling PC series of all time**.

The Sims also assisted in moving strategy and simulation games beyond the traditional PC format, penetrating further than ever into the console and handheld markets. This repositioning has recently been consolidated with the release of the console-focused *Civilization Revolution* (2008), an iPhone version of Will Wright's *Spore* (2008) and Microsoft's RTS addition to the *Halo* universe, *Halo Wars* (2009).

Despite the prevalence of strategy and simulation titles in the gaming consciousness, the mainstream has arguably yet to truly embrace the genre – most people would be more familiar with *Warcraft* from the MMORPG phenomenon *World of Warcraft* than the original RTS. However, with *The Sims 3*, *StarCraft II* and *Civilization V* all currently in development, the future continues to appear healthy for strategy and simulation gaming and its fans.

KEY GAME
AGE OF EMPIRES

RTS series *Age of Empires* is based around past military campaigns and real historical events. The first game was such a hit that it spawned several sequels and multiple expansion packs, and the series has sold over 20 million copies as a whole, earning developer Ensemble Studios a fearsome reputation within the genre. Ensemble also went on to produce the recent *Halo* RTS, *Halo Wars* (2009).

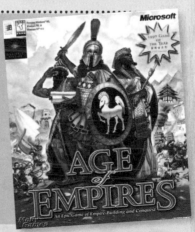

1997	2000	2005	2008

GT Interactive's futuristic space RTS *Total Annihilation* brings 3D terrain and units to the genre, winning great critical praise and a loyal fanbase.

EA releases *The Sims*, a life-simulator that goes on to become the **best-selling PC game of all time**, with worldwide sales of over 16 million copies.

Civilization IV (left) is the fourth game in Sid Meier's turn-based franchise, which goes on to become the world's **most critically acclaimed strategy series**.

Allowing players to develop a species from micro-organism to super-culture, Will Wright's *Spore* and *Spore Creatures* (left) are instant hits.

TURN-BASED STRATEGY

TURN TO P.146 FOR THE LATEST IN RPG GAMING.

✳ MOST PROLIFIC TURN-BASED STRATEGY SERIES

Holder: YU-GI-OH!
(Konami, 2000 to present)
Prolific Japanese trading card series *Yu-Gi-Oh!* has spawned a vast array of spin-offs, including a plethora of anime, manga and, of course, videogames (*Yu-Gi-Oh! World Championship 2008* pictured). The videogame series features 36 turn-based strategy titles, including five exclusive to Japan, across 10 platforms. What's more, this total doesn't include the recent release for Wii, which focuses more on racing than strategy.

> Strategy games require putting more blood to your brain than adrenalin to hand and eye.
>
> Mark H Walker, strategy guide author

TEN GAMES YOU SHOULD PLAY IN THIS GENRE

	GAME
1	Sid Meier's Civilization (1991)
2	Empire: Total War (2009)
3	Sid Meier's Civilization IV (2005)
4	Advance Wars: Dual Strike (2005)
5	Heroes of Might and Magic (1995)
6	Galactic Civilizations II: Dread Lords (2006)
7	Rome: Total War (2004)
8	Magic: The Gathering (1997)
9	Sid Meier's Civilization Revolution (2008)
10	Worms: Open Warfare 2 (2007)

✳ NEW RECORD
◻ UPDATED RECORD

[**350,000...** the number of *Magic Online* accounts registered between 2002 and 2008, making it the world's **most popular online collectible card game**.]

OVERVIEW

▶ The turn-based strategy game has been a staple of the wider strategy genre since its inception, predating even the development of the IBM PC. Controlling and managing their units sequentially and/ or simultaneously with their opponent, players are allowed a predetermined allocation of time, resources or unit actions to complete the desired gameplay steps that make up any given turn. Probably the best-known example of the turn-based strategy game is the Civilization series, a widely acclaimed franchise that has sold in excess of 8 million copies since the first iteration arrived in 1991.

✳ MOST CRITICALLY ACCLAIMED HANDHELD TURN-BASED STRATEGY GAME

Holder: ADVANCE WARS: DUAL STRIKE (Nintendo, 2005)
According to review aggregator websites Metacritic and GameRankings, *Advance Wars: Dual Strike* for the DS is the top-rated strategy game on any current handheld, with an average review score of 90%. Following on the heels of two successful outings on the

Game Boy Advance, *Dual Strike* was the popular franchise's first DS entry and won several awards, including IGN's Best Strategy Game for the DS.

✳ FIRST TURN-BASED STRATEGY GAME

Holder: TANKTICS: COMPUTER GAME OF ARMORED COMBAT ON THE EASTERN FRONT
(Avalon Hill, 1978)
Tanktics, by noted games designer Chris Crawford (USA), is widely regarded as the first ever turn-based strategy game. Initially released in 1978 for the Commodore PET, *Tanktics* was subsequently published for other systems, including the Apple II, TRS-80 and the Atari 8-bit family. The game sees players take command of a lone German Panzer Group of up to eight tanks, with orders to make a last stand against an overwhelming computer-controlled Soviet tank force.

✳ FIRST AUGMENTED REALITY GAME FOR A CONSOLE

Holder: THE EYE OF JUDGMENT
(Sony, 2007)
Augmented Reality (AR) games combine real-world data with computer data, enabling players to interact with computer-generated characters on screen. The first console game to feature such technology was *The Eye of Judgment* for PS3. The game used the console's PSEye camera to gather real-world images and read the coded information on small physical trading cards. This information allowed the game to bring the characters on the trading cards to life on the screen.

✳ MOST GAMES HEADLINED BY A DESIGNER

Holder: SID MEIER
Legendary strategy game designer Sid Meier (Canada) has had his name featured in the title of 18 separate games and a total of 51 releases between *Sid Meier's Pirates* in 1987 and *Civilization Revolution* in 2008. Some suspect that Meier is now trying to get himself into the games themselves, noting his likeness to Grey Wolf, the Barbarian from *Civilization Revolution* (pictured).

Greetings from Grey Wolf of the Barbarians...
You have captured my favorite village.
This village is skilled in horsemanship, but I have many others.

Ok

FACT

▶ In Civilization Revolution, *many civilizations can develop unique units relating to a particular national history, such as T34 tanks for Russia and Spitfire fighter planes for the British.*

▶ As in the physical version of the game, there are a certain number of special "foil" cards in Magic Online. These feature a kind of "shiny" animation to differentiate them from normal cards. In the videogame, these special cards mark your character as being rare or special.

TRIVIA

▶ Brad Wardell (USA), the lead designer of Galactic Civilizations II: Twilight of the Arnor, has admitted that he is addicted to Blizzard's World of Warcraft.

▶ Civilization Revolution, the fourth major sequel in the long-running franchise, was in fact only the first to be designed by the series' renowned creator, Sid Meier (pictured below).

REAL-TIME STRATEGY

! FOR MORE *HALO* ACTION, TURN TO CONSOLE FPS ON P.48.

✳ BEST-SELLING CURRENT GENERATION CONSOLE RTS GAME

Holder: HALO WARS (Microsoft, 2009)

The Xbox 360's *Halo Wars*, the first non-FPS in the *Halo* series, is the most successful RTS on the current generation of consoles. With sales of 1.21 million as of May 2009, it easily beats previous top-seller *Tom Clancy's EndWar*, which shifted 730,000 units. *Halo Wars* is set 20 years before the events of *Halo: Combat Evolved* and does not feature the Master Chief.

> ≪ We're going to make Ensemble's last game the most kick-ass Microsoft game ever, and they're really going to regret closing us down. ≫
>
> Halo Wars lead developer Graeme Devine

NEW RECORD ▪ UPDATED RECORD

TEN GAMES YOU SHOULD PLAY IN THIS GENRE

	GAME
1	*Warcraft III: Reign of Chaos* (2002)
2	*StarCraft* (1998)
3	*Populous* (1989)
4	*Command & Conquer* (1995)
5	*Age of Empires II: The Age of Kings* (1999)
6	*Total Annihilation* (1997)
7	*Company of Heroes* (2006)
8	*Dungeon Keeper* (1997)
9	*Patapon* (2007)
10	*The Lord of the Rings: The Battle for Middle-earth* (2004)

OVERVIEW

> *Emphasizing time management, unit control and resource gathering, real-time strategy (RTS) games allow opponents to operate against each other concurrently rather than consecutively, and are viewed as the format of choice for the strategy-game purist. In recent years, RTS titles have proved to be more popular than their turn-based counterparts in terms of sales, with many of the genre's most successful franchises – such as* Age of Empires, Warcraft *and* Command & Conquer *– continuing to dominate the release calendars and sales charts year after year.*

* MOST TOP 3 FINISHES IN WARCRAFT III WORLD CHAMPIONSHIPS

Holder: **MANUEL "GRUBBY" SCHENKHUIZEN** (Netherlands)

Since the release of *The Frozen Throne* expansion pack in 2003, Blizzard Entertainment's *Warcraft III: Reign of Chaos* has been the subject of numerous individual and team World Championships. The player who has finished in the most Gold, Silver and Bronze positions in these tournaments is Dutch gamer Manuel "Grubby" Schenkhuizen, who has achieved 44 podium placings. Grubby is recognized as one of the best *Warcraft* players currently playing and was the star of a gaming documentary entitled *Beyond The Game* (2008).

* FIRST UNIVERSITY TO OFFER A COMPETITIVE VIDEOGAMING QUALIFICATION

Holder: **UNIVERSITY OF CALIFORNIA, BERKELEY** (USA)
The first university qualification in competitive gaming is "Game Theory in *StarCraft*", a 14-week course covering the theory and practice of high-level gaming in *StarCraft* (Blizzard, 1998). The course, which began at UC Berkeley in 2009, includes lectures on timing, resource-management and base layout, and requires students to produce detailed analyses of previous games to better understand the strategy of world-class players. The reading list features *The Art of War* by Sun Tzu and *Crazy as Me* by the professional *StarCraft* player Lim Yo Hwan.

HIGHEST CASH PRIZE FOR A FAN MOD TOURNAMENT

Holder: **SENDI MUTIARA MULTIMEDIA GRAND NATIONAL DOTA TOURNAMENT** (Malaysia)
The largest prize fund for a tournament on a fan modification is 120,000 Malaysian Ringgits (£21,000, $35,000), for the Sendi Mutiara Multimedia Grand National DotA Tournament. The tournament saw players from seven countries compete on the *WarCraft III* mod *Defense of the Ancients* in Berjaya Times Square, Kuala Lumpur, Malaysia, on 22-23 November 2008.

* TOP SCORE ON AGE OF BOOTY (XBOX 360)

Holder: **PFX984** (Italy)
The overall top score on the Xbox Arcade version of Capcom's pirate strategy game *Age of Booty* (2008) is held by Italian PFX984, with a total of 5,620 wins out of 6,060 games. The player puts his success down to practice and adapting to the speed of the game during combat. The title is also available as a PC download, and on the PlayStation Network.

* FIRST RHYTHM/ STRATEGY GAME

Holder: **PATAPON** (Sony, 2007)
Perhaps the strangest addition to the RTS sub-genre is the PSP game *Patapon*, released in February 2007. During the game, players take control of a tribe of cartoon creatures, guiding their actions against opposing armies by rhythmically pressing buttons in time to a musical beat.

SIMULATION GAMES

TAKE A LOOK AT RPG TITLES FROM P.146 ONWARDS.

* NEW RECORD
* UPDATED RECORD

TEN GAMES YOU SHOULD PLAY IN THIS GENRE

	GAME
1	Spore (2008)
2	SimCity 2000 (1993)
3	Nintendogs (2005)
4	Viva Piñata: Trouble in Paradise (2008)
5	Sid Meier's Railroad Tycoon (1990)
6	Theme Park (1994)
7	Flight Simulator X (2006)
8	Black & White (2001)
9	SimCity 4 (2003)
10	Viva Piñata (2006)

* MOST USER-GENERATED CREATIONS FOR A VIDEOGAME

Holder: SPORE (EA, 2008)
As of 27 July 2009, the community for *Spore* had uploaded 113,719,430 user-generated creatures to the game's web presence, Sporepedia, the most individual pieces of user-generated content ever produced for a videogame. The closest competition is from Sony's 2008 release *LittleBigPlanet*, which has just over 1 million different user-created levels available.

OVERVIEW

> Described by some as a "super category" of gaming, owing to the great diversity of their settings – cities, theme parks, zoos, homes – simulation games allow control over almost any imaginable societal system or life process. Players make progress in simulation games through the subtle manipulation of elements, often not in order to complete any set goal but to produce merely the best outcome as the player sees it. From SimCity to Flight Simulator and beyond, designers such as the legendary Will Wright (USA) are constantly striving to put as much power as possible in the hands of the player.

* MOST ILLEGAL DOWNLOADS OF A GAME
Holder: SPORE (EA, 2008)
Following controversy surrounding bundled Digital Rights Management software and the resultant registration difficulties, EA's simulation game *Spore* – which allows a player to control the evolution of species from their uni-cellular beginnings to the development of fully blown civilizations – was illegally downloaded on 1.7 million occasions in 2008, a record for a videogame. This huge level of illegal downloading eventually resulted in EA removing the controversial copy protection from the game.

* MOST POWERFUL FLIGHT SIMULATOR
Holder: SIMUSPHERE HD WORLD (Link, 2009)
The most powerful flight simulation system is the *Simusphere HD World*, produced by Link Simulation and Training (USA) for clients including the United States Air Force. The Air Force version simulates an F 16 fighter jet and runs on 120 dual core PCs, each of which contains a $400 (£250) graphics card, allowing for 10,000 on-screen objects to be displayed simultaneously.

WEALTHIEST INDIVIDUAL TO HEADLINE A VIDEOGAME
Holder: DONALD TRUMP (USA)
The richest person to appear in and endorse a videogame is the US billionaire Donald Trump, who appeared in *Donald Trump's Real Estate Tycoon* in 2002.

FIRST SIMULATION GAME RELEASED ON XBOX LIVE ARCADE
Holder: OUTPOST KALOKI X (Microsoft, 2005)
Surviving the next gen update from Xbox to Xbox 360, the Xbox Live Arcade is an opportunity for players to download new arcade titles or updates of some old classics. The first simulation game released on the service was *Outpost Kaloki X*, an update of the Games for Windows title, which was made available for download on 22 November 2005, the day the service was launched on the Xbox 360.

* BEST-SELLING HANDHELD SIMULATION GAME
Holder: NINTENDOGS (Nintendo, 2005)
Nintendogs, originally released in 2005, is a real-time videogame for the Nintendo DS designed to simulate dog ownership. There are various versions of the game offering several different breeds of dog. The combined sales of all of these versions makes *Nintendogs* the biggest-selling simulation videogame for a handheld console, with sales totalling more than 22 million copies.

> In the right circumstances, we can be encouraged to examine our own values by seeing how we behave within virtual space.
> Prof. Henry Jenkins, MIT, USA

TRIVIA

> In January 2008, publisher EA released the original source code for SimCity, one of the best-selling games series of all time. The only restriction on usage of the code relates to trademark issues, such as the use of the SimCity name. Titled Micropolis, the release was EA's contribution to the One Laptop Per Child project under the GNU General Public License.

> Commercial tie-ins with videogames are not unusual, but unique on the list is a furniture partnership! The Sims 2: Ikea Home Stuff was an expansion pack for the famous simulation game, which was released in 2008.

> The Nintendogs phenomenon is so vast that the game has inspired toys, trading cards and even an appearance by a dog in Super Smash Brawl for the Wii.

> In 1999, Sid Meier (USA), creator of many seminal simulation games, such as Railroad Tycoon and Civilization, became just the second person to be inducted into the Academy of Interactive Arts and Sciences' Hall of Fame. The first person to receive that honour was Nintendo's legendary Shigeru Miyamoto, creator of Mario, Donkey Kong, Zelda and many more.

STRATEGY RPG

CHECK OUT THE TOP RPGS ON PP.146-155. !

✳ HIGHEST EXPERIENCE LEVEL IN AN RPG

Holder: DISGAEA (Nippon Ichi, 2004)

Most RPGs use a system of experience levels to give players an idea of their power relative to enemies in the game – and to encourage them to keep playing. The RPG series that has taken this idea to its most extreme is *Disgaea* (*Disgaea 3: Absence of Justice* pictured), which allows players to take their characters from a lowly level 1 up to an incredible level 9,999. Many players are competing online to discover the fastest way to achieve this feat.

> If I only had one game with me on a deserted island, I'd want it to be a Disgaea game.
> Daemon Hatfield, IGN.com

TEN GAMES YOU SHOULD PLAY IN THIS GENRE

	GAME
1	*Disgaea: Afternoon of Darkness* (2006)
2	*Tactics Ogre: Let Us Cling Together* (1995)
3	*Final Fantasy Tactics* (1997)
4	*Valkyria Chronicles* (2008)
5	*Final Fantasy XII: Revenant Wings* (2007)
6	*Makai Kingdom: Chronicles of the Sacred Tome* (2005)
7	*Disgaea 3: Absence of Justice* (2008)
8	*Final Fantasy Tactics A2: Grimoire of the Rift* (2007)
9	*Phantom Brave* (2004)
10	*Disgaea 2: Dark Hero Days* (2009)

✳ **NEW RECORD**
◇ **UPDATED RECORD**

220,000... worldwide sales achieved by *Disgaea 3: Absence of Justice* since the game's PS3 release on 31 January 2008.

OVERVIEW

> Combining elements of turn-based strategy and Japanese RPG, the strategy RPG is a hybrid sub-genre that occupies a small but perfectly formed niche in the market, particularly for Japanese gamers. Players usually control a group of warriors who can be customized and levelled up in a way similar to traditional RPGs, but the action normally takes place on a grid-style map, as in a strategy game. Stand-out titles such as Tactics Ogre and Final Fantasy Tactics *provide incredible depth and customization as well as twisting plots for gamers to really sink their teeth into, while the likes of* Disgaea and Makai Kingdom *offer the ultimate in level grinding for the ultra-hardcore.*

* FIRST STRATEGY RPG

Holder: FIRE EMBLEM: ANKOKU RYU TO HIKARI NO TSURUGI (Nintendo, 1990)
Released in 1990 for the NES, the first strategy RPG was Nintendo's *Fire Emblem*. The game popularized many of the gameplay elements that are associated with modern strategy RPGs, and the series now has 12 entries. Two characters from the game, Marth and Roy, have even made it into the Nintendo crossover fighter game *Super Smash Bros. Melee* (2001).

* MOST PROLIFIC DEVELOPER OF STRATEGY RPGs

Holder: NIPPON ICHI (Japan)
As of May 2009, Nippon Ichi has brought a record 14 strategy RPGs to the videogame market, not including regional variations. Memorable examples include the *Disgaea* series and *Rhapsody* (DS version pictured).

* FASTEST SEGMENTED COMPLETION OF FINAL FANTASY TACTICS

Holder: JOHN "CHESSJERK" KEARSLEY IV (USA)
The fastest segmented completion of the PlayStation version of *Final Fantasy Tactics* (Square, 1997) took 4 hr 45 min, and was achieved by John Kearsley IV in 37 segments, on 21 June 2007. Kearsley's run makes extensive use of glitches and the "Math Skill" ability, which allows the player to clear an entire battlefield in one turn – essential for completing the game's 50-plus levels quickly.

* BEST-SELLING STRATEGY RPG FOR THE DS

Holder: FINAL FANTASY XII: REVENANT WINGS (Square Enix, 2007)
With estimated global sales of over 1.2 million, *Final Fantasy XII* is the DS platform's top-selling strategy RPG.

* MOST CRITICALLY ACCLAIMED STRATEGY RPG FOR THE PS3

Holder: VALKYRIA CHRONICLES (SEGA, 2008)
According to critics, SEGA's *Valkyria Chronicles* is the best strategy RPG for the PS3. In its year of release, the game won several accolades, including Game of the Year and Strategy Game of the Year, and achieved average review scores of 86% and 86.83% on Metacritic and GameRankings, respectively.

FACT

> While strategy RPGs are most popular in Japan, there have been notable Western additions to the canon, such as the X-com series (1993 to present) from Mythos Games and MicroProse. In these games, the player takes control of an Earth-based organization seeking to gather the technology of invading alien species in order to develop it against them. Gameplay varies from strategy-like researching and developing of technology, to shooting down alien spacecraft, to turn-based recovering of alien technology.

TRIVIA

> Strategy RPG is also known as simulation or tactical RPG – definitions that emphasize the varied nature of the sub-genre.

> Players of the original Final Fantasy Tactics (Square, 1997) should handle the weapons very carefully, particularly the elemental guns. On playing the game for the first time, unsuspecting gamers soon discover that, despite the names, the Blaze gun actually fires a stream of ice, while the evocatively titled Glacier gun unleashes a ball of fire. This glitch was fixed by the time the PSP version was released in 2007.

INSTANT GAMING

1,500... the number of machines in the initial production run of 1971's *Computer Space*, the **first commercial coin-operated videogame** and ancestor to the coin-ops that were to follow.

GUINNESS WORLD RECORDS

CONTENTS:

INTRODUCTION

! CHECK OUT ALL THE HOTTEST TITLES FOR YOUR MOBILE PHONE ON P.38.

TORU IWATANI

Toru Iwatani (Japan) is the man behind *PAC-Man* – videogaming's iconic pellet guzzler. Iwatani joined software developer Namco in 1977, and it was there that he came up with the idea for the character, inspired by the shape of a pizza from which he had taken a slice. Released in 1980, *PAC-Man* was hugely successful, particularly in the USA, and Iwatani's famous yellow character went on to become a cultural icon. Iwatani left Namco in 2007 after 30 years' service, and he now works as a lecturer at Tokyo Polytechnic University, Japan.

ALTHOUGH ARCADES STILL OFFER THE ULTIMATE INSTANT FIX, RAPID ADVANCES IN MOBILE PHONE TECHNOLOGY MEAN GAME FANS NOW HAVE MANY OF THEIR FAVOURITES AT THEIR FINGERTIPS

The **first coin-operated videogame** was 1971's space-blaster *Galaxy Game*, which proved so popular that players would queue for more than an hour to have a go. Later that same year, young programmers Nolan Bushnell and Ted Dabney (both USA) developed their own space-based coin-op, *Computer Space*. Though the game enjoyed only limited success, it was the **first commercially sold coin-operated videogame** and inspired the pair to to set up Atari. Then, in 1972, Atari released the mighty *Pong* – and the arcade industry never looked back.

By the late 1970s, arcade games were a fairly common sight in pubs and bars, and, despite the arrival of consoles, their popularity continued throughout the 1980s, with titles such as *PAC-Man* (1980), *Donkey Kong* (1981) and the cinematic *Dragon's Lair* (1983) leading the way.

One of the reasons to pump coins into arcade machines, other than the promise of graphics that couldn't be matched at home, were the unique control methods. Many cabinets had specially tailored controls to suit the game: Namco's *Pole Position* (1982) used a steering wheel, Atari's *Paperboy* (1984) had bicycle handlebars, while Taito's 1987 hit *Operation Wolf* wielded a menacing Uzi submachine gun.

As the 1980s were drawing to a close and console and PC gaming took hold, games arcades in the West began to see a decline in popularity. However, a welcome shot in the arm came with the arrival

KEY GAME
DANCE DANCE REVOLUTION

Konami's highly original dance mat series arrived in Japan in 1998. Players use their feet to beat out a rhythm to the game's mix of original and licensed music. *DDR*, as it is known, has been praised as an exercise tool and has millions of fans.

NEW RECORD
UPDATED RECORD

TIMELINE

1971	1978	1980	1983	1986	1987
Galaxy Game and *Computer Space* lay the foundations of the coin-op industry, while a year later, Nolan Bushnell's *Pong* ensures its future success.	The popular 2D shooter *Space Invaders* causes a shortage of coins in Japan and goes on to earn a cool $500 million (£300 million) for its publisher, Taito.	The 1980s get off to a great start, first with *PAC-Man*, and then, a year later, with *Donkey Kong*, the game that saves Nintendo of America from bankruptcy.	Three years in the making, the sensational *Dragon's Lair* boasts laserdisc technology and graphics never before seen in a videogame.	Everyone's favourite driving game, *OutRun* puts gamers in the hot seat with a hydraulic cockpit cabinet, some great tunes and a wide open road.	One of the first ever side-scrolling beat-em-ups, *Double Dragon* is released in arcades and impresses gamers with its co-operative two-player gameplay.

293,822... the number of *PAC-Man* coin-operated cabinets sold in the USA between 1980 and 1987, making it the **most successful arcade machine of the 1980s**.

OVERVIEW

> The idea behind instant gaming is pure "pick up and play" – no complex controls, lengthy cutscenes or tutorial missions, just unadulterated gameplay with no strings attached. The best place to find this kind of action has always been the arcade, but the exponential growth of mobile phone gaming over the last few years has provided fertile new ground for this style of gameplay to grow a brand new audience. As arcades experience a resurgence through games such as Street Fighter IV, and the iPhone comes to dominate mobile gaming, fans of instant gaming will have more choice than ever before.

of two-player fighting games such as 1991's *Street Fighter II*, which became the **best-selling arcade fighting game**. Although by the mid-1990s consoles had started to match the sophistication of coin-ops, some innovative new titles helped keep the arcades competitive. Blockbusters such as Namco's light-gun series *Time Crisis* (1995) boosted the

traditional format, while the advent of dance mat games such as Konami's *Dance Dance Revolution* (1998) created fresh interest.

It was around this time that instant gaming took an unexpected new turn. In 1997, Finnish mobile phone company Nokia began shipping their phones with *Snake*, the **first mobile phone game**, which was based on the earlier, almost identical worm game *Nibbler* (1982). This simple move put games in the palms of millions of people who

traditionally would not have seen themselves as gamers, and opened the door to a whole new market – games that could be downloaded to mobile phones. In 2003, Nokia took things further, launching the N-Gage (pictured below left), the **first mobile phone designed for games**, but a lukewarm reception suggested this was a step too far, too soon.

Today, while the mobile gaming market continues to develop apace, the future of the arcade is less certain. In Japan, where appeal has remained relatively strong, Namco Bandai and SEGA SAMMY have announced a number of closures. In response, some cabinet makers have started to look to the consoles for inspiration, with BMI Gaming launching *Guitar Hero Arcade* in 2009. Its success suggests there may well be life in the arcades yet.

> "People who didn't really play games became avid fans of PAC-Man."
> *Toru Iwatani*

EXPERT

> David Crookes began writing about computers in 1993 for Amstrad Action. He has since written for a wide range of games magazines including Games™, Retro Gamer, X360 and Total PC Gaming. In 2009, he curated the Videogame Nation exhibition at Urbis in Manchester, UK.

TRIVIA

▸ PAC-Man was originally to be called "Puck-Man", but Namco feared that vandals would alter the "P" to an "F".

▸ Arcade games have always been designed so that they are easy to play straight away. However, difficulty levels increase sharply as play progresses, ensuring that unskilled players quickly lose and have to insert more coins.

▸ Good games are good forever, and now it is possible to play older arcade games on the Nintendo Wii. Games such as Gaplus, Mappy, Star Force and The Tower of Druaga are available on the Wii's Virtual Console service.

✳ LARGEST MOBILE PHONE

Holder: SAMSUNG SCH-R450

While most mobiles are a fair bit smaller than the average arcade machine, this scaled-up version of Samsung's SCH-R450 is the exception. Measuring a whopping 24.28 ft (7.4 m) long, it was created by Cricket Communications and Samsung Mobile, and features fully playable versions of the games that appear on the standard-sized model.

1991		1997	1998	2003	2009
Capcom's *Street Fighter II* (right) sparks a coin-op comeback and paves the way for the glut of fighting games that hits arcades during the 1990s.		Nokia takes the decision to include *Snake* on its handsets, establishing the mobile phone as a viable gaming platform for the first time.	*Dance Dance Revolution* pioneers the dance mat sub-genre, inspiring a number of clones and helping to bring a new breed of gamer into the arcades.	Nokia boldly launches its mobile phone gaming platform, the *N-Gage*, but despite the hype, the device fails to impress and achieves disappointing sales.	Based on the *Guitar Hero III* game, *Guitar Hero Arcade* is ported from console to coin-op, becoming one of those rare titles to make the leap in this direction.

CLASSIC ARCADE

 FOR ARCADE CLASSICS IN YOUR POCKET, CHECK OUT BEST OF MOBILE PHONES ON P.38.

✱ MOST RECOGNIZABLE VIDEOGAME CHARACTER

Holder: PAC-MAN (Namco, 1980) According to a May 2008 poll by the Davie-Brown Index (DBI), *PAC-Man* is the best-known of all videogame characters, recognized by 94% of American consumers. Mario comes a close second with 93%, while other notable characters who make it into the index include Lara Croft, Donkey Kong, Sonic the Hedgehog and Link from *The Legend of Zelda*.

■ **NEW RECORD**
■ **UPDATED RECORD**

	TEN GAMES YOU SHOULD PLAY IN THIS GENRE	
		GAME
1		*Space Invaders* (1978)
2		*PAC-Man* (1980)
3		*Donkey Kong* (1981)
4		*Asteroids* (1979)
5		*Defender* (1980)
6		*Galaga* (1981)
7		*Gauntlet* (1985)
8		*OutRun* (1986)
9		*Pong* (1972)
10		*Robotron 2084* (1982)

OVERVIEW

> The arcade classics of the 1970s and 1980s were the start of videogames as we know them. Although they began as fairly simple affairs with quite primitive graphics, in those days it was all about gameplay. Pong and Space Invaders captured imaginations and, in time, spawned more complex games with huge cockpit cabinets – SEGA's Afterburner and OutRun being classics of the day. These coin-op giants helped bring arcade gaming into the home, with many top titles being ported to home computers and consoles.

FIRST ARCADE DRIVING GAME TO FEATURE FORCE FEEDBACK

Holder: OUTRUN (SEGA, 1986)
When driving off-road in SEGA's *OutRun*, the cabinet controls shake in response to the rougher terrain. This was the first time an arcade driving game had incorporated force feedback, and the feature was built into all four versions of the game cabinet – two with sit-in cockpits and two stand-up versions.

LARGEST VIDEOGAMES ARCADE

Holder: FUNSPOT (USA)
Weirs Beach, New Hampshire, USA, is home to the largest games arcade in the world – Funspot. It has more than 500 classic and new games over three floors, and was founded in 1952 by Bob Lawton. The venue also includes the Classic Arcade Museum, which holds over 250 working arcade machines dating from the early 1970s to 1987, including *Computer Space* (1971) and *Pong* (1972).

FIRST GAME TO APPEAR ON A POSTAGE STAMP

Holder: DEFENDER (Williams Electronics, 2000)
In 2000, the USA postal service's *Celebrate the Century* series included a 33-cent stamp showing two children playing the Atari 2600 version of *Defender* – "the hardest significant game there is", according to *Gamasutra*.

LONGEST CONTINUOUS PLAY ON AN ARCADE MACHINE

Holder: JAMES VOLLANDT (USA)
James Vollandt played the game *Joust* (Williams Electronics, 1982) for 67 hr 30 min at Johnny Zee's Family Fun Center, in Victoria, Canada, starting on 8 July 1985. Vollandt achieved the longest official recorded time playing one arcade game and, in the process, set a high-score record of 107,216,700.

MOST VALUABLE ARCADE MACHINE

Holder: BLASTER
(Williams Electronics, 1983)
Williams' *Blaster* cockpit is believed to be the world's most valuable arcade machine, with an estimated worth of $12,000 (£7,388). Released in 1983, only five cockpits were ever created.

SMALLEST CONVERSION OF AN ARCADE GAME

Holder: MATHIEU HENRI
Produced over the course of three nights in July 2008, *Defender of the Favicon* is a fully playable conversion of retro space shooter *Defender* (1980), reduced to 16 x 16 pixels in the icon of Mathieu "Poi" Henri's web page.

TRIVIA

> *Futurama* episode "Anthology of Interest II", which aired on 6 January 2002, features classic arcade characters Donkey Kong, Mario, PAC-Man and the Brain from *Robotron 2084* (1982).

> *Space Invaders* (1978) was so popular in Japan that it led to a shortage of 100¥ coins, forcing the Japanese mint to produce more.

> *Mario* was originally known as "Jumpman" in Nintendo classic *Donkey Kong* (1981).

TALKING TO...

NOLAN BUSHNELL

Nolan Bushnell (USA) is a founding father of the videogames industry, being the brains behind 1972's *Pong*, the arcade industry's first commercial success. Bushnell also started Atari the same year and was a key player in the production of the pioneering Atari 2600 console. On 10 March 2009, Bushnell was awarded BAFTA's prestigious Academy Fellowship at the British Academy Video Games Awards, in recognition of his outstanding contribution to the industry.

Do you feel proud to have been a videogames pioneer?
Videogames had already been invented and that is why I became so fascinated by them. I just made them commercial.

What is the most important game you've played?
SpaceWar! (1961) on a PDP-1, while at college. I really enjoyed it – it was such great fun and very challenging. The game inspired me to start Atari, but it was only playable on a very expensive computer and I would have to stay up late to play it.

Did you expect *Pong* to be as successful as it has been?
Not at all, because when I put together the *Pong* concept and asked Al Alcorn to produce it, I only intended it as a training project. It's the reason I chose tennis – it's so simple. What I really wanted to do was a driving game, but we soon realized *Pong* was amazing.

MODERN ARCADE

! EXCHANGE THE CABINET FOR THE COUCH – CHECK OUT THE BEST OF HOME GAMING FROM P.26 TO P.33.

◆ NEW RECORD
◆ UPDATED RECORD

MOST PROLIFIC PRODUCER OF ARCADE MACHINES
Holder: SEGA

SEGA has produced more arcade games than any other company, with 530 games on 23 different arcade system boards since 1981 (2008's *Harley Davidson: King of the Road* is pictured). To date, a total of 76 SEGA franchises have made it into the arcades.

> ≪ To be this good takes AGES, to be this good takes SEGA.
> SEGA Europe's 1993 "Pirate TV" campaign slogan ≫

SCORE 120560   TIME 54   RANK 75th/100

TEN GAMES YOU SHOULD PLAY IN THIS GENRE

	GAME
1	Sega Rally Championship (1995)
2	Ridge Racer (1993)
3	Dance Dance Revolution (1998)
4	Tekken (1994)
5	Daytona USA (1993)
6	Guitar Hero Arcade (2009)
7	OutRun 2 (2003)
8	Virtua Cop (1994)
9	Time Crisis (1995)
10	DrumMania (1999)

OVERVIEW

While many claim that the brief spark of super-innovation and popularity from 1982 to 1986 represents the true golden era of the arcade, it is impossible to ignore the still successful longer burn between the 1970s and the early 1990s. Since then, while it would be untrue – particularly in the West – to say that arcades have flourished, they have struggled on, albeit with a greater reliance on control methods and sociability to distinguish them from home consoles. In recent years, modern-day classics have continued to emerge – from Ridge Racer *to* SEGA Rally *to* Tekken – while the 2009 crop boasts some head-turners of its own, including Namco's H2Overdrive, *SEGA's* Harley Davidson, *and Nirin/Konami's* Guitar Hero Arcade.

FIRST ARCADE GAME WITH A HARD DISK

Holder: KILLER INSTINCT (Midway, 1994)
Killer Instinct was the first arcade videogame to include a hard disk drive. The extra digital storage was used to include pre-rendered backgrounds, allowing for more realistic graphics.

MOST PLAYED COIN-OPERATED VIDEOGAME FRANCHISE

Holder: GOLDEN TEE GOLF
(Incredible Technologies, 1989 to present)
The arcade golf series *Golden Tee Golf* has been played by an estimated 1 billion people on more than 100,000 units in bars and pubs across more than 12 countries.

LONGEST SUPPORT FOR AN ARCADE SYSTEM

Holder: NEO GEO MVS
The first game made for the Neo Geo MVS arcade hardware, *Magician Lord*, was released in 1990, with the last game on the system, *Samurai Shodown V Special,* released in 2004, 14 years later. No other arcade system has been in active use for a longer period of time.

TALKING TO...

KEVIN WILLIAMS

English-born Kevin Williams is a leading member of the emerging Out-of-Home (OOH) leisure entertainment industry.

What are the most exciting recent developments in arcade gaming?
The use of network gaming systems with prize-based tournament events is a major aspect of the amusement revolution, offering a level of sociability and direct competitor contact that home consoles are simply unable to match.

The need to keep pushing the envelope means that video amusement has now far outstripped the wildest dreams of early coin-op developers. That said, Nolan Bushnell's 1972 mantra "easy to learn but difficult to master" is still driving game design.

What will be big in the arcade scene in 2010?
Metal Gear Solid Arcade will generate big interest with its 3D visuals, while some consumer game publishers will follow the likes of EA and Activision by developing their own cross-over titles to publicize their popular brands.

How does modern amusement gaming differ from the golden age of arcades?

What can arcade fans look forward to in the longer term?
The original arcade concepts, such as the dancing stage and motion capture, are just the tip of the iceberg of what immersive gaming will offer the future amusement venue visitor.

FASTEST COMPLETION OF SEGA RALLY 3

Holder: MATTHEW PAGE (UK)
The fastest completion of Championship Mode on *SEGA Rally 3* (SEGA, 2008) is 6 min 34.47 sec, achieved by Matthew Page at the Arcades Trade Exhibition International (ATEI) in London, UK, on 27 January 2009.

TRIVIA

▷ *The first Mario Kart game to feature playable non-Nintendo characters was Mario Kart Arcade GP in October 2005. It allowed people to control PAC-Man, Ms PAC-Man and the PAC-Man ghost, Blinky. This arcade-only version of Nintendo's popular franchise was developed in conjunction with Namco. Gamers could also insert their own likeness into the game, captured by a camera built into the cabinet.*

▷ *To date, more than 500 songs have featured in the arcade versions of DrumMania – a music videogame similar to Guitar Hero and Rock Band. Although there are many covers of songs by US bands, the majority of tracks are Japanese pop and rock titles.*

▷ *There are a number of different styles of arcade cabinet: upright; cocktail or table; cockpit and environmental; sit-down; deluxe (such as a driving game with pedals, a bucket seat and steering wheel); mini; and countertop.*

▷ *Refurbishing or building arcade cabinets from scratch is a very popular pastime, with hundreds of project tips and ideas available on the Internet.*

MOBILE PHONE GAMING

! WHY NOT TAKE A LOOK AT THE BEST OF MOBILE PHONES ON P.38?

* MOST SUCCESSFUL MOBILE PHONE GAME

Holder: TETRIS (Alexey Pajitnov, 1984)

The first mobile phone version of *Tetris*, the legendary falling-blocks puzzle game, was released on 25 April 2008 for Nokia's N-Gage. It has since topped the charts in every country that offers mobile phone games and also features highly in the iPhone's top 10 best-sellers. In July 2009, US mobile phone provider Verizon Wireless announced that EA Mobile's *Tetris* was its best-selling game in the first half of 2009.

Some of the games are getting pretty fantastic. There is something here for everyone.

Apple co-founder Steve Jobs discusses the potential of the iPhone for gaming

NEW RECORD
UPDATED RECORD

$176,400 (£87,723)... the price of the world's **most expensive iPhone**. Called the iPhone Princess Plus, it boasts 13 "princess cut" diamonds, with another 180 being "brilliant cut".

[ ]

TALKING TO...

VINCENT DONDAINE

We caught up with Vincent Dondaine, who was the Senior Producer of *Crash Bandicoot Nitro Kart 3D* on the iPhone.

Are you pleased *Crash Bandicoot Nitro Kart 3D* continues to sell so well?
Definitely. It's amazing to see *Crash Bandicoot* still in the top 50 of nearly all App Stores around the world 10 months after the release. I'm proud to have produced this game with Polarbit [the studio that handled the development]. They are brilliant and experienced.

Why do you think it is so popular?
Crash Bandicoot Nitro Kart 3D is simple to control, the graphics are really good and everybody can enjoy playing it, even non-gamers. For example, we decided to have an auto acceleration function combined with accelerometer handling. Many people said to us, "You're mad, it will never work"... but check out all the racing games on the App Store now!

Will mobile phone games take over from handheld consoles?
I'm not sure, because some people don't want a phone at all, while others want to have all functionalities in one device. What is sure for me is that phones will have at least the same capacity as handheld consoles (it's already the case with the iPhone).

TEN GAMES YOU SHOULD PLAY IN THIS GENRE

	GAME
1	Tap Tap Revenge (2008)
2	Snake (Nokia) (1998)
3	Crash Bandicoot Nitro Kart 3D (2008)
4	Playman Extreme Running (2007)
5	Tetris (original) (1984)
6	Puzzle Quest: Challenge of the Warlords (2008)
7	Rally Master Pro (2008)
8	Boom Blox (2008)
9	Tom Clancy's Splinter Cell: Chaos Theory (2005)
10	Playman Summer Games 3 (2008)

TRIVIA

On 11 July 2008, Daniel Bowmen Simon (USA) became the first person to buy an iPhone 3G from New York's Fifth Avenue Apple Store. As the head of an organization calling itself TheWhoFarm, Daniel had queued for seven days, establishing a new record for the **longest time queuing for a product launch**.

FACT

The billionth application to be downloaded from Apple's App Store for the iPhone and iPod Touch was Bump – a program that makes it easy to transfer contacts between handsets. It was downloaded first by 13-year-old Connor Mulcahey, of Weston, Connecticut, USA, on 23 April 2009. As a reward, he received a $10,000 iTunes gift card, an iPod Touch, a Time Capsule and a MacBook Pro. The App Store is the **largest applications store in the world**.

OVERVIEW

Ever since Snake arrived on Nokia handsets in 1998, gamers have become accustomed to playing videogames on their mobile phones. Over the years, the games have quickly matured and they are now comparable to handheld consoles. With a mixture of ports and original titles available, the variety of games on offer is vast. But while Nokia's N-Gage platform has dozens of titles, some of them award winners, it is Apple's successful iPhone and iPod Touch that many experts believe will prove most successful.

✳ FASTEST-SELLING IPHONE GAME

Holder: SUPER MONKEY BALL
(SEGA, 2008)
Super Monkey Ball sold 9,029 units in 24 hours when it was released for the iPhone in July 2008. The game went straight to No.1 in the iPhone App Store on release, making the publisher, SEGA, a reported $63,112.71 (£31,872.70) in one day.

✳ MOST PLAYED VIDEOGAME OF ALL TIME

Holder: SNAKE (NOKIA)
(Nokia, 1998 to present)
Originally a 1970s arcade hit, *Snake* is now the most played videogame ever, thanks to its incorporation into successive Nokia mobile phone handsets since 1998. Estimates put the total number of people who have played it at over 1 billion. Since the first version on the Nokia 6110, there have been many updates, the latest being *Snakes Subsonic*, released in May 2008 for the second-generation N-Gage.

NOKIA N96

00000730

JAPANESE ARCADE

! IF YOU ENJOY THE BRIGHT LIGHTS OF THE ARCADE, CHECK OUT THE TOP COIN-OP RACING GAMES ON P.80.

>> *The users in America just don't go to arcades any more, because they don't see why they should invest the effort when they have games at home.* >>
Makoto Osaki, head of SEGA's AM2 arcade division

* MOST OFFICIAL TOURNAMENTS HELD FOR A VIDEOGAME

Holder: MUSHIKING: KING OF THE BEETLES (SEGA, 2003)

With 110,240 officially sanctioned competitions held in Japan between May 2003 and July 2009, *Mushiking: King of the Beetles* holds the record for the most official tournaments held. *Mushiking* is a combination of an arcade game and a collectible card game developed by SEGA (pictured is the *Mushiking* development team in April 2008).

* NEW RECORD
▪ UPDATED RECORD

OVERVIEW

With close to 500,000 machines in 9,000 game centres, Japan is a shining light when it comes to arcade gaming – but it's not just about the latest fighters or shoot-em-ups. In Japan, one of the most popular types of arcade machine is the claw game, in which players extract physical prizes from the cabinet using a joystick-controlled mechanical arm with a claw at the end. Other favourites include purikura (photo-sticker booths) and games that reward players with print-out collectible cards, such as Mushiking. Also attracting strong interest is the pachislot game, a kind of slot machine that allows players to use their skill and judgement to stop the spinning reels, rather than leaving it to chance.

TEN GAMES YOU SHOULD PLAY IN THIS GENRE

	GAME
1	Mushiking: King of the Beetles (2003)
2	UFO Catcher (1985 to present)
3	Print Club 2 (1996)
4	Street Snap (1998)
5	Mahjong Fight Club (2002)
6	World Club Champion Football (2002)
7	Oshare Majo: Love and Berry (2004)
8	Sangokushi Taisen (2005)
9	Robo Catcher (2007)
10	Kido Senshi Gundam: Senjo no Kizuna (2006)

✳ MOST SUCCESSFUL CLAW GAME PLAYER

Holder: YUKA NAKAJIMA (Japan)
Having liberated over 3,500 teddy bears from arcade cabinets, Yuka Nakajima is the undisputed champion of the claw game – and her success has not gone unnoticed. Nakajima's skills have earned her celebrity status in Japan, where she has even appeared on television to showcase her talent.

✳ BEST-SELLING PACHISLOT MACHINE

Holder: HOKUTO NO KEN
(SEGA SAMMY, 2003)
In terms of sales, the most successful pachislot machine is *Hokuto No Ken*, which has sold over 620,000 units – a staggering number, considering that a game is generally deemed to be a hit when sales reach 20,000. The game is themed on the popular anime and action videogame series of the same name, which translates as "Fist of the North Star".

✳ MOST PEOPLE IN A PURIKURA BOOTH SIMULTANEOUSLY

Holder: JAPANTOWN, SAN FRANCISCO, USA
Depending on their design, purikura booths can accommodate up to 10 people at the same time. However, on 1 January 2009, a record 27 purikura fans managed to squeeze into a single booth in Japantown, San Francisco, USA.

MOST BROKEN BONES CAUSED BY A SIM GAME

Holder: ARM SPRINT (Atlus, 2007)
In August 2007, Atlus was forced to recall all 150 units of its arm-wrestling sim *Arm Sprint*, after three people broke their arms while playing it. The company claimed that users must have become over-excited and twisted their arms in an unusual way.

JAPANESE ARCADE: THE KEY PLAYERS

▶ **KONAMI**
Back in 1969, Konami was a jukebox company, only moving into videogames in the late 1970s. The company has many hits to its name, including the dance mat sensation *Dance Dance Revolution* (1998) and *DrumMania* (1999). Konami has also produced a number of successful pachislot titles.

▶ **NAMCO**
The Nakamura Manufacturing Company began life in Tokyo in 1955, making children's rides for retail stores. The company became Namco in 1972 and, two years later,

acquired Atari's Japanese division. This paved the way for entry into the arcade market and, in 1980, Namco released *PAC-Man* to great acclaim. In 2005, Namco merged with Bandai to become the third largest videogames entity in Japan.

▶ **NINTENDO**
Founded in 1889, Nintendo started out making handmade "hanafuda" playing cards. However, the company made the leap to videogames in 1974, when it secured the rights to distribute the Magnavox Odyssey in Japan. Nintendo's first arcade game was 1978's *Computer Othello*, but it

was *Donkey Kong* in 1981 that gave the company its first real success. Other hits include *Mario Bros.* (1983) and *Mario Kart Arcade GP* (2005).

▶ **SEGA**
Once the arch rival of Nintendo on the hardware front, SEGA now concentrates on developing software and arcade games. The company has enjoyed great success with its *UFO Catcher* – a version of the claw game machine – and is behind some of the biggest arcade heavyweights of all time, including *Virtua Fighter* (1993).

CONTENTS:

GUINNESS WORLD RECORDS

CERTIFICATE

The most popular videogame series of all time, as voted for by visitors to the official website of Guinness World Records Gamer's Edition, is...

GUINNESS WORLD RECORDS LTD

www.guinnessworldrecords.com

APPROVED WORLD RECORD

THIS YEAR'S GUINNESS WORLD RECORDS GAMER'S EDITION TOP 50 HAS BEEN CHOSEN BY YOU, OUR READERS. BETWEEN JANUARY AND AUGUST 2009, OVER 13,000 OF YOU VISITED OUR WEBSITE TO TELL US ABOUT YOUR FAVOURITE GAMES, AND WE USED YOUR VOTES TO COMPILE THIS LIST OF THE 50 BEST VIDEOGAMES EVER. AS THE TITLE SUGGESTS, THIS ISN'T A LIST OF INDIVIDUAL GAMES, BUT RATHER A LIST OF THE TOP SERIES, INCLUDING ALL ENTRIES AND SPIN-OFFS, AND SERVES AS A SNAPSHOT OF THE BIGGEST NAMES IN GAMING IN 2010.

50 TO 26

WHAT WERE THE KEY GAMING EVENTS OF THE PAST YEAR? CHECK OUT PP. 16–21 TO FIND OUT.

50 PRO EVOLUTION SOCCER
(Konami, first release 2001)
The main rival to EA's *FIFA* soccer sim, *Pro Evo* commands fierce loyalty among its fans. People who like it, like it a lot.

49 CRASH BANDICOOT
(Sony, 1996)
3D platforming at its best, with a great sense of humour. A genuine must-have for PlayStation owners.

48 BURNOUT (Acclaim/EA, 2001)
The stylish street racer just keeps getting better, with the latest entry *Burnout Paradise* still going strong.

47 MARIO KART (Nintendo, 1992)
With its unbeatable multiplayer mode, this classic console racer has shown its lasting appeal for hardcore and casual gamers alike.

46 LEGO BATMAN (Warner, 2008)
The Dark Knight cleans up Gotham City, one brick at a time. Great two-player co-op and memorable characters.

■ NEW RECORD
● UPDATED RECORD

45 DIABLO (Blizzard, 1996)
The action RPG that turned frantic mouse-clicking into a compelling gameplay element. Another sequel is in the works for 2010.

44 BATTLEFIELD (EA, 2002)
Blending fact and fiction, past and future, EA's multiplayer FPS series retains a solid fanbase that continues to grow with spin-offs *Bad Company* and *Heroes*.

43 STAR WARS: BATTLEFRONT
(LucasArts, 2004)
The only *Star Wars* game to make it into the Top 50 this year, *Battlefront* lets gamers re-enact the sci-fi series' greatest conflicts.

42 TOM CLANCY'S (Red Storm/Ubisoft, 1997)
Tom Clancy is the most successful author in videogaming history. His is the name behind big franchises including *Ghost Recon*, *Rainbow Six* and flight sim *H.A.W.X.*

41 PONG (Atari, 1972)
The oldest title in this year's list, Atari's seminal tennis arcade game shows that developers still have a lot to learn from the old-school.

40 RATCHET & CLANK (Sony, 2002)
A slick slice of 3D platforming that has kept its trademark humour and outrageous weaponry through 11 releases.

39 STARCRAFT (Blizzard, 1998)
The definitive real-time strategy game, still beloved by gamers all over the world but adored by Koreans in particular.

38 GRAN TURISMO (Sony, 1997)
The driving sim by Polyphony Digital has been a figurehead of great PlayStation games design for over 12 years.

37 CHRONO TRIGGER (Squaresoft, 1995)
The Japanese RPG classic, with the development "dream team" of Sakaguchi, Horii and Toriyama, shows how timeless great game design can be.

36 NEED FOR SPEED (EA, 1994)
After more than 15 years on the circuit, the massively popular street-racing series has become one of videogaming's brightest and most adrenalin-fuelled stars.

2.76 MILLION... sales of *Bioshock* across all platforms as of 24 September 2009, according to vgchartz.com.

35 LEFT 4 DEAD (Valve, 2008)
Live together or die alone in this zombie apocalypse shooter, with tense co-op play and a dark sense of humour.

34 SKATE (EA, 2007)
Great visuals and responsive, innovative controls make *skate* the newly crowned best skateboarding series ever.

33 KILLZONE (Sony, 2004)
The best multiplayer FPS on PS3, *Killzone 2* blends gritty HD action with great level design.

32 BIOSHOCK (Take-Two, 2007)
A stunning underwater city gone mad provides the backdrop for this philosophical FPS.

31 GOLDENEYE 007 (Nintendo, 1997)
The original console FPS, *GoldenEye 007* was the frantic multiplayer shooting game of choice for an entire generation of gamers.

30 GOD OF WAR (Sony, 2005)
Sony's hack-and-slash masterpiece stays true to what the genre is all about: giant, unbelievable boss fights.

29 THE ELDER SCROLLS (Bethesda/Take-Two, 1994)
The series that brought open-world role playing to the masses, with gorgeous visuals and enormous amounts of depth.

28 SAINTS ROW (THQ, 2006)
A gangster sandbox title that excels in free-roaming mayhem and holds its own against the *GTA* series.

27 LITTLEBIGPLANET (Sony, 2008)
Media Molecule's beautiful 2D platformer, now better than ever with over 1 million user-generated levels.

26 ROCK BAND (EA, 2007)
The critics' choice in band simulators, *Rock Band*'s hugely varied setlist caters to the most esoteric of musical tastes. *The Beatles: Rock Band* is the latest release in the series.

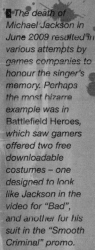

Killzone 2 will be one of the most cinematic and immersive games ever produced on a console.
BBC News, August 2007

TRIVIA

❯ The first racing game to feature Mario was not *Super Mario Kart*, but *Famicom Grand Prix: F-1 Race*, a top-down racer released in Japan in 1987 for the Famicom.

❯ *Ratchet & Clank* developer Insomniac ran a competition for players to design a new weapon for the game. The "Captain Qwark's My Blaster Runs Hot" competition was won by Jackson Finley (USA) with his "Spiral of Death" gun.

❯ The death of Michael Jackson in June 2009 resulted in various attempts by games companies to honour the singer's memory. Perhaps the most bizarre example was in *Battlefield Heroes*, which saw gamers offered two free downloadable costumes – one designed to look like Jackson in the video for "Bad", and another for his suit in the "Smooth Criminal" promo.

25 TO 11

TO FIND OUT HOW TO BECOME A RECORD-BREAKER, TURN TO P.5.

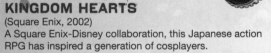

25 WWE SMACKDOWN VS. RAW (THQ, 2000)
This annually updated brawler is a must-have for sports entertainment fans, bringing the definitive pro-wrestling experience to home console owners.

24 TOMB RAIDER (Eidos, 1996)
The series that gave us gaming's most famous pin-up, Lara Croft, blends shooting, platforming and puzzling with gorgeous character graphics.

23 THE SIMS (EA, 2000)
Maxis' legendary lifestyle simulation demonstrates that to be successful, games don't have to be about anything other than the humdrum of everyday life.

19 KINGDOM HEARTS
(Square Enix, 2002)
A Square Enix-Disney collaboration, this Japanese action RPG has inspired a generation of cosplayers.

22 MADDEN NFL (EA, 1989)
EA's evergreen gridiron simulation is the most accurate representation of NFL action that doesn't involve buying tickets to the Super Bowl.

18 FIFA (EA, 1993)
Soccer gaming's apex in terms of sales as well as critical reception, FIFA has established itself as the beautiful game's definitive sim.

21 PAC-MAN (Namco, 1980)
The original and best maze game, PAC-Man is the highest placed Golden Age arcade game in this year's Top 50.

17 RUNESCAPE (Jagex, 2001)
The free browser-based MMORPG has been quietly taking over the world since its launch in 2001.

* NEW RECORD
◦ UPDATED RECORD

20 FINAL FANTASY
(Square Enix, 1987)
The most successful Japanese RPG series of all time, Final Fantasy has grown a dedicated fanbase with its vivid fantasy worlds and tireless innovation.

60... the number of countries that *The Sims* has been shipped to. Along the way, the game has been translated into 22 different languages, including Russian and Thai.

TRIVIA

16 COUNTER-STRIKE (Valve, 1999)
The first-person shooter that brought professional gaming to the masses, *Counter-Strike* is still the standard against which other FPS games are judged.

15 SONIC THE HEDGEHOG (SEGA, 1991)
The Blue Dude with the 'tude remains a hit with gaming fans almost 20 years after his glory days in the 1990s.

14 HALF-LIFE (Valve, 1998)
The perfect single-player FPS series, *Half-Life*'s blend of frantic action, brilliant set-pieces and engaging characters has yet to be matched.

13 FALLOUT (Interplay/Bethesda, 1997)
With its stunning depiction of a nuclear wasteland infused with a wicked sense of humour, *Fallout* is essential gaming for fans of RPGs and shooters.

> We wanted a game that didn't feel like a doll being controlled, but to give life to a world stuck inside the television.
>
> *Naoto shima*, Sonic the Hedgehog character designer

12 RESIDENT EVIL
(Capcom, 1996)
The classic survival horror series' continued success proves that gamers will never get tired of having the snot scared out of them.

11 POKÉMON (Nintendo, 1996)
Gotta catch 'em all! The ultimate collect-em-up that has turned millions of casual gamers into hardcore otaku.

The only character to appear in all three main entries in the *Fallout* series is Harold, a severely mutated human with a plant called Bob growing out of his head. By *Fallout 3*, Bob has grown into a full-sized tree and taken over much of Harold's body, leaving him rooted to one spot and extremely depressed as a result. In one of the game's possible endings, the player character puts Harold out of his misery by killing him at his request, so appearances in future games seem unlikely.

Every year during Wrestlemania, real WWF superstars take part in a tournament to see who is the best at the latest WWE videogame. The winner of the 2009 event was Kofi Kingston (Ghana), who played as himself and chose Jimmy Hart as his manager in the final against Cody Rhodes (USA).

SEGA's Sonic the Hedgehog has starred in a number of bizarre offshoots from his main role as a platform game hero. Some of the Blue Blur's more unusual spin-offs include Sonic Spinball (a pinball game where Sonic is the ball), Sonic Eraser (a falling blocks puzzle game) and Waku Waku Sonic Patrol Car (an arcade game that casts Sonic as a traffic warden).

XBOX

HALF-LIFE²

10 TO 4

! CHECK OUT P.22 FOR THE LATEST DEVELOPMENTS IN THE WORLD OF PRO-GAMING.

10 GRAND THEFT AUTO
(Rockstar, 1997)
The undeniable king of open-world crime simulations, Rockstar Games' most popular series has never been afraid of courting controversy.

9 SUPER SMASH BROS. (Nintendo, 1999)
The fantastic platform/fighter/party game crossover that finally lets you solve the age-old question: who would win in a fight between Mario and Solid Snake?

8 GEARS OF WAR (Microsoft, 2006)
Epic's ultra-violent shooter is a must-have for Xbox 360 owners, although squeamish gamers need not apply.

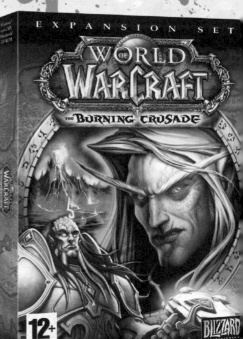

EXPANSION SET

WORLD OF WARCRAFT
THE BURNING CRUSADE

12+
www.pegi.info

BLIZZARD

7 WORLD OF WARCRAFT (Blizzard, 2004)
The biggest MMORPG in history makes an appearance at No.7 to remind us of its stranglehold on the genre.

[**$100 MILLION (£62 MILLION)...** the estimated development budget for *Grand Theft Auto IV.*]

* **NEW RECORD**
* **UPDATED RECORD**

6 SUPER MARIO BROS. (Nintendo, 1985)
Gaming's most famous icon, the Italian plumber has starred in an unbroken streak of phenomenal games since his console series debuted in 1985.

5 METAL GEAR (Konami, 1989)
Hideo Kojima's (Japan) elaborate, complicated and beautifully balanced tactical espionage series has been the granddaddy of the stealth genre for 20 years.

> « What I'm doing is creating a game. I'm not making a movie. To make the game more enjoyable and captivating… we need the cinematic element. »
>
> Hideo Kojima,
> Metal Gear Solid creator

4 GUITAR HERO (RedOctane/Activision, 2005)
The people's choice when it comes to rhythm games, the *Guitar Hero* series has gone from small-time pastime to multi-media phenomenon in five short years.

TRIVIA

> *Azeroth is the planet on which much of Blizzard's World of Warcraft is set. As the game has over 12 million registered players, this means that the "population" of Azeroth is greater than the population of Belgium.*

> Metal Gear Solid creator Hideo Kojima (Japan) and his team used LEGO blocks to prototype levels in the game. They stopped this practice with MGS2, though, due to the complexity of the level designs.

> Hideo Kojima has said that he came up with the idea for Metal Gear while playing hide and seek with his son.

> Rockstar Games, the controversial studio behind Grand Theft Auto, has continued its tradition of shocking the gaming world by including a full frontal male nude in GTAIV: The Lost and Damned, the first of two episodic expansion packs developed for the Xbox 360 version of GTAIV.

TOP 3

TURN BACK TO P.18 FOR THE GAMING YEAR IN REVIEW.

3 THE LEGEND OF ZELDA (Nintendo, 1986)

Always a reliable entry in lists of great games, *The Legend of Zelda* franchise remains a classic in every sense of the word. The series' ability to constantly push boundaries while remaining accessible and compelling to players of all ages and gaming abilities shows that *The Legend of Zelda* thoroughly deserves its place in this year's Top 3.

2 CALL OF DUTY (Activision, 2003)

Although the series has its roots in World War II, it's only since making the transition to *Modern Warfare* that *Call of Duty* has become the bastion of great game design and towering monolith of popularity that it is today. A combination of beautifully balanced gameplay, jaw-dropping set pieces and an almost matchless multiplayer mode, *Call of Duty* is currently the most important multi-format shooter in the world.

◆ NEW RECORD
◇ UPDATED RECORD

39,000... the number of lines of dialogue featured in Bungie's *Halo 3*, resulting in more audio than 20 feature films combined as well as around 13,000 sound effects.

GUINNESS WORLD RECORDS

HALO (Microsoft, 2001)

The flagship game on Microsoft consoles, *Halo*'s influence on modern gaming can be judged by the number of games that have been promoted as "*Halo* Killers" and the fact that none of them have succeeded. The *Halo* series reads like a checklist of great videogame design: an iconic character, excellent level design, perfect controls and unparalleled multiplayer options. With credentials like those, it's easy to see why Bungie's FPS masterpiece was chosen by our readers as the best videogame series ever.

YOUR CHOICE

« We've never said that we're finished with Halo 3; in the Edge acceptance video, we confirmed that the ride isn't over.

Studio Bungie's weekly update on 22 August 2008, shortly after winning the Edge Award for Interactive Innovation 2008

TRIVIA

At a Bungie press event in the summer of 2009, Bungie's Brian Jarrard said that nearly two years after Halo 3's release, there are still around 1 million unique users playing the game online every day – that's more people than the population of San Francisco, California, USA.

EXPO
'09

A highlight of E3 2009, held in Los Angeles, USA, on 2 June 2009, was Steve Wiebe's (USA) attempt to reclaim the coveted *Donkey Kong* high-score record, under the watchful eyes of Twin Galaxies officials.

CONTENTS:

A TO C

WHICH GAMES ARE EXCLUSIVE TO WHICH CONSOLES? FIND OUT IN OUR HARDWARE SECTION, STARTING ON P.24.

TRIVIA

Despite its name, 1941: Counter Attack was not the first game in Capcom's popular series of World War II top-scrolling shoot-em-ups. That honour goes to 1942, which was released in arcades in 1984. Its prequel didn't arrive until 1990, three years after the release of the second game in the series, 1943: The Battle of Midway.

Dubbed as SEGA's answer to Shigeru Miyamoto (Japan), games designer Yu Suzuki (Japan) created the After Burner arcade series as well as a host of other titles, including Space Harrier, OutRun and Hang-On.

Released for the Gameboy and Game Boy Advance by Acclaim in 1991, Bart Simpson's Escape from Camp Deadly (below) saw the yellow troublemaker facing up to the perils of a summer camp run by a relative of Mr Burns, and featured a plot that was very similar to the "Kamp Krusty" TV episode, aired in 1992.

First announced in January 2009, rhythm game Bit.Trip Beat had already spawned two sequels by that September.

THOUSANDS OF GAMING RECORDS HAVE FALLEN SINCE OUR LAST EDITION. HERE, WE PRESENT A SELECTION OF TWIN GALAXIES' NEWEST SCORES – AND SOME OF THE CLASSICS, TOO...

GAME	PLATFORM	NOTES/ SETTINGS	RECORD	PLAYER (NAT.)	DATE
1941: Counter Attack (World)	MAME	No Continues	2,455,800	Vicente Morales (Brazil)	8 Jun 09
		Two-Player Team	1,225,500	Antonio Filho & Suzan Araujo (both Brazil)	13 Sep 08
1942	Arcade		13,360,960	Martin Bedard (Canada)	19 Nov 06
Absolute Pinball	PC	Balls 'n' Bats	2,627,010,736	Ralf Wernery (Germany)	5 May 05
		Desert Run	575,233,590	Nashua Nashua (USA)	5 May 05
		Dream Factory	147,810,110	Kiril Statev (Belgium)	5 May 05
After Burner	MAME	Japanese Arcade Version	66,000	Vicente Morales (Brazil)	28 Nov 08
After Burner II	Arcade		5,083,740	David C Hernly (USA)	30 May 09
	Mega Drive/ Genesis		30,213,110	Dan Lee (USA)	11 Jun 04
Alien Crush Returns	WiiWare	Arcade Mode, First Stage	38,246,500	William Willemstyn III (USA)	22 Nov 08
		Second Stage	9,977,500	William Willemstyn III (USA)	18 Jan 09
		Third Stage	47,243,000	William Willemstyn III (USA)	1 Jan 09
Apache 3	MAME		388,200	Robert Flynn (USA)	15 Jun 06
Arkanoid DS	DS	Clear Mode	164,630	Daniel M Phillips (USA)	11 Sep 09
Asteroids	Arcade		41,336,440	Scott Safran (USA)	13 Nov 82
Bad Dudes vs. DragonNinja	MAME	TGTS	999,999	Magnus Andersson (Sweden)	11 Jul 09
Bart Simpson's Escape from Camp Deadly	GB/GBC		19 min 50 sec	Rudy J Ferretti (USA)	20 Feb 08
Beatmania CompleteMIX	Arcade	TGTS, Most Cash	$3,461.67	Justin Goeres (USA)	22 Aug 04
Beats	PSP	Hip Hop, Extreme Difficulty	62,540	Blaine Locklair (USA)	17 Jan 08
		Inflated Plains, Extreme Difficulty, Longest Chain	31	Blaine Locklair (USA)	17 Jan 08
Biohazard: Gun Survivor	PS2		38 min 29 sec	Shin Sato (Japan)	1 Apr 04
BioShock	PS3	Medium Difficulty	3 hr 25 min 10 sec	Ben Greenman (USA)	24 Apr 09
Bit.Trip Beat	WiiWare	Descent	829,420	William Willemstyn III (USA)	1 May 09
		Transition	954,141	William Willemstyn III (USA)	17 Apr 09

89... the impressive number of cars that can be unlocked by completing the various game modes in *Burnout Legends*.

GAME	PLATFORM	NOTES/ SETTINGS	RECORD	PLAYER (NAT.)	DATE
Bomberman	NES	Marathon	1,000,093,700	Kristina Sakundiak (Canada)	18 Jun 05
Boom Blox	Wii	Explore Challenge, Master Challenges, Complex	200	Marc Cohen (USA)	31 Aug 09
		Explore Challenge, Expert Challenges, Shiny Tower, Least Throws	3	William Willemstyn III (USA)	19 Jul 09
Burnout Legends	DS	Airport, Most Cash	$78,792	Tee Jester (USA)	17 Aug 09
	PSP	Three Ways to Fly, Most Cash	$558,473	Tom Duncan (USA)	1 July 08
		Advanced, Traffic	2 min 55.79 sec	Jason DeHeras (USA)	15 Jan 99
		Expert, Traffic	3 min 21.14 sec	Jorge Abreu (USA)	9 Sep 98
	Dreamcast	Time Attack, Dinosaur Canyon, Reverse Track	3 min 21.5 sec	Magnus Andersson (Sweden)	28 Aug 09
Burnout 2: Point of Impact	Xbox	Pursuit Mode, Ocean Spirit, Reverse Track	1 min 6.75 sec	Tee Jester (USA)	13 Sep 09
Burnout 3: Takedown	PS2	Frozen Peak Southbound, Takedowns	57	Tom Duncan (USA)	28 Jun 09
Capcom Classics Collection	PS2	1941: Counter Attack, Hardcore Difficulty	314,100	Ryan Sullivan (USA)	28 Dec 08
Capcom Classics Collection Remixed	PSP	1941: Counter Attack, Hardcore Difficulty	121,500	Ryan Sullivan (USA)	19 Jan 08
Carnival Games	Wii	Super Alley Ball	650	Marc Cohen (USA)	21 Jun 09
Castlevania	NES		13 min 8 sec	Ian D Greenwood (USA)	11 May 09
	Wii Virtual Console	NES, Fastest Completion	16 min 40 sec	Andrew D Furrer (USA)	22 May 09
Castlevania II: Simon's Quest	NES		45 min 57 sec	Ian D Greenwood (USA)	9 Feb 09
Castlevania III: Dracula's Curse	NES	No Partners, Fastest Completion	32 min 59 sec	Tom Votava (USA)	12 Apr 04
Castlevania: Aria of Sorrow	GBA	Boss Rush Mode, Fastest Completion, Soma Cruz	2 min 15.3 sec	Kelly R Flewin (Canada)	17 May 07
Chrono Trigger	SNES	Fastest Completion	15 hr 41 min 12 sec	Bob Taylor (USA)	15 Apr 09
Crash Bandicoot 3: Warped	PlayStation	Time Trial 01, Toad Village	41.63 sec	Paulo Valmir (Brazil)	17 Mar 09
		Time Trial 02, Under Pressure	1 hr 18.2 sec	Fabiano G Souza (Brazil)	2 May 06
		Time Trial 26, Ski Crazed	41.63 sec	Alexander T Trammell (USA)	22 Aug 05
Crash Bandicoot: The Wrath of Cortex	Xbox	Time Trial 01, Arctic Antics	34.75 sec	Paulo Valmir (Brazil)	27 Feb 09

NOTES

E Emulator software allows gamers to play old arcade machines without the need for the original cabinet and hardware. The standard emulator for arcade machines is **MAME**: the Multiple Arcade Machine Emulator. The **e** symbol in a table entry indicates that the game has been played on a different, non-MAME, emulator. Please contact Twin Galaxies for a list of approved emulators.

E **TGTS** stands for Twin Galaxies' Tournament Settings. These vary from game to game, so please contact Twin Galaxies for full details of the settings required for each record category.

E Unless otherwise specified, all gaming machines and consoles are on default settings, and records are for **points earned** or **completion times**.

TRIVIA

E The star of his own action-adventure series, Crash Bandicoot (below) is based on the Eastern Barred Bandicoot species.

HEAD OVER TO P.12 TO FIND OUT WHICH RECORD-BREAKING GAMES BECAME AWARD-WINNING GAMES.

HEAD OVER TO P.12 TO FIND OUT WHICH RECORD-BREAKING GAMES BECAME AWARD-WINNING GAMES.

TRIVIA

▷ A title renowned for its difficulty, the original Defender arcade game was the breakthrough hit for Williams Electronics. The game's sequel was titled Stargate for its arcade release but was renamed Defender II for the home console market.

▷ The innovative animation-like adventures of Dirk Daring (below) in Don Bluth's (USA) Dragon's Lair were made possible by the large storage capacity of the laserdiscs used in its arcade cabinet. Unfortunately, the laserdisc players weren't designed for the intensive use and jostling of the arcade. Consequently, many Dragon's Lair cabinets spent a lot of time with "Out of Order" signs on them.

▷ The genre-blending Dr. Mario Online RX, the WiiWare remix of Dr. Mario, sees the plump plumber attach his name to a match-the-colour Tetris clone in which players attempt to match the coloured halves of a variety of different pills.

GAME	PLATFORM	NOTES/SETTINGS	RECORD	PLAYER (NAT.)	DATE
Crash Nitro Kart	PS2	Time Trials, Android Valley	1 min 17.95 sec	Alexander T Trammell (USA)	28 Jun 06
Dance Dance Revolution: Extreme (8th Mix)	Arcade	Difficulty 4 (Medium), 3 Songs	487,065,570	Sterling C Franklin (USA)	24 Oct 07
		Difficulty 4 (Medium), Doubles Mode	223,403,725	Luke C Wiebe (USA)	14 Jan 06
		TGTS, Difficulty 4 (Medium), 5 Songs	680,808,465	Jason T Gilleece (USA)	5 Aug 05
		Marathon, Single Player	13 hr 9 min 40 sec	Airy Peterson (USA)	1 Jan 07
Defender	Arcade	TGTS	543,950	Bill Jones (USA)	19 Sep 08
Defender II	Atari 2600	Game 1, Difficulty B	79,700	Stephen Knox (USA)	9 May 01
Depthcharge	Arcade		4,770	Martin Bedard (Canada)	
Destruction Derby	PSP	Championship, Division 1	406	Terence O'Neill (USA)	3 Jan 08
	PlayStation	Championship, Division 1	426	Terence O'Neill (USA)	25 Jan 08
Dig Dug	Arcade	TGTS	1,340,840	Ken House (USA)	13 Jun 09
Digger	Arcade		17,400	Mark Peterson (USA)	13 Feb 83
Dr. Mario Online RX	WiiWare	Classic, Multiple Levels	643,000	Patrick Scott Patterson (USA)	12 Dec 08
Donkey Kong	Arcade	TGTS, Hammer Allowed	1,050,200	Billy L Mitchell (USA)	26 Jul 07
	MAME	TGTS, US Set 1	1,051,500	Dean Saglio (USA)	8 Jul 09
		No Hammer	421,200	Scott Kessler (USA)	2 Feb 09
Donkey Kong 3	Arcade	TGTS	473,400	Dwayne Richard (Canada)	22 Oct 05
Donkey Kong Jr.	Arcade	TGTS	1,139,800	Steve J Wiebe (USA)	15 Apr 09
Double Dragon	Arcade	Two Player	102,310	Jérôme Pastorel & Regis Martzel (both France)	7 Jun 09
Dragon's Lair	Arcade	3 Men	374,954	Greg R Sakundiak (Canada)	11 Jun 04
		5 Men	558,724	Judd Boone (USA)	31 Oct 83
	Commodore 64		4,911	Ron Corcoran (USA)	26 May 03
	Commodore 64		3,170	Paulo Valmir (Brazil)	1 Feb 09
Dynamite Duke	MAME	Japanese Arcade	136,730	Ryan Sullivan (USA)	5 May 09
Dynasty Warriors 4	Xbox	Yellow Turban Fortress, Hard, Fastest Completion	2 min 54.7 sec	Mike K Morrow (USA)	10 Apr 05
Fatal Fury: King of Fighters	MAME	TGTS	476,000	Alan Fraser (USA)	18 Mar 07
FIFA Street	PS2	Easy, Biggest Blowout (PAL)	36 goals	Jonathan Pete Mee (UK)	16 Mar 08
	Xbox	Easy, Biggest Blowout (PAL)	22 goals	Jonathan Pete Mee (UK)	12 Sep 07

860,630... the high score the character George Costanza is supposed to have racked up on a game of *Frogger* in an episode of the hit TV comedy series *Seinfeld*.

GAME	PLATFORM	NOTES/SETTINGS	RECORD	PLAYER (NAT.)	DATE
		Easy (PAL)	222,774	Andrew Pete Mee (UK)	11 Sep 07
	GameCube	Easy, Biggest Blowout	12 goals	Steffan M Fazzari (USA)	17 Jun 08
		Easy	78,600	Steffan M Fazzari (USA)	17 Jun 08
Final Fantasy	NES	Fastest Completion	5 hr 25 min 49 sec	Caner M Cooperrider (USA)	11 Dec 08
Final Fantasy III	NES	Fastest Completion	8 hr 24 min 50 sec	Rodrigo Lopes (Brazil)	11 Oct 04
Frogger	Arcade	TGTS	771,060	Pat Laffaye (USA)	22 Jul 09
	ColecoVision	Slow	53,150	Tom Duncan (USA)	22 Apr 08
		Fast	47,810	Ron Corcoran (USA)	12 Aug 08
	GB/GBC		20,550	Tom Duncan (USA)	6 Aug 09
	MAME		881,150	Donald Hayes (USA)	2 Jan 09
	SNES		99,990	Marc Merica (USA)	1 Aug 09
	Xbox 360 Live Arcade		13,680	Rusty Nunnelee (USA)	25 Apr 09
Gauntlet	Arcade	Single Player, Single Credit	4,401,169	Charles Nagle (USA)	28 Mar 03
Galaga	Arcade	Rapid Fire	205,690	Jerry Dixon (USA)	10 Jul 99
		TGTS	2,729,350	Andrew B Laidlaw (USA)	21 Dec 07
		Marathon	15,900,000	Stephen Krogman (USA)	1 Jun 89
	MAME	Rapid Fire	20,518,900	Stephen Krogman (USA)	8 Feb 05
	NES	Game C: Balloon Trip	507,070	Kyle M Orland (USA)	25 Nov 05
		Marathon	20,233,769	Todd Rogers (USA)	1 Oct 04
		TGTS	1,033,880	Tom Votava (USA)	6 Oct 07
	Wii Virtual Console	Marathon	666,670	Cody A Corley (USA)	14 Oct 08
	Xbox 360 Live Arcade		102,790	Patrick Scott Patterson (USA)	10 Sep 09
Geometry Wars: Galaxies	DS	Alpha, Claeis, Single Player	691,962,000	Ginger Stowe (USA)	10 Apr 09
Geometry Wars: Retro Evolved	Xbox 360 Live Arcade	Evolved	408,960	Dennis M Weaver (USA)	16 Aug 09
		Retro	104,845	Dennis M Weaver (USA)	16 Aug 09
Geometry Wars: Retro Evolved[2]	Xbox 360 Live Arcade	Deadline	7,504,025	Dennis M Weaver (USA)	16 Aug 09
		King	5,085,310	Dennis M Weaver (USA)	16 Aug 09
		Evolved	13,960,230	Dennis M Weaver (USA)	16 Aug 09
		Pacifism	28,820,000	Dennis M Weaver (USA)	16 Aug 09
		Waves	3,277,640	Dennis M Weaver (USA)	16 Aug 09
		Sequence	16,506,670	Dennis M Weaver (USA)	16 Aug 09
Grand Theft Auto: Vice City	PS2	Fastest Minimalist Completion	3 hr 20 min 58 sec	Shane E Aukerman (USA)	20 Jun 06
	Xbox	Alloy Wheels of Steel	1 min 13 sec	Mike K Morrow (USA)	10 Apr 05

TRIVIA

▶ *Frogger* has come a long way since its original classic arcade debut in 1981. By 2005, the series had evolved into a 3D platformer, and its froggy hero (above) had learned how to stand upright.

▶ First released in 2002, Grand Theft Auto: Vice City boasts a star-studded voice cast, ranging from Ray Liotta, who takes on the main role of Tommy Vercetti (below), through to Dennis Hopper and Burt Reynolds, who play Steve Scott and Avery Carrington, respectively.

WHAT ARE YOUR FAVOURITE GAMES OF ALL TIME? CHECK OUT OUR READER POLL FROM P.186.

GAME	PLATFORM	NOTES/SETTINGS	RECORD	PLAYER (NAT.)	DATE
Guinness World Records: The Video Game	Wii	Longest Motorcycle Jump	125.94 m	Troy Whelan (USA)	10 Sep 09
		Fastest Time to Pop 100 Balloons	9.54 sec	Troy Whelan (USA)	10 Sep 09
		Longest Balance of a Vehicle on Your Head	30.61 sec	Troy Whelan (USA)	10 Sep 09
		Fastest Time to Pluck 3 Turkeys	13.83 sec	Troy Whelan (USA)	10 Sep 09
Guitar Hero: Aerosmith	Wii	"Draw The Line", Easy	83,256	Dick Moreland (USA)	26 Jun 09
Guitar Hero III: Legends of Rock	PS3	"Hit Me With Your Best Shot", Easy	68,169	Nik Meeks (USA)	18 May 08
		"Lay Down", Easy	85,710	Nik Meeks (USA)	23 May 09
	Wii	"Hit Me With Your Best Shot", Easy	48,652	Jeffrey M Widzinski (USA)	28 Aug 09
		"Story Of My Life", Easy	158,158	Jeffrey M Widzinski (USA)	23 Aug 09
		"Knights Of Cydonia", Easy	119,836	Jeffrey M Widzinski (USA)	23 Aug 09
Gyrostarr	WiiWare		15,643,500	Dave W Vogt (USA)	25 Mar 09
Hang-On (Simulator)	Arcade	TGTS	40,715,030	Don Novak (USA)	22 Jun 04
The House of the Dead 2 & 3 Return	Wii	House of the Dead 2, Arcade Mode, No Continues	89,720	Ryan T Fenton (USA)	23 Aug 09
		House of the Dead 3, Arcade Mode, No Continues	65,500	Daniel Lee Strickland Perea (USA)	28 Jul 09
The Incredible Maze	WiiWare	1, Starting Off, Challenge Mode	13.000	William Willemstyn III (USA)	22 Feb 09
		2, Schematic Holes, Challenge Mode	16.000	William Willemstyn III (USA) Marc Cohen (USA)	22 Feb 09 1 Apr 09
Jet Moto	PSP	Blackwater Falls, Fastest Race	2 min 13.5 sec	Terence O'Neill (USA)	5 May 08
Joust	Arcade	Marathon	107,216,700	James Vollandt (USA)	8 Jul 85
		Tournament	1,489,250	Donald Hayes (USA)	11 Nov 08
	Atari 400/800/XL/XE	Skilled	279,300	Todd Rogers (USA)	30 Sep 04
	Commodore 64		1,007,500	Mike K Morrow (USA)	13 Jul 04
	NES	Difficulty A	215,750	Brent T Coffman (USA)	1 May 09
	Mega Drive/Genesis		134,000	Ron Corcoran (USA)	28 Jan 98
	Xbox 360 Live Arcade		55,580	Rusty Nunnelee (USA)	25 Apr 09

3,722... the number of notes in DragonForce's "Through the Fire and the Flames", the *hardest song on Guitar Hero III*.

GAME	PLATFORM	NOTES/SETTINGS	RECORD	PLAYER (NAT.)	DATE
Kingdom Hearts	PS2	Fastest Completion	11 hr 49 min 44 sec	Paul Gerver (USA)	13 Jul 08
Konami Classics Series: Arcade Hits	DS	*Shaolin's Road*	263,100	Jason C Dove (USA)	7 Jul 09
Konami Collector's Series: Arcade Advanced	GBA	*Frogger*, 3 Lives	11,660	Tee Jester (USA)	25 May 08
Kung-Fu Master	Arcade	TGTS	1,349,040	Mike Sullivan (USA)	30 Jun 85
	Atari 2600/VCS	Game 1, Difficulty B	1,000,000	Todd Rogers (USA)	14 Sep 02
				David B Yancey (USA)	18 Jan 03
				Douglas C Korekach (USA)	18 Jan 03
	Atari 2600/VCS e	Game 1, Difficulty B (PAL)	79,360	Andrew Pete Mee (UK)	13 May 03
	Atari 7800		537,300	David B Yancey (USA)	12 Nov 04
	Commodore 64 e	TGTS	242,160	Clay W Karczewski (Canada)	29 Dec 07
	MAME		386,680	Pete Topping (UK)	31 Aug 09
		Marathon	624,330	Mats R Ranlind (Sweden)	10 Jun 08
The Legend of Kage 2	DS	Kage or Chihiro	177,050	Steve T America (USA)	21 Nov 08
The Legend of Zelda	NES	Fastest Completion, First Quest, 1 Life	31 min 37 sec	Rodrigo Lopes (Brazil)	7 Sep 06
		Fastest Completion, Second Quest, 1 Life	39 min 59 sec	Rodrigo Lopes (Brazil)	31 Oct 06
The Legend of Zelda: Ocarina of Time	N64	Fastest Completion	5 hr 40 sec	Michael B Damiani (USA)	2 Oct 05
LEGO Racers 2	GB/GBC	Amazon Alley, Fastest Race	2 min 10.30 sec	Tom Duncan (USA)	20 Nov 08
Link's Crossbow Training	Wii	Level 1–1 (PAL)	100,209	Ben Townsend (UK)	15 Jan 09
		Level 1–1	92,749	Michael E Estep (USA)	23 Jun 09
Lode Runner	NES		146,300	Patrick Scott Patterson (USA)	31 Mar 08
		TGTS	59,400	Patrick Scott Patterson (USA)	31 Mar 08
	Wii Virtual Console		155,200	Patrick Scott Patterson (USA)	10 May 08
		TGTS	83,100	Patrick Scott Patterson (USA)	10 May 08
	ZX Spectrum e		1,008,050	Andrew Pete Mee (UK)	23 May 08
		TGTS	162,600	Patrick Scott Patterson (USA)	23 May 08
	Xbox 360 Live Arcade	Journey Mode	55,108	Charles Adams (USA)	24 May 09
Madden NFL 08	Wii	Exhibition	43 points	Jeffrey M Widzinski (USA)	22 Apr 09
	Xbox	Exhibition	102 points	Patrick Scott Patterson (USA)	9 Oct 08

TRIVIA

█ In 2005, the popular Japanese RPG Kingdom Hearts was adapted into manga based loosely on the videogame's plot by mangaka (manga maker) Shiro Amano (Japan).

█ One entry in the Zelda series that never saw the light of day was The Legend of Zelda: Mystical Seed of Courage for the Game Boy Color. The title was planned as part of a trilogy of games, but when this proved too problematic, the trilogy was scaled back to two games: The Legend of Zelda: Oracle of Seasons and The Legend of Zelda: Oracle of Ages.

█ American gamer Tom Duncan (USA) is the most prolific Twin Galaxies record-holder, with a total of 5,597 current records as of October 2009. His nearest rival is Swede Magnus Andersson, with a "mere" 1,028 current titles to his name.

█ Madden NFL 09 (below) was first in the series to feature the innovation of online league gameplay, which allows up to 32 players to compete with one another over the course of a season.

WANT TO KNOW MORE ABOUT MARIO'S MAKER? P.102 HAS OUR PROFILE OF SHIGERU MIYAMOTO.

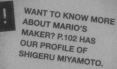

TRIVIA

Each year during Super Bowl weekend, EA, the makers of the Madden series of American football simulators, holds the "Madden Bowl", which sees NFL stars play each other on the latest version of the game. The winner of the 2009 Madden Bowl was Antonio Bryant (USA) of the Tampa Bay Buccaneers. Using the Dallas Cowboys, Antonio beat the New York Giants' Justin Tuck, who stayed loyal by playing as his own side. Antonio took advantage of some important interceptions to establish a big lead that was never seriously endangered. The final score was 28–7 to Antonio.

Since starting life as a Neo Geo arcade title, SNK's classic run and gunner Metal Slug has been adapted to 12 other platforms, including the Game Boy Advance (above) and Xbox 360.

As well as being the keeper of videogame records, Twin Galaxies also specializes in pinball records, making titles such as Metroid Prime Pinball doubly interesting to them.

GAME	PLATFORM	NOTES/ SETTINGS	RECORD	PLAYER (NAT.)	DATE
Madden NFL 09 All Play	PS2	Play Now Mode, 50% Penalty Level	38 points	Jeffrey M Widzinski (USA)	28 Aug 09
Major League Baseball	NES	Single Player, World Series, Points Difference	84 runs	Aaron Kimball (USA)	28 Nov 06
Maniac Mansion	NES	Play Any Two Characters, All Three Kids Remain Alive	10 min 24 sec	Christopher D Harrington (USA)	20 Feb 09
Mario Bros.	GBA	Super Mario Advanced Series	999,990	Terence O'Neill (USA) Isaiah TriForce Johnson (USA)	17 Feb 06 27 Jun 08
Mario Kart DS	DS	Airship Fortress, Best Lap	40.534 sec	Alex L Shepherd (UK)	10 Dec 07
Mario Party Advance	GBA	Amplifried	3,110	Tee Jester (USA)	27 May 08
Marvel Super Heroes vs. Street Fighter	PlayStation	TGTS	1,448,500	Paul Luu (USA)	11 Apr 99
Marvel vs. Capcom	PlayStation	TGTS	1,489,700	Bruno Augusto (Brazil)	3 Jan 07
Mega Man	NES	TGTS, Fastest Completion	22 min 57sec	Trevor Seguin (USA)	6 Aug 08
			5,111,100	Dominick Festagallo (USA)	19 Aug 09
Metal Gear	NES	Fastest Completion	48 min 41 sec	Ian D Greenwood (USA)	9 May 09
Metal Gear Solid	PlayStation	TGTS, Fastest Minimalist Completion	1 hr 55 min 31 sec	Rodrigo Lopes (Brazil)	30 Jun 00
		TGTS, VR Mission, Fastest Minimalist Completion	1 min 55.15 sec	Shin Sato (Japan)	21 Mar 04
Metal Gear Solid: VR Missions	PlayStation	TGTS, VR Survival Mission, Fastest Minimalist Completion	2 min 25.55 sec	Yoshihiro Ogihara (Japan)	31 Mar 03
Metal Slug: Super Vehicle-001	Arcade	Single Player	1,044,890	Cliff Reese (USA)	21 Sep 08
Metal Slug 2: Super Vehicle-001/II	Arcade	Single Player	1,655,059	Jim Brown (USA)	9 Aug 99
Metroid II: Return of Samus	GB/GBC	Fastest 100% Completion	1 hr 15 min 11 sec	Jonathan Fields (USA)	11 May 04
Metroid Prime Pinball	DS	Multi Mission, Normal Difficulty	12,538,070	William Willemstyn III (USA)	6 Oct 06
Micro Machines V4	PSP	Attic Ambush	43.233	Tee Jester (USA)	16 Jan 08
Midway Arcade Treasures: Extended Play	PSP	720°	73,110	Jason C Dove (USA)	29 Nov 08
		Defender	18,850	Ryan Sullivan (USA)	19 Dec 08
Mortal Kombat 4	N64	Fastest Completion	7 min 33 sec	Michael T Valenti (USA)	19 Dec 08
	PlayStation	TGTS, Hardest Difficulty, Fastest Completion	7 min 46 sec	Michael J Girard (USA)	9 May 09
Mortal Kombat: Deception	PS2	TGTS, Hardest Difficulty, Fastest Completion	14 min 59 sec	Michael J Girard (USA)	9 May 09

459,330... the number of points scored by Carlos Daniel Borrego Romero (Mexico) over two five-minute rounds to secure the title of *PAC-Man* World Champion in June 2007.

GAME	PLATFORM	NOTES/ SETTINGS	RECORD	PLAYER (NAT.)	DATE
Mortal Kombat: Armageddon	PS2	TGTS, Hardest Difficulty, Fastest Completion	13 min 16 sec	Michael J Girard (USA)	9 May 09
Need For Speed: Underground	Arcade	14th & Vine, Fastest Race	1 min 35.129 sec	Clinton L Abby (USA)	20 Sep 09
		Atlantica, Fastest Race	2 min 27.84 sec	Clinton L Abby (USA)	20 Sep 09
		Inner City, Fastest Race	2 min 54.872 sec	Clinton L Abby (USA)	20 Sep 09
		National Rail, Fastest Race	2 min 34.9 sec	Clinton L Abby (USA)	20 Sep 09
		Olympic Square, Fastest Race	2 min 41.648 sec	Clinton L Abby (USA)	20 Sep 08
Neo Mr. Do!	MAME	Single Player, No Continues	1,088,950	Robert Macauley (Australia)	12 Jul 09
New Super Mario Bros.	DS	Minimalist Speed Run, 5 Lives, Must Complete Game	44 min 2 sec	Chris Herrera (USA)	25 Aug 08
		Balloon Racing	11.53 sec	Victor M Delgado (USA)	23 Sep 08
		Mario's Slides	14	William Willemstyn III (USA)	6 Oct 06
		Whack-a-Monty	80	Ginger Stowe (USA)	29 Feb 08
		Which Wiggler?	14	Chris Horrora (USA)	25 Aug 09
Ninja Gaiden	Arcade	TGTS	19,100	Jason Wilson (USA)	2 Jun 99
The Ninja Warriors	Arcade	TGTS, Single Player	188,900	Brian Chapel (USA)	10 Nov 88
PAC-Land (Set 1)	MAME	Difficulty A	738,630	Peter Gatland (UK)	10 Sep 08
PAC-Man	Arcade	Perfect Game, Fastest Completion	3 hr 41 min 22 sec	David W Race (USA)	15 Aug 00
		TGTS, 5 PAC-Men, Bonus PAC-Man at 10,000 Points	3,333,360	Billy L Mitchell (USA) Rick D Fothergill (USA) Chris Ayra (USA) Tim Balderramos (USA) Donald Hayes (USA) David W Race (USA)	3 Jul 99 31 Jul 99 16 Feb 00 12 Dec 04 28 Aug 05 15 Aug 09
PAC-Man Championship Edition	Xbox 360 Live Arcade	TGTS, Championship Mode	169,440	Patrick Scott Patterson (USA)	10 Sep 09
PAC-Man World 2	PS2	Maze Mode (L8), Butane Pain	15,220	Troy Whelan (USA)	10 Sep 09
PAC 'N Roll	DS	Time Attack L1-1	27.33 sec	Tee Jester (USA)	19 Aug 09
Paperboy	Arcade	Easy Street	135,989	Eric Ahlers (USA)	15 Mar 09
		Middle Road	124,120	Pat Laffaye (USA)	5 Jun 05
		Hard Way	360,761	Brian Kuh (USA)	1 Jun 06
		TGTS, Grand Slam Score	1,136,435	Phil Britt (USA)	11 Jun 04
Paperboy (Rev 3)	MAME	Grand Slam Score	218,174	Tom Connell (USA)	31 Aug 09
Pigout	Arcade	Calories	101,910	Karl Last (USA)	12 Aug 07
	MAME	Calories	266,155	Ben Janto (USA)	20 Aug 09

TRIVIA

2 Need for Speed: Underground was the first game in the prolific racing game series to introduce car modification into the gameplay.

3 The first all-new 2D Mario platformer of the century, New Super Mario Bros. on the DS (2006, below) marked the 21st anniversary of Super Mario Bros., **the first side-scrolling 2D platformer.**

4 Ryu Hayabusa has a busy life as a ninja – not only does he star in the Ninja Gaiden series, but he is also one of the main characters in the Dead or Alive 3D fighter series.

5 Like a number of classic arcade games, the original PAC-Man had a "kill screen" that effectively marked the end of the game. Kill screens often arise due to an error in the way the game is programmed. In the early days of videogames, few programmers thought players would survive or persevere long enough to get to the game's kill screen. In the case of PAC-Man, the kill screen occurs on level 256, with the right-hand side of the screen obscured by garbled code.

! WANT TO BREAK SOME PARTY GAME RECORDS? TURN TO PP.118–31 TO CHECK OUT THE OPPOSITION FIRST.

TRIVIA

◾ The voice of character Ada Wong (above) in Resident Evil 2 and 4 was provided by Canadian actress Sally Cahill.

◾ According to a number of polls, SEGA's Sonic the Hedgehog (below) is one of the most recognizable of all videogame characters. The Blue Blur even stars in his own annual convention, the Summer of Sonic, which has been held in London each August since 2008.

GAME	PLATFORM	NOTES/ SETTINGS	RECORD	PLAYER (NAT.)	DATE
Pokémon Pinball: Ruby & Sapphire	GBA	Ruby	2,743,835,300	Kelly R Flewin (Canada)	13 May 08
		Sapphire	1,638,900,668	Mark L Bidegain (USA)	28 Nov 08
Pokémon Red	GB/GBC	Fastest Completion	2 hr 41 min	Ryan D Bahr (Australia)	6 Aug 08
Puzzle Bobble/ Bust-a-Move	Arcade		16,013,660	Kim Korpilahti (Sweden)	6 Jul 08
Puzzle Bobble 2/ Bust-a-Move Again	Arcade	Difficulty L6	75,275,450	Stephen Krogman (USA)	1 May 97
	MAME	Difficulty L6	108,840,020	Peter Gatland (UK)	30 Mar 09
	PlayStation		2,900,600	Paul Luu (USA)	11 Apr 99
R-Type	Arcade	TGTS	521,840	Jason Wilson (USA)	15 Jun 97
	MAME	Japanese Arcade Version	422,200	Jonathan A Hale (USA)	10 Jun 09
	Wii Virtual Console	TurboGrafx-16 Settings	191,700	Andrew D Furrer (USA)	31 Jul 08
R-Type II	MAME		209,400	Richard Piper (UK)	8 Mar 06
Rainbow Islands	MAME		9,999,990	Julien Delantes (France)	8 Feb 08
Rampage	Arcade	TGTS, Single Player	208,040	Jason Cram (USA)	21 Apr 07
Rampage Puzzle Attack	GBA	Marathon Mode	118,150	Kelly R Flewin (Canada)	12 Feb 09
Rayman Raving Rabbids TV Party	Wii	Groove On, Ladies Night	7,986	Julie M Mee (UK)	7 Feb 09
Resident Evil 4	Wii	Fastest Completion, New Round	3 hr 10 min 41 sec	Jeffrey M Widzinski (USA)	31 Aug 09
Resident Evil: The Umbrella Chronicles	Wii	Mansion Incident, Fastest Completion, Single Player	12 min 47 sec	Daniel Lee Strickland Perea (USA)	28 Jul 09
		Mansion Incident, Fastest Completion, Two Players	13 min 24 sec	Ginger Stowe & William Willemstyn III (both USA)	7 Mar 09
Return of the Jedi	Arcade	Easy	1,938,010	Mike Sullivan (USA)	11 Jun 04
Robotron: 2084	Arcade	TGTS, 5 Turns Per Player	945,550	Abdner Ashman (USA)	4 Dec 05
Snake Pit	Arcade	Default Setting	262,325	Kipp Howard (USA)	1 Sep 84
Sonic Rush	DS	Time Attack, Altitude Limit, Act 2	2 min 37.49 sec	Ben Townsend (UK)	17 Jul 08
Sonic the Hedgehog	Wii Virtual Console	Highest Score, 3 Lives	124,520	Patrick Scott Patterson (USA)	7 Sep 08
	Mega Drive/ Genesis		9,999,990	Brian Herrmann (USA)	11 Jun 04
		TGTS	280,780	William H Smith (USA)	2 Sep 06
		Full Completion, Must Collect All of the Emeralds	48 min 6 sec	Ashley Jackson (UK)	14 Dec 06

223... the number of issues of *Sonic the Comic*, a British comic book chronicling the adventures of Sonic and various other SEGA characters, published between 1993 and 2002.

GAME	PLATFORM	NOTES/SETTINGS	RECORD	PLAYER (NAT.)	DATE
		Fastest Minimalist Speed Run	37 min 38 sec	Ashley Jackson (UK)	14 Nov 06
Sonic the Hedgehog 2	Mega Drive/Genesis	Fastest Full Completion with Knuckles	1 hr 20 min 1 sec	Jared E Oswald (USA)	22 Aug 08
		Fastest Full Completion with Sonic	56 min 17 sec	Ashley Jackson (UK)	14 Dec 06
		TGTS (PAL)	721,540	Magnus Andersson (Sweden)	12 Jun 09
		Fastest Speed Run with Sonic	42 min 11 sec	Ashley Jackson (UK)	14 Dec 06
Sonic the Hedgehog 3	Mega Drive/Genesis	Fastest Full Completion with Sonic	53 min 04 sec	Ashley Jackson (UK)	20 Dec 06
		TGTS (PAL)	2,002,200	Magnus Andersson (Sweden)	26 Jun 09
SoulCalibur	Arcade	TGTS	1 min 33.48 sec	Corey A Sawyer (USA)	15 Jan 99
SoulCalibur II	Xbox	Extra Time Attack, Standard	3 min 35.4 sec	Anthony J Saputo (USA)	20 Jun 09
		Original Survival, Most Consecutive Wins	10	Anthony J Saputo (USA)	13 Jun 09
SoulCalibur IV	Xbox 360	TGTS	395,480	Lance M Eustache (USA)	18 Jun 09
Space Ace	Arcade		770,866	Steven Joseph (USA)	5 Feb 84
Space Firebird	Arcade		38,590	Tim Curtis (USA)	23 May 01
Space Harrier	Arcade		38,530,220	Philip Campbell (UK)	9 May 09
Space Invaders	Arcade		55,160	Donald Hayes (USA)	7 Jun 03
	GB/GBC		6,326	Tom Duncan (USA)	23 Oct 05
	GBA		389,080	Andrew Pete Mee (UK)	16 Mar 08
		Classic Mode, Marathon	27,690	Andrew Pete Mee (UK)	3 Jul 08
	MAME		222,940	Martin Bedard (Canada)	8 Feb 05
	N64		887,500	Troy Whelan (USA)	4 Oct 06
	PlayStation		880,010	Troy Whelan (USA)	12 Nov 05
Space Invaders Extreme	PSP	Multiple Stages	3,417,290	Douglas B Simpson (USA)	16 Aug 08
Space Invaders Pocket	PSP	Space Invaders '95	113,440	Terence O'Neill (USA)	22 Jul 07
Spider-Man 2	Xbox	Fastest Defeat of Rhino	48 sec	Mike K Morrow (USA)	10 Apr 05
Spider-Man and the X-Men: Arcade's Revenge	SNES	No Star Leeching	140,300	Adam E De Anda (USA)	9 Feb 09
Splatterhouse	MAME	TGTS, No Continues	266,400	Robbie J Shua (Canada)	11 Jul 09
	TurboGrafx-16	No Continues	265,000	Rudy J Ferretti (USA)	2 Feb 08

TRIVIA

The weapons of the popular SoulCalibur character Kilik (below) are named after the four ages of the world in Hindu scripture – from his sword, Krita-Yuga ("Age of Truth") to his staff, Kali-Yuga ("Age of Vice").

Lurid side-scrolling arcade beat-em-up Splatterhouse (below) owes a large debt to the horror movie genre, with Rick, the hero, wearing a mask similar to that of Jason Voorhees in Friday the 13th (USA, 1980). Its initial console port for the Turbo Grafx-16 even carried a warning label claiming: "The horrifying theme of this game may be inappropriate for young children... and cowards."

S TO T

! SEE HOW TO BREAK COMBAT RECORDS WITHOUT BREAKING BONES, IN OUR FIGHTING GAMES SECTION ON PP.104–17.

> Inspired by the gadget-laden cars and chases of the James Bond films, Spy Hunter successfully mixes shoot-em-up action with driving simulation and has been ported to many consoles including the GameCube (below). The strangest port of all, though, must be that found in a version of Microsoft Excel 2000, which featured the game as a hidden "Easter egg".

> Despite playing the original arcade version of Star Wars non-stop for 54 hours, taking no break longer than the 7 seconds between levels, Brandon Erickson (USA) could "only" manage a score of 283,779,000 – significantly short of Robert Mruczek's 25-year-old record on the game.

> Super Mario Kart was originally developed as a generic kart-racing game – Mario and friends were only added two months into development as a means to make the similar-looking karts more distinctive.

GAME	PLATFORM	NOTES/ SETTINGS	RECORD	PLAYER (NAT.)	DATE
		Fastest Completion, No Continues	16 min	Rudy J Ferretti (USA)	2 Feb 08
	Wii Virtual Console	No Continues	306,400	Preston A Fassel (USA)	31 Aug 09
		No Continues (PAL)	230,000	James Paul Billingsley (UK)	20 Jun 07
	Commodore 64		28,570	Stig Remnes (Norway)	26 May 03
Splatterhouse 2	Mega Drive/ Genesis		280,813	Rudy J Ferretti (USA)	2 Feb 08
Spy Hunter	Arcade	TGTS, Factory Default	9,512,590	Paul Dean (USA)	28 Jun 85
	Atari 2600/VCS e	Game 1, Difficulty B	530,350	Mike K Morrow (USA)	18 Aug 02
	Atari 2600/VCS	Game 1, Difficulty B	95,200	Robert T Mruczek (USA)	29 Nov 03
	Atari 400/800/ XL/XE		23,800	Tom Duncan (USA)	1 Sep 05
	PS2	Midway Arcade Treasures	25,325	Shaun P Michaud (USA)	10 Feb 09
	PSP	Midway Arcade Treasures, Extended Play	45,555	Ryan Sullivan (USA)	19 Dec 08
	ZX Spectrum	Novice (PAL)	70,940	Andrew Pete Mee (UK)	16 Mar 08
Sssnake	Atari 2600	Difficulty B	909	Todd Rogers (USA)	30 Sep 04
Star Wars	Arcade	Bonus Shields For Destroying The Death Star	300,007,894	Robert T Mruczek (USA)	22 Jan 84
		TGTS, No Bonus Shields For Destroying The Death Star	31,660,614	David Palmer (USA)	4 Aug 04
Super Castlevania IV	Wii Virtual Console	SNES, 5 Lives, No Backtracking To Former Screens For Candles	815,830	Dave W Vogt (USA)	29 Mar 09
Super Contra	Arcade	TGTS, No Continues	10,645,580	Hector T Rodriguez (USA)	10 Jul 09
	MAME	No Continues, 3 Lives	10,714,560	Rudy Chavez (USA)	16 Aug 08
Superman	Arcade	TGTS, Single Player	1,914,900	Rudy Chavez (USA)	31 May 09
		TGTS, Two-Player Co-op	876,800	Isaiah Triforce Johnson & Jeron Grayson (both USA)	31 May 08
	NES	Must Complete Game, Fastest Completion	31 min 29 sec	Jonathan T Plombon (USA)	19 Apr 08
Super Mario Kart	SNES	Bowser Castle 3, Fastest Race	1 min 41.04 sec	Brandon M Skar (USA)	24 Aug 09
Super Princess Peach	DS	Puzzle A	17.42 Sec	Jennifer B Carmichael (Canada)	19 Jul 06
Super Smash Bros. Brawl	Wii	Boss Battles Mode, Fastest Completion	3 min 21.85 sec	Rocky L Rose (USA)	1 Jun 08

$431 MILLION (£273 MILLION)... the worldwide lifetime gross takings for the first two *Tomb Raider* movies. A prequel movie is currently under development.

GAME	PLATFORM	NOTES/SETTINGS	RECORD	PLAYER (NAT.)	DATE
		10-Man Brawl, Fastest Completion	12.11 sec	Rocky L Rose (USA)	18 May 08
Tekken 3	Arcade	TGTS, Fastest Completion	4 min 4.3 sec	Troy Towers (USA)	18 Feb 99
	PlayStation	Survival Mode, Most Consecutive Wins	384	Mike K Morrow (USA)	10 Apr 05
		Time Attack Mode, Fastest Completion	1 min 8.21 sec	Kelly G Campbell (USA)	5 Feb 03
Tetris DS	DS	Marathon, Endless	99,999,999	Isaiah TriForce Johnson (USA)	18 Jun 08
Tetris Party	WiiWare	Beginner, Marathon, 150 Lines	240,461	Patrick Scott Patterson (USA)	22 Dec 08
		Beginner, Marathon, Endless	15,179,595	Jeffrey M Widzinski (USA)	14 Jul 09
Tetris Worlds	Xbox	*Tetris*, Highest Level Cleared	10	Patrick Scott Patterson (USA)	27 Apr 09
		Cascade Tetris, Highest Level Cleared	6	Anthony J Saputo (USA)	14 Jun 09
Tiger Woods PGA Tour 2004	Xbox	Easy Difficulty, 18 Holes	46 strokes	Tom Duncan (USA)	30 Aug 09
Tomb Raider II	PlayStation	Lara's Obstacle Course, Fastest Completion	1 min 3.9 sec	Wolff K Morrow (USA) Shin Sato (Japan) Niral Shah (USA) Nobuyuki Takebe (Japan) Matthias De Scheerder (Belgium)	13 Aug 02 1 Apr 04 5 Mar 05 5 Mar 05 5 Mar 05
Tomb Raider III	PlayStation	Jungle, Fastest Minimalist Completion	1 min 17 sec	Mike K Morrow (USA)	29 May 05
		All Hallows, Fastest Minimalist Completion	6 min 26 sec	Shin Sato (Japan)	1 Apr 04
		Nevada Desert, Fastest Minimalist Completion	12 min 49 sec	Mike K Morrow (USA)	28 Jun 05
		Thames Wharf, Fastest Minimalist Completion	25 sec	Mike K Morrow (USA)	20 Feb 05
Tom Clancy's Ghost Recon 2	Xbox	Quick Mission, Firefight Mode, Airfield	2,854	Patrick Scott Patterson (USA)	25 Feb 09
Track & Field	Arcade	TGTS	95,350	Hector T Rodriguez (USA)	23 Jan 09
	MAME	TGTS	95,930	Tommi J Tiihonen (Finland)	8 Feb 05
Tron (Set 1)	MAME		2,608,140	Tommi J Tiihonen (Finland)	8 Feb 05
Tunnel Hunt	Arcade	TGTS	821,330	Chris Randall (USA)	11 Jun 04
	MAME		47,520	Sami Virtanen (Finland)	31 Aug 09
Tutankham	Arcade	Marathon Setting, Default Mode	2,791,880	Rob Barrett (USA)	5 Jun 04

TRIVIA

> At the centre of the Tekken series (above), which literally translates as "Iron Fist", is the Mishima Zaibatsu financial corporation. Control of the company is determined by the winner of each Tekken tournament – a novel way for a company to choose its CEO.

> Tomb Raider III features a secret level entitled "All Hallows". To access it, players must first locate all 59 secrets hidden throughout the rest of the game.

> Classic arcade sports title Track & Field features some obscure ways to score bonus points. For example, if you manages to throw the javelin off the top of the screen and hit a bird, you are rewarded with 1,000 extra points.

> First released in 1982, Tutankham was one of six games featured in an article about Twin Galaxies and videogame world records published by LIFE magazine that same year. In 2007, a follow-up documentary, Chasing Ghosts, revisited the lives of the players featured in the article.

FOR A WALK DOWN MEMORY LANE TO THE ARCADES OF YESTERDAY, CHECK OUT CLASSIC ARCADE ON P.178.

TRIVIA

We Love Katamari, the second entry in the strange, yet compelling Katamari series of games, sees our hero, the prince, tasked with fulfilling the requests of his fans by collecting materials with which to make new planets. This time around, it's possible to unlock some of the prince's cousins (below and right) as playable characters.

With a total of 66 instruments to simulate in Wii Music (above) – from guitars to cowbells and dog barks – the Wii Remote and Nunchuk are put to a staggering array of uses. Even the Balance Board plays its part, simulating a set of drums!

Shigeru Miyamoto first demonstrated Wii Music at E3 2008, using it to play The Legend of Zelda Overworld Theme.

GAME	PLATFORM	NOTES/ SETTINGS	RECORD	PLAYER (NAT.)	DATE
		TGTS	622,440	Rob Barrett (USA)	25 Jul 03
Ultimate Ghosts 'n Goblins	PSP	Novice Mode	420,900	Terence O'Neill (USA)	2 Sep 07
Ultimate Mortal Kombat 3	SNES	Very Hard Difficulty, Fastest Completion	12:10	Michael J Girard (USA)	9 May 09
Virtua Fighter	MAME	TGTS	2 min 10.63 sec	Gavin Carper (USA)	27 Aug 09
Virtua Fighter 2	Arcade	TGTS	2 min 40.79 sec	Brandon Smith (USA)	11 Jun 04
Virtua Fighter Remix	Arcade	TGTS	7 min 43 sec	Lamont Coleman (USA)	20 Apr 97
Wardner	MAME		9,999,990	Clay W Karczewski (Canada)	11 Sep 07
We Love Katamari	PS2	As Large As Possible 5 (Diameter)	3,572.02 m	Ben Greenman (USA)	21 Mar 08
		Roll Up The Sun (Number Of Celestial Bodies)	3,531	Ben Greenman (USA)	21 Mar 08
		Save The Pandas (Dollars)	$101,097.42	Geoffrey Lin (USA)	28 Aug 09
Whac-a-Mole	DS	Arcade	25,550	William Willenstyn III (USA)	6 Oct 06
WWE Legends of WrestleMania	PS3	Fastest Victory, Legendary Difficulty	55 sec	Carmelo P Consiglio (USA)	4 May 09
Wii Fit	Wii	Aerobics, Advanced Step	672	Jonathan R Shemansky (USA)	13 Mar 09
		Balance Games, Penguin Slide (PAL)	99	Julie M Mee (UK)	12 Sep 09
		Body Test, Agility	21	William Willemstyn III (USA)	21 Feb 09
		Body Test, Stillness	79	Ginger Stowe (USA)	28 Mar 09
		Ultimate Balance Test	16.92 sec	Marc Cohen (USA)	12 Aug 09
		Ultimate Balance Test (PAL)	10.95 sec	Julie M Mee (UK)	19 Sep 09
Wii Music	Wii	Mr. Maestro, Legend of Zelda Theme	100	Blaine Locklair (USA) Marc Cohen (USA)	11 Jun 09 20 Jun 09
		Pitch Perfect, L8	95	Marc Cohen (USA)	20 Jun 09
Wii Sports	Wii	Baseball, Biggest Blowout	18	Lance M Eustache (USA) Kevin M Conner (USA)	15 Jan 09 27 Apr 09
		Training: Baseball, Swing Control	78	Kevin M Conner (USA)	27 Apr 09
		Training: Bowling, Power Throws	701	Carl Aspinwall (USA)	13 Feb 07
		Training: Tennis, Returning Balls	113	Gregrey S Hall (USA)	16 May 09
Wii Sports Resort	Wii	Air Sports, Island Flyover, Balloons	110	Marc Cohen (USA)	31 Aug 09
		Air Sports, Island Flyover, iPoints	3	Ronald F Loch (USA)	22 Aug 09

GAME	PLATFORM	NOTES/ SETTINGS	RECORD	PLAYER (NAT.)	DATE
		Air Sports, Sky Diving	113	Marc Cohen (USA)	12 Aug 09
		Archery, Expert	105	Brandon M Skar (USA)	24 Aug 09
		Basketball, 3-Point Contest	26	Lance Eustache (USA)	29 Aug 09
		Basketball, Pick-Up Game	20	Lance Eustache (USA)	29 Aug 09
		Bowling, 100-Pin Game, Wall-Strike Cheat Not Allowed	2,098	Marc Cohen (USA)	31 Aug 09
		Bowling, Full Game	221	Marc Cohen (USA)	31 Aug 09
		Bowling, Spin Control	144	Marc Cohen (USA)	31 Aug 09
		Canoeing, Expert	409.24 m	Lance Eustache (USA)	29 Aug 09
		Cycling, 6-Stages	15 min 53.86 sec	Lance Eustache (USA)	29 Aug 09
		Frisbee, Dog, Manual Style	1,010	Marc Cohen (USA)	31 Aug 09
		Frisbee, Golf, Manual Style	64	Marc Cohen (USA)	31 Aug 09
		Power Cruising, Beach	183.2 m	Marc Cohen (USA)	13 Aug 09
		Power Cruising, Cavern	209.3 m	Marc Cohen (USA)	13 Aug 09
		Power Cruising, Lagoon	157.6 m	Marc Cohen (USA)	13 Aug 09
		Power Cruising, Lighthouse	145.6 m	Marc Cohen (USA)	13 Aug 09
		Power Cruising, Marina	144.4 m	Marc Cohen (USA)	13 Aug 09
		Power Cruising, Shoals	186.6 m	Marc Cohen (USA)	13 Aug 09
		Table Tennis, Match	1,388	Brandon M Skar (USA)	24 Aug 09
		Table Tennis, Return Challenge	999	Brandon M Skar (USA)	24 Aug 09
		Swordplay, Duel	1,054	Marc Cohen (USA)	13 Aug 09
		Swordplay, Showdown	722	Lance Eustache (USA)	29 Aug 09
		Swordplay, Speed Slice	1,358	Lance Eustache (USA)	29 Aug 09
		Wakeboarding, Expert	1,581	Brandon M Skar (USA)	24 Aug 09
Wipeout Fusion	PS2	Area 1	35,317,633	Alexander T Trammell (USA)	22 Aug 05
World of Goo	WiiWare	TGTS, Tallest Structure	20.6 m	William Willemstyn III (USA)	15 Jan 09
X-Men vs. Street Fighter	Arcade	TGTS	2,098,100	Clarence E Leung (USA)	16 Mar 99
Zoo Keeper	DS	Tokoton	4,943,370	Ginger Stowe (USA)	7 Jun 08

TRIVIA

■ Few can resist the appeal of Wii Sports. Police in Polk County, Florida, USA, even stopped to play some Wii Sports: Bowling during a raid on the home of a suspected drug dealer in September 2009. Unfortunately for them, the suspect had security cameras fitted in his house and released the footage to the media, leaving the officers involved red-faced and facing disciplinary action.

■ Unlike real cyclists, Wii Sports Resort cyclists have to use their arms rather than their legs to simulate pedalling, with the Wii Remote and Nunchuk.

■ Along with Ken, Ryu (pictured below in Super Street Fighter II Turbo HD Remix) has appeared in every release of a Street Fighter game, including X-Men vs. Street Fighter.

PICTURE CREDITS

ACKNOWLEDGEMENTS

Guinness World Records would like to thank the following individuals, groups and websites for their help in the creation of *Guinness World Records Gamer's Edition 2010*:

Sarah-Jane Allen, Asda Media Relations, Brian Ashcraft, Polly Atherton, Dan Bendon, Paul Benjamin, Pete Bouvier, Phil Brannelly, Bjarne Brunsgard, Jonnie Bryant, Fay Burgin, Rob Burman, Hugo Bustillos, Carly Byron, Simon Byron, Alison Carroll (Lara Croft Official Model), Fiona Cherbak, Letty Cherry, Edd and Imogen China, Gunther Comploj, Bryan Coney (MCM Expo), Beckie Cooper and Tim Levell (*Blue Peter*), George Costi,

Brian Crecente, Taynor Darn, Fraser Davidson, Victor De Leon and "Lil Poison", Lewis Digby, Jesse DiMariano, Jane Douglas, Eidos Interactive Limited, Roxana Etemad, Jonathan Fargher, Moe Farley, Alex Fierek, Tom Foy, Jonathan Goddard, Christopher Grabowski, Hannah Grant, Emma Green, Sarah Hartland (Barrington Harvey), Kathleen Heinz, Anita-Lynne Henderson, Jon Hicks, Jonas Holm Hansen, Jon Hurrell, Morley John, Chris Jones, Sara Kaplan, Kirsten Kearney (Ready Up), Joe Korsmo, Christian Kruse, Joe Lee, Kristina Levsky, Rebecca Liburd (Asda Press Office), Paddy Lynch, Katy McNeill, Laura McTurk (Taylor Herring PR), Mike Mantarro,

Chris Marsh, Kristy Marshall (TFL), Johnny Minkley (Eurogamer TV), Edward Newby-Robson, Michael O'Dell, Ai Ogata, Alan O'Grady, Sophie Orlando, Cathy Orr, Patrick Scott Patterson, Rasmus Pedersen, Francesca Pipe (Westminster City Council), Patricia Pucci, Christophor Rick, Mark Robins, Taina Rodriguez, David Rutter, Fran Shergold, Iain Simons, Pamela Simpson, Charlotte Skinner, Nick Smith, Tom Smith, Martin Snelling, John Swatton, Kate Szlendak, Tommy Tallarico, Leo Tan, Stuart Taylor, Louise Thomsen, Adam Tuckwell, Stuart Turner, Britta Wackerman, Mark Ward, Peter Webber, Alex Weller, Kate White, Kevin Williams, Oz Wright.